Flesh
as Transformation Symbol
in the Theology
of
Anselm of Canterbury

Flesh
as Transformation Symbol
in the Theology
of
Anselm of Canterbury

Historical and
Transpersonal Perspectives

James Gollnick

Texts and Studies in Religion
Volume 22

The Edwin Mellen Press
Lewiston/Queenston

Library of Congress Cataloging in Publication Data

Gollnick, James.
    Flesh as transformation symbol in the theology of Anselm
of Canterbury.

    (Texts and studies in religion ; v. 22)
    Bibliography: p.
    1. Flesh (Theology)--History of doctrines--Middle Ages, 600-1500.
2. Anselm, Saint, Archbishop of Canterbury, 1033-1109--Contributions
in theology.
I. Title. II. Series: Texts and studies in religion : 22.
BT741.2.G64 1985   233   85-10502
ISBN 0-88946-810-9 (alk. paper)

This is volume 22 in the continuing series
Texts and Studies in Religion
Volume 22 ISBN 0-88946-810-9
TSR Series ISBN 0-88946-976-8

The Edwin Mellen Press   The Edwin Mellen Press
Box 450   Box 67
Lewiston, New York   Queenston, Ontario
USA 14092   L0S 1L0 CANADA

Printed in the United States of America

To the Memory of
Isabelle and Albert Gollnick
My Mother and Father

CONTENTS

ACKNOWLEDGMENTS

I wish to thank Professors Walter Principe, Eugene Fairweather and Jasper Hopkins for their helpful comments in the preparation of this work, and Father Donald Finlay, librarian of the Pontifical Institute of Medieval Studies, for access to many of the sources for this research.

I am also grateful to my colleagues in the Department of Religious Studies at the University of Toronto, especially Professors Lawrence Elmer and Roger Hutchinson, for their support and encouragement in this project.

Finally, I am indebted to my mentor, Professor Herbert Richardson, for many years of warm friendship and wise guidance in my work on St. Anselm.

ABBREVIATIONS

Anselm's Works

CDH	*Cur Deus Homo*
DCD	*De Casu Diaboli*
DCP	*De Concordia Praescientiae et Praedestinationis et Gratiae Dei cum Libero Arbitrio*
DCV	*De Conceptu Virginali*
DG	*De Grammatico*
DLA	*De Libertate Arbitrii*
DPS	*De Processione Spiritus Sancti*
DV	*De Veritate*
E	*Epistola*
EDSA	*Epistola de Sacrificio Azimi et Fermentati*
EDSE	*Epistola de Sacramentis Ecclesiae*
EDIV	*Epistola de Incarnatione Verbi*
Ep. ad Urbanum	*Epistola ad Urbanum Papam II*
Med.III	*Meditatio Redemptionis Humanae*
Mon.	*Monologion*
Orat.	*Oratio*
Pros.	*Proslogion*

Translations of Anselm's Works

AC	J. Hopkins and H. Richardson, *Anselm of Canterbury*. 3 volumes
PAM	B. Ward, *The Prayers and Meditations of Saint Anselm*

Other Works

AA	*Analecta Anselmiana*, ed. F.S. Schmitt. Frankfurt, 5 volumes.
SB	*Spicilegium Beccense*. Vol. I. Paris, 1959
SR	*Sola Ratione*, ed. H. Kohlenberger.
VSA	*Vita Sancti Anselmi: The Life of St. Anselm by Eadmer.* Edited and translated by R. W. Southern.
DZ	Denzinger, *Enchiridion Symbolorum*. Friburg, 1957.

In this study, textual references will indicate the title and chapter of Anselm's work and the location of the text in F. S. Schmitt's edition. When the English translation of the text appears, precise reference to the translation will also be given. For example, *Mon.* XVI; S I, 30, 8-31; AC I, 25 refers to chapter sixteen of Anselm's *Monologion*; the Latin text is located in the first volume of Schmitt's edition on page thirty, lines eight through thirty-one; the English translation used is J. Hopkins and H. W. Richardson, *Anselm of Canterbury*, volume one, page twenty-five.

Flesh

as Transformation Symbol
in the Theology
of
Anselm of Canterbury

Historical and
Transpersonal Perspectives

INTRODUCTION: RECENT LITERATURE

The history of twentieth-century Anselm scholarship can be seen as an attempt to recover the real
Anselm and to understand his distinctiveness and
importance in the history of western theology. In the
history of Christian thought, Anselm, recognized as a
Father of Scholasticism, is an important transitional
figure between the Neoplatonic tendencies of St. Augustine and the Aristotelian synthesis of St. Thomas
Aquinas. Many Anselm scholars have attempted to understand Anselm's thought by reading him against the background of these two intellectual giants.1 Although
these studies have made important contributions to
Anselm research, they have not always allowed the distinctiveness of Anselm's own thought to surface. The
most recent Anselm scholarship, however, tries to get at
the singularity of his theological system.

Twentieth-century Anselm scholarship can be
roughly divided into three periods: The first, extending from the beginning of the century until the
appearance of Barth's _Fides Quaerens Intellectum_ (1931),
was characterized by its interest in Anselm's intellectual and metaphysical thought. The next period began
in the 1930s with the critical studies of F. S. Schmitt
and culminated in the International Anselm Congress in
Normandy in 1959, which celebrated the nine hundredth
anniversary of Anselm's arrival at the monastery of
Bec. This period is characterized by a growing awareness of the authentic works that constitute the Anselm
corpus and by an increased interest in the historical
context of his theology. The most recent period began
in the 1960s and was no doubt stimulated by certain new
proposals that surfaced at the Anselm Congress of 1959,
for example, J. McIntyre's "Premises and Conclusions in
the System of St. Anselm's Theology."2 This period is
marked by a growing interest in the character of Anselm's distinctive theological system.

This division of modern Anselm scholarship is only
schematic, yet it serves to classify important materials
and to highlight shifts in emphasis within the body of

literature. During the first period, there was a
tendency to focus attention on the philosophical import
of Anselm's thought or on isolated doctrines in his
theology. With regard to the philosophical interest, we
cite C. Filliatre's La philosophie de saint Anselme as a
fairly typical example. While this work demonstrates
concern for the historical setting of Anselm's thought,
it does not seriously consider the relationship of that
thought to its foundation in Anselm's religious life.
Filliatre also gives preference to Monologion and Proslogion and pays almost no attention to Anselm's prayers
and meditations. The same point can be made regarding
A. Koyré's L'idée de Dieu dans la philosophie de st.
Anselme. Anselm's religious life and his prayers are
not given sufficient emphasis in these works precisely
because there is a tendency to view his thought as
separate from lived context and devotional meaning.

          E. Lohmeyer's study, Die Lehre von Willen bei
Anselm von Canterbury, is an example of the interest in
particular doctrines found especially in this first
period. Lohmeyer's work draws mainly on De Concordia
and De Libertate Arbitrii in this philosophical analysis
of Anselm's doctrine of will. He carries out this
rather abstract analysis on the basis of a limited
number of Anselm's works without examining the life
setting that moved Anselm to arrive at this particular
doctrine of will.

          K. Barth is an important transitional figure be-
tween the first and second periods. Barth is especially
important because he attempts to characterize Anselm's
method as being primarily theological, showing that even
those works that have often been considered philosophical can be understood only in the context of Anselm's
overall theological program, namely, fides quaerens
intellectum. Barth makes it clear that one must not
consider certain works of the Anselm corpus in isolation
from his other works since all are directly related to a
single methodological program.

          Another important figure in the second period is
A. Stolz. He is in general agreement with Barth that
Anselm's thought must be considered in relation to the
general thrust of his theological method, but Stolz
further specifies that method as "mystical." He emphasizes that even Proslogion, which contains the ontological argument, should not be seen apart from Anselm's
quest for the vision and experience of God. Stolz characterizes Anselm's Proslogion as "essentially a piece of
mystical theology," calling attention to the unity of

mysticism and theology that proceeds directly from the
devotional context of Anselm's writing.3

   The second period in the twentieth- century Anselm
scholarship, marked by an interest in the authenticity
of his works, was anticipated in the 1920s by the work
of A. Wilmart. Wilmart exposes the confusions and
inadequacies of the Gerberon edition of Anselm's prayers
and meditations, removing from the Anselm corpus over
fifty prayers, nearly twenty meditations, and sixteen
homilies that had been erroneously attributed to Anselm
by Th. Raynaud in the seventeenth century.

   F. S. Schmitt prepared his critical edition of the
Anselm corpus over a period of years. Although Schmitt
wrote critical articles in the 1920s and early 1930s,
the several volumes of his critical edition did not
appear until later (volume I in 1938, II in 1940, III in
1946, IV in 1949, and V in 1951). Before Schmitt's
critical edition of Anselm's texts, scholars had relied
upon the edition produced by Migne in 1853, which, in
turn, was based on G. Gerberon's judgments about the
authenticity of Anselm's works. Gerberon, apparently
misled by the previous uncritical collection of Th.
Raynaud, included in his 1675 Paris edition of Anselm's
works a great number of prayers and meditations that had
not been written by Anselm.4 Without wishing to dispar-
age the work of Gerberon, whose edition served for well
over two hundred years, it must be said that all Anselm
scholars are indebted to Schmitt for producing his
critical edition. With reference to Schmitt's important
contribution to Anselm studies, we should also note that
he provided helpful guidelines for the chronology of
Anselm's treatises and dialogues, giving us a clearer
picture of the life setting in which these works arose.
Although the exact dates of composition are uncertain,
Schmitt has arrived at the following judgment about the
years in which Anselm's main theological works were
composed:5 Monologian, 1076; Proslogion, 1077-1078; De
Grammatico, 1080-1085; De Veritate, 1080-1085; De
Libertate Arbitrii, 1080-1085; De Casu Diaboli, 1085-
1090; Epistola de Incarnatione Verbi, 1092-1094; Cur
Deus Homo, 1094-1098; De Conceptu Virginali, 1099-1100;
De Processione Spiritus Sancti, 1102; De Concordia
Praescientiae et Praedestinationis et Gratiae Dei cum
Libero Arbitrio, 1107-1108.

   The papers presented at the Anselm Congress in
1959 evinced a real concern for the life setting of Anselm's theology. Perhaps something of the living force
of Anselm was present in that gathering of scholars,

some of whom had studied Anselm and his works for a
lifetime. The concentration of so much scholarly energy
on this great figure at a conference held in his own
monastery has given new impetus to the study of the
historical context of Anselm's thought. This attention
to the historical context can be observed in a number of
the articles that appear in Spicilegium Beccense I.6
For example, J. Mason's "St. Anselm's Relations with
Laymen" examines a small selection of Anselm's letters
to determine some of the matters that occupied him
during his period as archbishop.7 All of the letters
considered were sent to members of the aristocracy in
Northern France. This study paints a vivid picture of
Anselm's concern with the spiritual and temporal welfare
of the Church. Mason's main interest is that these
letters give a better idea of the type of man Anselm was
and of the problems that beset him in administering his
office. In this article and others like it, increased
attention is given to the writings of Anselm that had
previously received little notice.

The Anselm Congress in 1959 provides a transition
to the most recent period in Anselm scholarship. An
important discussion took place at the conference regarding the systematic character of Anselm's theology,
exemplified by J. McIntyre's article "Premises and
Conclusions in the System of St. Anselm's Theology."8
In the fourth chapter of this study we shall discuss the
principal contributors to our understanding the nature
of Anselm's system; so here we shall discuss only
briefly the most important studies on Anselm's theological system that have appeared since 1959. They are R.
Pouchet's La rectitudo chez Saint Anselme, H. Kohlenberger's Similitudo und Ratio, and J. Hopkins's A Companion to the Study of St. Anselm. Although the
approaches of these three works are quite different,
they are all concerned with the nature of Anselm's
theological system. Pouchet is primarily interested in
the way Anselm's entire theology is guided by a vital
concern with rectitude, a concern that extends beyond
theoretical considerations and into Anselm's own spiritual and pastoral experience. Kohlenberger, on the other
hand, examines the way in which Anselm's concern for
language is the foundation for his entire theological
system. Hopkins takes yet a different approach to
Anselm's system in that he characterizes it not so much
by its relation to a fundamental inspiration, but rather
by its overall logical coherence.

These three important studies represent a growing
interest in the character of Anselm's theological
system.9 In this work, we propose to consolidate the

gains made by these studies and to contribute to the most recent body of literature through an analysis of one of the central ideas in Anselm's system, the concept of flesh or the "transformation complex." This term represents a whole range of words, concepts and symbols dealing, both directly and indirectly, with the physical, fleshly aspects of man. We shall also speak of this transformation complex as "flesh" and as the "flesh complex." Anselm himself, of course, did not use the term "transformation complex" in his writing; rather, he used the Latin words <u>caro, corpus,</u> and <u>concupiscentia</u>.

Not only is the concept of flesh a significant key to unlocking the nature of Anselm's theological system, it also highlights the dynamics of transformation, a crucial aspect heretofore unexplored by Anselm scholars. Past studies of Anselm's theology also lack a systematic analysis of Anselm's preoccupation with the flesh concept.10 Throughout this study, we shall attempt to emphasize this major concern of Anselm's theology by stressing the monastic context and the devotional logic that guided his life and his work.

The connection between the concept of flesh, the monastic setting, and the process of transformation merits exploration. For Anselm, it is through the flesh that the individual person gains access to a realm of human experience that is properly called "transpersonal," that is, to a region where one encounters and is transformed by realities communicated in ancient universal symbols that are not merely aspects of the individual's mind. The monastic context expresses the immediate life setting within which Anselm meets and is transformed by these spiritual realities. So the concept of flesh and the monastic-devotional context are vital to a deeper understanding of the transformational intent of Anselm's entire theology.

The goal of Anselm's own religious quest was spiritual transformation, and his purpose in writing was to engage the reader in a personal journey where one encounters and is transformed by the major spiritual forces at work in the world. This attempt to engage the reader can be seen in the form that his writing takes: dialogues, discourses, meditations, prayers, and letters. Anselm's works contemplate and wrestle with the ultimate structures of human reality. When we read Anselm we are invited to embark upon a journey toward powerful and ancient spiritual realities: God's existence, presence, wisdom, power, and justice; the trinitarian structure of God; the mysterious and powerful

forces of evil, of the angels, and of the saints; the
two-nature doctrine of the God-man, and the dilemma of
the human condition.

        Anselm considers the flesh itself to be the essen-
tial point of contact between the individual and this
realm of God, angels, saints, and demons. By means of
the flesh, human nature was initially corrupted and by
means of the flesh, it was later restored. To follow
the vicissitudes of the flesh as they are described in
Anselm's theology is to observe the course of human
transformation, the transformation both of the race and
of the individual. In this sense, the concept of flesh
provides a hermeneutical perspective that exposes this
basic transformational goal of Anselm's life and work.

NOTES

1. A few notable examples: the Augustinian interpretation includes K. Flasch, "Der philosophische Ansatz des Anselm von Canterbury im Monologion und sein Verhaeltnis zum augustinischen Neuplatonismus," in AA II (1970), pp. 1-43 , and J. Hopkins, A Companion to the Study of St. Anselm, (Minneapolis, 1972); the Thomistic interpretation includes F. S. Schmitt, "Anselm und der (Neu-)Platonismus," (Analecta Anselmiana I, Frankfurt, 1969, pp. 39-71) and can be seen in M. Charlesworth's introduction to St. Anselm's Proslogion (London, 1965). Some of the discussions in this book will illustrate the impact of this type of scholarship on the state of certain questions in contemporary Anselm research.

2. J. McIntyre, SB, pp. 95-101.

3. A. Stolz, "Anselm's Theology in the Proslogion," in The Many-Faced Argument ed. J. Hick and A. McGill (New York, 1967), p. 186. This essay first appeared in 1933 in Catholica.

4. A. Wilmart offers a brief account of the stages leading up to the Migne edition in the article "Une prière au saint patron attribuée à saint Anselme," in Auteurs spirituels et textes devots du moyen age latin (Paris, 1932), pp. 147-61: "J'entends les derniers editeurs: Th. Raynaud, S. J., Lyon 1630, et le mauriste bien connu G. Gerberon, Paris 1675 (et, de nouveau, 1721). Migne a reproduit l'édition de Gerberon (1854). Avant Raynaud, de 1491 à 1612 (Nuremberg 1491, Paris 1510, Venise 1512, Paris 1544, Cologne 1573, Lyon 1610, Cologne 1612) on n'avait publié que quelques pièces où déjà l'apocryphe apparaissait. Le vrai coupable est bien Raynaud. Quant à Gerberon, ayant entre les mains des manuscrits de toute espèce qui lui permettaient de voir clair, il eut la malheureuse idée de recevoir la masse indigest des morceaux admis par Raynaud d'après de mauvais témoins" (p. 148).

5. For more information on Schmitt's dating of Anselm's works see "Zur Chronologie der Werke des hl. Anselm von Canterbury," Revue Bénédictine, 44 (1932), pp. 322-50.

6.   Some of the articles in <u>Spicilegium Beccense</u>, Vol. I, which indicate this increased interest in the life context of Anselm's theology include P. Cousin "Les relations de saint Anselme avec Cluny," J. Laporte "Saint Anselme et l'ordre monastique," J. Pouchet "La componction chez saint Anselme," P. Salmon "L'ascèse monastique dans les lettres de saint Anselme de Cantorbéry," and J. Dickinson "Saint Anselm and the First Regular Canons in England."

7.   J. Mason, <u>SB</u> pp. 547-60.

8.   McIntyre, <u>SB</u>, pp. 95-101.

9.   Even those who have not devoted lengthy studies to various aspects of Anselm's theological system have called attention to the interrelation of the works of Anselm's entire <u>corpus</u>.   For example, R. Herrera warns those interpreting the <u>Proslogion</u> that: "the entire Anselmian work and the monastic culture from which it proceeds must be seriously considered. The argument, without this preliminary investigation, is, as often happens, interpreted out of context, isolated from the ground that gives it substance and meaning" ("St. Anselm's <u>Proslogion</u>:   A Hermeneutical Task" in <u>AA</u> IV/2, p. 141). More recently, D. Duclow has pointed out that to understand the ontological argument, Anselm's view of truth in other works must also be consulted ("Structure and Meaning in Anselm's <u>De Veritate</u>," <u>American Benedictine Review</u> 26 (1975), pp. 406-17.

We may also consider the appearance of the English translations of all Anselm's treatises, dialogues, prayers, and meditations as an indication of the recent interest in Anselm's entire theological system.   J. Hopkins and H. Richardson are responsible for the translation of those treatises and dialogues of Anselm which remained until 1965 untranslated into English: see <u>Truth, Freedom, and Evil</u> (New York, 1967) and <u>Trinity, Incarnation and Redemption</u> (New York, 1970). In 1973, B. Ward published the complete prayers and meditations of Anselm: see <u>The Prayers and Meditations of Saint Anselm</u> (Middlesex, 1973).   These new English translations focus attention on these writings of Anselm which shed important light on the nature of his theological system.

10. At the end of chapter 3 we shall review the secondary literature on the concept of flesh in Anselm's theology to indicate how little material has actually been devoted to this area of his thought.

2

THE MONASTIC CONTEXT OF ANSELM'S THEOLOGY

St. Anselm was first and foremost a monk. His
intellectual growth and the formation of his theological
system took place while he was a member of the Benedictine monastic community of Bec in Normandy (1059-1093).
He entered the monastery as a novice of twenty-six and
left Bec thirty-four years later when he was appointed
archbishop of Canterbury. Anselm spent his prime as a
monk at Bec, dedicated to the spiritual life and the
quest for God.

Anselm was born in northern Italy. He attended a
primary school conducted at a nearby monastery and later
studied at a church school taught by Benedictines. By
the age of fifteen, Anselm had decided that he wanted to
join the monastery. When Anselm asked the abbot for
permission, he refused to admit him without his father's
approval. Anselm prayed that he would become ill because he thought he would then be allowed to enter the
monastery. Although his prayers for an illness were
answered, the abbot still refused him. Anselm recovered
from his illness and waited a number of years for his
wish to be fulfilled.

According to L. Merton, Anselm's monastic orientation is the essential point Eadmer emphasizes in his
biography of Anselm: "The main purpose of Eadmer's _Vita
Anselmi_ is to portray Anselm not as a miracle worker and
a charismatic figure, but rather as a perfect monk, a
father and friend to his monks, a man of profound humility, full of love for his vocation and his brethren,
totally absorbed in that charity of Christ which was
constantly pressing him to struggle for the truth and
rectitude which formed the heart of his teaching."[1]
Throughout his life, Anselm's principal theological
concerns were related to the monastic setting and the
liturgical life of the Church. Even in his later years
as archbishop he was still mainly concerned with devotion and the proper form of the sacraments. The monastic life provided the dominant setting and the devotional content for Anselm's thought.

The primary concern in the medieval monastery is
the transformation of human beings. In fact, the

Benedictine monastery can be viewed as an attempt to create another world set apart from the physical life outside the monastery. This is evident even in the organization of the monastery; it is a self-contained economic, political, and social unit. The monks grow their own food, establish their own schedule of work and prayer, and govern their own internal affairs. This independence from the outside world, especially as the monastic life is centered around the contemplation and worship of God, is already one step toward transforming human life. It is the creation of an intermediate cosmos that is somewhere between the life of earth and that of heaven. Because the monastery is organized around the liturgy, the worship of God, and the veneration of Mary, the apostles, the angels, and the saints, it is, in a sense, more like life in heaven than life on earth. Monastic life establishes an image of what life will be like after death; it symbolically anticipates heavenly existence.

Initially we can discern the fundamental difference between the earthly life and the monastic life in the vows that the Benedictine monk makes: poverty, chastity, obedience, and enclosure. The major structures of the earthly life--property, family, freedom, and movement--are renounced in order to enter into another reality. We can interpret this renunciation as an attempt to wean a person from his physical body, the flesh of Adam. This transformation might also be described as one's turning one's life away from the mind and will of Adam towards a refocusing on the mind and will of Christ. From this perspective, the physical, mental and spiritual discipline of the monastery can be considered as the means to bring about this transformation from the old Adam to the new Adam. Anselm says in his "Prayer to God": "Give me heart-piercing goodness and humility; discerning abstinence and mortification of the flesh."2

In the monastery the structures of earthly life become symbols of transformation. For example, the physical senses represented in sexual activity, in eating, and in drinking are transformed into a relationship with God and the saints. This transformation is especially evident in Anselm's prayers. In "Prayer to Christ," Anselm directs the powerful passion of human love to the divine: "I praise and thank you for the desire that you have inspired. . . . Most merciful Lord, turn my lukewarmness into fervent love of you. . . . I thirst for you, I hunger for you, I desire you, I sigh for you I covet you. . . . Lord, meanwhile, let my

tears be my meat day and night, until they say to me,
'Behold your God,' until I hear, 'Soul, behold your
bridegroom.'"3   Here we can observe the tremendous
psychological energy that Anselm invests in the spiritual realm, energy which, in the earthly realm, would
naturally be directed toward human beings.

A well-known twentieth century monk, Thomas Merton, describes the goal of monastic transformation:

> Our monastic life . . . is a life which is
> nourished by constant spiritual contact with
> the glorified humanity of Christ the saviour,
> who lives in us by His grace and is thus the
> principle of our supernatural life--life-
> giving spirit.
>
> Contact with the risen humanity of Christ
> is true holiness. Growth in holiness is
> growth in our union with the risen Christ.
> But Christ lives and acts in His Church.
> Growth in union with the Church, deeper par-
> ticipation in the prayer life of the Church,
> in her sacramental life, in her other activi-
> ties, gives us a deeper sharing in the life
> and mind and prayer of Christ Himself. The
> life of a monk is immersed in the depth of the
> Church's life in Christ. The monk is essen-
> tially a vir ecclesiae.4

This description of the monastic transformation process
stresses the degree to which a new existence is created,
one that participates in the life of the risen Christ.
It also emphasizes that this new life is brought about
in a spiritual union with the Church as the Body of
Christ.

We can observe how life in the monastery is a
school of transformation by considering Anselm's own experience. Each stage of his development in the monastery was step toward perfection. He entered the monastery of Bec in 1059 when he was twenty-six years old.
His was not a life of abstract speculation or a search
for empirical knowledge for its own sake but a fully
engaged emotional and spiritual quest.5   In the monastery, Anselm studied and discussed important theological
matters with others and, most importantly, he prayed.
Anselm's prayers contributed to an important development
in the history of spirituality. B. Ward notes that
Anselm's prayers were "the answer to a new demand for
personal and more intimate forms of prayer," adding that

the fact that his friends requested him to write and
publish his prayers indicates "the reputation of Anselm
even as a young monk as a man of prayer, from whom
others were eager to learn."6

Anselm was at Bec only four years when he was
appointed prior or master over the novices. In this
position he assumed greater authority which presupposes
a higher degree of perfection and wisdom. Then, in
1078, following the death of Herlwin, the founder of the
monastery of Bec, Anselm was chosen to be abbot. He
became Father (and Mother) to the entire community.7 He
was renowned for the compassion and wisdom with which he
governed the monastery. In his conversation with the
monks, Anselm constantly emphasized the importance of
knowing God personally and directly rather than merely
knowing about God.8 So, in our reflection on Anselm's
path through the monastic hierarchy, we can see a change
in his functions--and his person--which indicates a
growing closer to God, Anselm's own self-transformation.

However, Anselm's most important transformation
occurred through the eucharistic spirituality that is
central to monastic life.9 The monastic discipline is
both a physical and spiritual preparation for human
transformation through the eucharist. Obedience, discipline, and fasting prepare the body for the change that
is to take place. Prayer and meditation also prepare
the soul for the move from the earthly to the heavenly
state. This preparation for transformation is seen
especially in Anselm's "Prayer Before Receiving the Body
and Blood of Christ: May I be worthy to be incorporated
into your body, 'which is the church,' so that I may be
your member and you may be my head, and that I may
remain in you and you in me. Then at the Resurrection
you will refashion the body of my humiliation according
to the body of your glory."10 The eucharist is the central focus of this transformation that occurs between
life on earth and life in heaven. For Anselm, the eucharist is the body of Christ; it is by eating Christ's
body that humans are being transformed from the earthly
to the heavenly state.

A major theological dispute took place in the
eleventh century that eventually led to the definition
of the change in the eucharistic elements as "transubstantiation." Lanfranc, Anselm's teacher and immediate
predecessor both as prior of the monastery at Bec and as
archbishop of Canterbury, was an important figure in
this debate. Lanfranc emphasized the complete objectivity of Christ's presence in the eucharist, main-

taining that even those who are sinners still receive the true body of Christ, i.e., the body that is the same as the fleshly body of Christ, who was born of Mary. This issue of the real presence of Christ is crucial because it prefigures the transformation that is at the heart of monastic life.

The description of eucharistic change as transubstantiation means that transformation is central to the liturgical mystery. Just as the bread and wine are changed into the body and blood of Christ, so the monks are changed from the image of the earthly man, Adam, into the image of the transformed man, Christ. Even in earthly existence, the body of Christ is available as the physical bread of heaven, and the words and teaching of Christ are present as the spiritual bread of heaven. In this devotional setting, the monks contemplate the physical and spiritual bread of heaven that is already in their midst. Their concentration is as much focused on heaven as it is focused on earth, and their future participation in the heavenly state is already anticipated in the eucharistic transformation that is occurring.

Anselm lived at the point in time where the eucharist was becoming the central sacrament.11 Baptism had been primary in the life of the early Church, when Christians were few in number. In the medieval Church, where the main concern was no longer conversion, the eucharist became primary in order to perfect the life of those who were already in the Church. From this perspective we can see why the eucharist, as a ritual of transformation and perfection, had such a great impact on Anselm's development as a monk and on his theology.

We have noted in general terms that the monastery is a school of transformation, an attempt to create another world. We have also considered briefly the important role that the eucharist plays in establishing the atmosphere of this setting and in bringing about the monastic transformation. These introductory comments are designed to place Anselm's thought in its proper context and to alert us to elements in his theology which are often overlooked. We have already indicated that the traditional emphasis placed on the best-known period of Anselm's life tends to overshadow the primary context of his theology, the medieval monastery. However, another factor divorces Anselm's work from its proper context. Anselm's nickname, the "Father of Scholasticism," should not lead us to imagine that his thought emerged as a product of "the schools." While it is true that Anselm was a prominent teacher at Bec, and that he turned the monastery into an even more famous intellectual center than it had been under Lanfranc, Anselm fit studies into the time left over from religious exercises. For Anselm, study was structured into the day of prayer. M. Charlesworth gives this description of a typical day at the monastery of Bec:

> Bec was a monastery following the Benedictine Rule and teaching, and learning had to be fitted into the time left over from the religious exercises (the Opus Dei) that occupied a good deal of the day. Thus the monks rose between midnight and 2 a.m. to chant the collection of psalms, lessons, and prayers known as Nocturns (later as Matins). This was followed by the office of Lauds, the whole night office taking about two hours. The monks then returned to bed until the first office of the day, known as Prime, which was said at about 6 a.m. in the summer and at daybreak in winter. The monks would then wash and go about their tasks until the time for the monastic or chapter Mass. Just before this Mass a light breakfast (mixtum) of bread with a little beer or wine would be taken. The chapter Mass was followed by the office of Terce, three hours after sunrise, and then the monks would assemble for half an hour in the chapter house for spiritual instruction and correction from the abbot and for the discussion of monastic business. The various manual and intellectual tasks would then be done. At about 12 a.m. High Mass would be sung, this being the most important part of the monastic day, and after the Mass, at about 2 p.m., the principal meal (cena) would be taken. The Benedictine Rule forbade the eating of meat, and for the most part the monks ate bread, fish, eggs, and cheese. After dinner the office of None was sung, and then the afternoon was given over to manual labour and to study and the copying of manuscripts in the scriptorium and reading room, which were usually in the walk attached to the monastery church, this being partially screened against the weather and having the floor covered with straw. At 5 p.m. the Office of Vespers was sung and then a small supper was served before the last office of the monastic day, Compline. The monks retired a little before 7 p.m.[12]

Charlesworth concludes from this schedule that "study and scholarly research were very much a secondary concern of twelfth-century monastic life."

In Vita Sancti Anselmi, Eadmer gives us a sense of Anselm's monastic life. He recounts the holiness and devotion of a great saint--his bodily discipline, his fasts, his prayers, and his vigils. Eadmer constantly reminds us of the depth of Anselm's feelings for matters of the spirit--the tears he shed in longing for union with God and bitter weeping over his sins and the sins of others.14 He also tells of Anselm's pastoral dedication, providing us with various accounts of Anselm's skill as a counselor, of his sensitivity to the spiritual needs of those he met. We see Anselm using holy guile to tame the unbridled spirit of a young man, leading him gradually to a mature and upright way of life.15 We see Anselm advising an abbot to deal more lovingly with the weaker souls in his charge, urging him to adapt his manner to their level of development. Anselm urges gentleness, kindness, compassion, cheerful encouragement, and a loving forbearance toward these weak souls.16 Eadmer describes how Anselm would spare nothing to make his guests at Bec comfortable, generously providing for their every need, sometimes to the point where he himself would have to do without food.17

Besides furnishing us with this general view of the life and character of the man who produced an extraordinary theological system, Eadmer also gives us an idea of how intimately Anselm's theology was related to his monastic life. According to Eadmer, it was while being "given up to God and to spiritual exercises" that Anselm struggled with the deep mysteries of faith. Eadmer offers the following description of the setting in which Anselm composed his theology after becoming prior of the monastery:

> And so it came about that, being continually given up to God and to spiritual exercises, he attained such a height of divine speculation, that he was able by God's help to see into and unravel many most obscure and previously insoluble questions about the divinity of God and about our faith, and to prove by plain arguments that what he said was firm and catholic truth. For he had so much faith in the Holy Scriptures, that he firmly and inviolably believed that there was nothing in them which deviated in any way from the path of solid truth. Hence he applied his whole

mind to this end, that according to his faith
he might be found worthy to see with the eye
of reason those things in the Holy Scriptures
which, as he felt, lay hidden in a deep
obscurity. Thus, one night it happened that
he was lying awake on his bed before matins
exercised in mind about these matters; and as
he meditated he tried to puzzle out how the
prophets of old could see both past and future
as if they were present and set them forth
beyond doubt in speech or writing. And, behold, while he was thus absorbed and striving
with all his might to understand this problem,
he fixed his eyes on the wall and-- right
through the masonry of the church and dormi-
tory--he saw the monks whose office it was to
prepare for matins going about the altar and
other parts of the church lighting the can-
dles; and finally he saw one of them take in
his hands the bell-rope and sound the bell to
awaken the brethren. At this sound the whole
community rose from their beds, and Anselm was
astonished at the thing which had happened.
From this he saw that it was a very small
thing for God to show to the prophets in the
spirit the things which would come to pass,
since God had allowed him to see with his
bodily eyes through so many obstacles the
things which then were happening.18

In this remarkable passage we see how, for Anselm,
spiritual exercises, meditation on Scripture, and
theological speculation merged inextricably into each
other. The spiritual exercises of the monastery form
the framework within which Anselm puzzles over the
mysteries of faith revealed in the Bible. Because of
his confidence in the reasonableness of the Scriptures
around which the spiritual exercises are centered, he
devotes himself night and day to seeing "with the eyes
of reason" the mysteries revealed to the Church in the
Bible. Here we perceive that Anselm's monastic life
helps to explain the unity of his method--a method that
does not recognize a gap between the truths of Scripture
and the truths arrived at by reason. This unity of
faith and speculation is grounded in Anselm's life as a
monk.

In the monastic setting, the liturgy is primary.
Devotion is the life context of thought, and thought at
its most profound level bursts into prayer. Prayer is
not opposed to thought; rather, it is the beginning and

end of Anselm's thought. It is not mere private prayer
that is the alpha and omega of Anselm's theological
thinking, but rather sacramental prayer in the context
of the monastic setting. For Anselm, prayer is a
liturgically inspired activity.

G. H. Williams has pointed out the liturgical and
sacramental character of Anselm's prayer as follows:
(1) Anselm's Orationes are influenced by the "I-style"
of the personal prayers of the priest which were beginning to appear in the missal as a result of the increase
in private masses; (2) in "Oratio ad sanctum Iohannem
Baptistam," Anselm describes the interrelationship of
the sacraments of baptism, eucharist, and penance; (3)
in "Oratio ad sanctum crucem," Anselm quotes the introit
from the Mass of the Holy Cross and speaks of the "rebirth into the new life of justice" as a result of the
daily eucharist rather than as the single event of baptism; (4) in "Oratio ad accipiendum corpus domini et
sanguinem," Anselm applies the key passage for Paul's
theology of baptism (Rom. 6:3 ff.) as dying, being
buried and being resurrected to his own theory of eucharistic redemption; (5) in "Oratio ad sanctum
Mariam," Anselm prays to Mary in her role as the media-
trix of redemption, who dispenses sacramental grace in
the Church; (6) in De Conceptu Virginali, Anselm sees
the sacrament of baptism as removing the sin of man's
nature (original sin), and he implies that the eucharist
incorporates the Christian into the sinless universal
humanity of Christ; (7) in "Meditatio redemptionis
humanae," Anselm describes the effect of baptism in
words placed in the mouth of Christ, and Anselm speaks
of the sacraments of eucharist and penance as removing
man's "personal" sins. This meditation also has vivid
language about eating the eucharistic bread, something
which we shall see more fully later.[19] From Williams's
observation, we gain a sense of the liturgical and
sacramental character of Anselm's prayer. This is important because it helps us to bear in mind the broadest
context of Anselm's theology; therefore, when we speak
of prayer as being the origin and goal of Anselm's
theology, we should remember that the prayer we are
talking about is itself shaped by the liturgy which
structured Anselm's religious life.

Fortunately, we do not have to speak only in general about the intimate relationship between Anselm's
theology and his life of prayer. Anselm furnishes us
with a very powerful instance of this close relationship
in Proslogion. In this work, Anselm's proof for the
existence of God is set in the context of prayer, pro-

viding us with a concrete example of how prayer and
thought are related. For example, the opening words of
the first chapter of <u>Proslogion</u> are an exhortation of
the mind to the contemplation of God:

> Come now, insignificant man, leave behind for
> a time your preoccupations; seclude yourself
> for a while from your disquieting thoughts.
> Turn aside now from heavy cares and disregard
> your wearisome tasks. Attend for a while to
> God and rest for a time in Him. Enter the
> inner chamber of your mind; shut out all else
> except God and whatever is of aid to you in
> seeking Him; after closing the chamber door,
> think upon your God. Speak now, my whole
> heart; speak now to God: I seek your coun-
> tenance; your countenance, O Lord, do I seek.
> So come now, Lord my God, teach my heart where
> and how to seek You, where and how to find
> you.20

From this introductory exhortation, we can see that the
atmosphere of devotion is the starting point even for
Anselm's most speculative intellectual endeavors, e.g.,
for his ontological argument for the existence of God.
Withdrawal from the burdens and cares of life's activity
is the prerequisite for thinking about God. And before
one moves into discursive thought about God's nature and
existence, it is necessary to spend some time quietly in
the presence of God to "rest for a little time in him."
It is necessary to pray before thinking, while thinking
and after thinking.

In this <u>Proslogion</u> prayer, Anselm goes on to
express his longing for the presence of God by asking
why the divine presence cannot be sensed if it is
everywhere. Anselm's passion and depth of feeling are
especially evident when he addresses this inaccessible
God whom he adores. Anselm is overwhelmed by the
reality of God and feels himself unworthy of the God he
loves. He also feels miserable because he is forced to
remain apart from the one he longs for. The powerful
language that Anselm employs here is that of a lover.
Here there is no uninvolved speculator, puzzling over an
insoluble riddle; Anselm cries out as one who is in
exile. Here we encounter the monk who feels "cast out
afar" (<u>longe projectus</u>) from the face of his lover whom
he "pants to see" (<u>anhelat videre</u>), to whom he "longs to
come" (<u>desiderat accedere</u>), whom he is "eager to find"
(<u>cupit invenire</u>), whom he "desires to seek" (<u>affectat</u>

quaerere).   Anselm goes from the heights of   this
passionate longing to the borderline of despair:

> O the wretched fate of man when he lost that
> end for which he was made!   O that hard and
> ominous fall! Alas, what he lost and what   he
> found, what vanished and what remained! He
> lost the happiness for which he was created
> and found a wretchedness for which he was not
> created. The necessary condition for happi-
> ness vanished and the sufficient condition for
> wretchedness remained. Man then ate the bread
> of angels for which he now hungers; and now he
> eats the bread of sorrows, which then he did
> not know.   Alas, the common mourning of all
> men, the universal lament of the sons of
> Adam! Adam burped with satiety; we sigh with
> hunger.   He abounded; we go begging.   He
> happily possessed and wretchedly deserted; we
> unhappily lack and wretchedly desire, while
> alas, remaining empty.21

Eadmer informs us about this period of turmoil as his
master struggled with the Proslogion argument, telling
us that Anselm was so troubled that he lost his desire
for food, drink, and sleep, and that it distracted him
from his religious exercises.   He feared that his pur-
suit might be a temptation of the devil and tried to
banish it from his mind.   It is too easy for us to
imagine only the serenity of monastic life when we think
of Anselm writing those profound works that have given
him such an important place in the history of theology
and philosophy. How quickly we can forget his prayers
of longing and confusion which express the condition of
his heart at the time he was struggling with the deep
mysteries of faith. Anselm's own words should constantly serve to remind us of the pain of love and the
agony of loss which surround even the most seemingly
abstract speculation.

     In this blackest hour, when he was so close to
despair, he still struggled to believe in the God whose
presence he no longer felt. At this point, some may
object that the sorrow and grief Anselm expresses in
Proslogion have to do more with the intellectual frustration than with the loss of his sense of the loving
presence of God.   For Anselm, there can be no clear
distinction between the volitional, emotional, and the
intellectual realms.   He approaches God through acts of
will, feeling, and intellect.   To Anselm, God is never
"a problem" but always his beloved,   whether he be

kneeling silently in the presence of God or actively trying to comprehend more about his beloved.

Thus, Anselm not only prays for insight into the mysteries of faith; he also prays to be rescued from the bitterness and despair that surround him. In this dark hour, Anselm speaks of himself as one in hunger, in poverty, in misery, in emptiness, bowed down. In this state of confusion, at the point of losing hope and struggling to banish tormenting thoughts, Anselm's mind suddenly becomes clear. Eadmer tells us that it was during matins that "the grace of God illuminated his heart" and "a great joy and exultation filled his inmost being."22 Now we have come full circle, seeing how Anselm's heart was fully engaged in every step of the Proslogion argument. He moved from the serenity of contemplation through the longing for an absent love through the pain of loss through the dryness of loneliness through the bitterness of despair to the exultation of reunion. Anselm's intellectual journey to theological insight was at the same time the spiritual journey to union with God.

This, then, is a concrete example of how thought and devotion are intimately joined in Anselm's life. There is no question of dispassionate speculation here. Anselm's entire life was involved in his struggle to arrive at the Proslogion argument. Devotion was both the origin and the goal of Anselm's thought; any interpretation that overlooks this life context will fail to appreciate the living force of Anselm's theology.

An awareness of the monastic setting is the prerequisite for grasping the transformation theme in Anselm's theology. Anselm's writing should first be viewed as a product of the monastic search for God guided by the liturgical life of the Church. The monastery as a devotional community whose members were dedicated to disciplines aimed at transformation is the necessary precondition for understanding Anselm's theology.

NOTES

1. L. Merton, "Reflections on Some Recent Studies of St. Anselm" _Monastic Studies_, v. 3 (1965), p. 234.

2. _PAM_, p. 91.

3. Ibid.

4. T. Merton, _The Monastic Journey_ (Kansas City, 1977), p. 23.

5. G. Olsen describes Anselm's spirituality as primarily contemplative in contrast to one of sentiment: "Anselm's approach is specifically Benedictine, for God is approached not through ecstacy nor through sentiment, but through monastic contemplation, contemplative reason (_ratio contemplatio_). This is a 'praying reason' in dialogue with the Truth, which moves unceasingly from meditation to prayer," ("Hans Urs von Balthasar and the Rehabilitation of St. Anselm's Doctrine of the Atonement," _Scottish Journal of Theology_, 34 [1981], p. 53). Here Olsen may be urging a too-sharp separation between contemplative reason and sentiment in Anselm's spiritual life.
R. Herrera appears to be more accurate when he says "St. Anselm makes no clear distinction between prayer, theology, logic and mysticism, but by including all, appears to transcend each one, taken individually," (_AA_ III, p. 143). B. Ward's observation about Anselm's prayers support Herrera's interpretation and would caution against a too-clear distinction between contemplation and sentiment _PAM_, pp. 58-59.

6. Ward, _PAM_, pp. 276-77. She adds that "it was through these prayers, and therefore as a spiritual guide, that Anselm first became known as a writer."

7. C. Bynum notes how maternal imagery was applied in the Middle Ages to male religious authority figures, especially the abbot, as well as to God and to Christ. She also observes that Anselm possibly influenced later writers in their use of maternal imagery.

Bynum says such maternal imagery expresses "a need for affectivity in the exercise of authority and in the creation of community, and a complex rhythm of renouncing ties with the world while deepening ties within the community and between the soul and God" (see "Jesus as Mother and Abbot as Mother: Some Themes in Twelfth-Century Cistercian Writing," Harvard Theological Review, 70 (1977), pp. 257-84).

8.   See G. R. Evans "St. Anselm and Knowing God" Journal of Theological Studies, 28 (1977), pp. 430-444.

9. In his article on Anselm and the liturgy, R. Amiet speaks eloquently of how Anselm stressed the importance of the eucharist in developing a profound sense of God. He sees the eucharist at the heart of the liturgy and the Church. Amiet summarizes the centrality of the eucharist in these words: "Or, pour nous chrétiens, la liturgie est essentiellement la célébration de l'Eucharistie, car, selon la forte parole de mon maître le Père de Lubac, 'si l'Eglise fait l'Eucharistie, c'est l'Eucharistie qui fait l'Eglise'" (AA III, p. 294).

10.   Anselm's "Prayer Before Receiving the Body and Blood of Christ" (S III, 10, 18-21; PAM 101).

11. This point will be discussed at length in chapter 8.

12.   St. Anselm's Proslogion (Oxford, 1965), pp. 12-13.

13. In 1079, when Eadmer was only nineteen years old, he met Anselm for the first time. At that time Anselm had recently become abbot of Bec and was visiting Canterbury in this capacity. After this meeting they were not to meet again for another thirteen years; thus, Eadmer was not with Anselm at the time he wrote the Proslogion. Nevertheless, R. Southern holds in high regard Eadmer's account of the origin of Proslogion, calling it "one of his most valuable contributions to the history of Anselm's philosophical development" (VSA p. 29). Southern says that the account of Anselm's difficulties in composing Proslogion could only come from Anselm himself.

14.   VSA, pp. 13-14.

15.   Ibid., pp. 16-17.

16.   Ibid., pp. 37-40.

17. Ibid., pp. 46-48.

18. Ibid., pp. 12-13.

19. For Williams's substantiation of the points listed here, see Anselm: Communion and Atonement, pp. 26-62.

20. "Eia nunc, homuncio, fuge paululum occupationes tuas, absconde te modicum a tumultuosis cogitationibus tuis. Abice nunc onerosas curas, et postpone laboriosas distentiones tuas. Vace aliquantulum deo, et requiesce aliquantulum in eo. Intra in cubiculum mentis tuae, exclude omnia praeter deum et quae te iuvent ad quaerendum eum, et clauso ostio quaere eum. Dic nunc, totum cor meum, dic nunc deo: Quaero vultum tuum; vultum tuum, domine, requiro.
Eia nunc ergo tu, domine deus meus, doce cor meum ubi et quomodo te quaerat, ubi et quomodo te inveniat" (Pros. I; S I, 97, 4-98, 2; AC I, 91).

21. "O misera sors hominis, cum hoc perdidit ad quod factus est. O durus et dirus casus ille! Heu, quid perdidit et quid invenit, quid abscessit et quid remansit! Perdidit beatitudinem ad quam factus est, et invenit miseriam propter quam factus non est. Abscessit sine quo nihil felix est, et remansit quod per se nonnisi miserum est. Manducabat tunc homo panem angelorum quem nunc esurit, manducat nunc panem dolorum, quem tunc nesciebat. Heu publicus luctus hominum, universalis planctus filiorum Adae! Ille ructabat saturitate, noc suspiramus esurie. Ille abundabat, nos mendicamus. Ille feliciter tenebat et miser deseruit, nos infeliciter egemus et miserabiliter desideramus, et heu, vacui remanemus" (Pros. I; S I, 98, 16-25; AC I, 91-92).

22. VSA, p. 30.

3

TRANSFORMATION AND THE FLESH MOTIF

A Childhood Dream

Chapter 2 established the context within which certain fundamental, though often overlooked, elements in St. Anselm's theology emerge into clearer view. Anselm's principal concern is that of a monk in search of God. His theology seeks a vision of God that lies somewhere between earthly faith and heavenly realization. Anselm's spiritual quest expresses the monastic goal of a transformed way of life, especially as that new life is formed by the eucharist, the flesh of Christ. For many modern people it is difficult to understand what Anselm's preoccupation with human transformation means. Today we tend to describe the soul's life not in terms of the sacraments and salvation but in terms of "psychological transformation." Hence, a brief digression into the modern psyschology of transformation shall bring into clearer focus what is at stake in this central motif of Anselm's theology. Since the thought of Carl Jung is so important in the twentieth-century psychology of human transformation, it might be helpful to consider how he would interpret what Anselm is doing at the monastery of Bec and how that eleventh-century transformation process might be understood today. Let us imagine for a moment how Jung would describe Anselm's monastery and transformation teaching:

Dr. Jung. "The first thing that is evident here in Anselm's monastery is the great amount of time devoted to religious exercises. The monks chant the psalms and say prayers in the night. They say the office at daybreak; there is a mass three hours after daybreak and again at noon. In the evening they say vespers and compline. It is clear that their entire day is structured by their life of prayer. The world of God and the saints is at the center of their consciousness. I would say that this structuring of their day is the externalization of the mental life of these monks. To put it another way, the monastery represents the constellation of the monastic psyche as it is reflected in the external world. And at the center of this psychological constellation is the mass and eucharist.

As I see it, the eucharist symbolizes the goal of transformation (becoming one mind with Christ) and is the symbolic center of the monastic day. This point is highlighted in Anselm's doctrine of transformation."

"Now, of course, our views of transformation differ, but there are basic, underlying similarities that I shall point out shortly. According to Anselm's view, the human will and flesh are at the heart of transformation. He speaks of the goal of life as that state of will which is upright for its own sake. This refers to a psyche that is oriented by and committed to the divine will. Human motivation in this case is not directed toward external goals but is focused on the integrity of the psyche itself and the divine presence therein. Anselm realizes that the human will is moved to act by certain dispositions that I would call 'attitudes.' There is the disposition toward happiness that is always associated with the will, and there is the disposition toward justice that can be separated from the will. This disposition of the will toward justice is an extremely important factor in understanding Anselm's goal of transformation, and it has a certain correspondence to my own concept of the collective unconscious. The disposition of the will toward justice represents a collective psychic element that influences favorably the individual's will and action. This disposition plays a role in the individual psyche that is comparable to what I have called the self-archetype, the God-image in man that orients and orders psychic activity.

"Now, for Anselm, when this disposition toward justice is absent from the will, the human being is in a state of unrighteousness where the will does not act correctly. That psychic state of disordered willing that Anselm attributes to the influence of Adam's sin is similar to the activity of the shadow-archetype (the negative and underdeveloped aspects of the psyche). More generally, the state of disordered willing that occurs when the will is not governed by the disposition toward justice is comparable to the activity of the autonomous complexes that interrupt and often subvert conscious intentions and goals. Thus, both in the case where the disposition toward justice is present and in the case where it is absent, we have an example of universal, collective psychic factors that influence the individual psyche. And the transformation process as understood by both Anselm and myself involves recognizing that the individual participates in a collective or transpersonal drama. Whereas I view the major fig-

ures in this drama as the archetypes that emerge from
the unconscious, Anselm understands these collective
figures as they appear in Christian doctrine. For him
transformation means moving from an identification with
the defective will of Adam (which does not possess the
disposition toward justice) to participation in the life
of Christ (which does possess the disposition toward
justice).

"Thus Anselm's understanding of human transformation is rooted in Christian doctrine and in his theory
of the human will. This is the theoretical foundation
of the discipline that is such an integral part of his
monastic experience. But there is an even more central
experiential element that finds expression in his transformation doctrine. As we observe the monastic day, we
see that the eucharist is at the core of Anselm's schedule. The eucharist is also essential to explaining how
the monastic transformation of the will occurs. The
process might be described like this:

"The body of Christ that the monks worship and
consume in the sacrament of the eucharist is the means
by which they acquire and strengthen the disposition of
will toward justice which is the key to transformation.
Consequently, the eucharist is the concrete method that
brings about human transformation for Anselm. Again, I
shall try to relate this aspect of transformation to my
theory of the collective unconscious. The sacrament of
the eucharist permits Anselm to participate in the upright will of Christ. This participation in the archetypal figure of Christ is in terms of psychological
function, equivalent to the goal of the individuation
process I have described where the self-archetype
emerges from the conscious confrontation of unconscious
contents. Of course, the method of the process that I
have described is considerably different from the meditative and sacramental process Anselm describes; yet in
both cases, a universal, collective factor influences
the individual person. For Anselm, Christ is actually
present in the eucharistic bread and so the real physical union with the body of Christ through sacramental
eating also effects the union of wills which is central
to his view of transformation. More specifically, the
eucharist adds to the will, or strengthens in the will,
the disposition toward justice. This is like sharing
Christ's own attitude, which is the essential factor
behind willing and doing the good. While Anselm's goal
of transformation is expressed differently from my own,
I also see that goal as an attitude of attention to the
God-image (self archetype) as it manifests itself in the

psyche. I see this expression of the divine numen in the individual's psyche as a type of participation in a universal psychological field that I have called the collective unconscious."

Because of Jung's work, we can better understand the essential elements of Anselm's view of transformation. We might also observe here that, in his study of human development, Jung looks at dreams as a guide to the inner life and to the process of transformation. According to Jung, childhood dreams can have great significance by foretelling in symbolic fashion the dreamer's future life course.1   We have already seen that Anselm was very young when he first displayed his interest in the monastic journey to God, but there is an even earlier experience recorded that reflects his spiritual longing, a childhood dream.

Again we have Eadmer to thank that this important early experience of Anselm was not lost to history. R. D. Church, an influential Anselm biographer, believes that this boyhood dream was doubtless from Anselm himself.   Here is the text in which Eadmer preserves this dream:

> Now Anselm, when he was a small boy, lent a ready ear to his mother's conversation, so far as his age allowed. And hearing that there is one God in heaven who rules all things and comprehends all things, he—being a boy bred among mountains—imagined that heaven rested on the mountains, that the court of God was there, and that the approach to it was through the mountains.   When he had turned this over often in his mind, it happened one night that he saw a vision, in which he was bidden to climb to the top of the mountain and hasten to the court of the great king, God.   But then, before he began to climb, he saw in the plain through which he was approaching the foot of the mountain, women—serfs of the king—who were reaping the corn, but doing so carelessly and idly. The boy was grieved and indignant at their laziness, and resolved to accuse them before their lord the king. Then he climbed the mountain and came to the royal court, where he found God alone with his steward. For, as he imagined, since it was autumn he had sent his household to collect the harvest.   The boy entered and was summoned by the Lord. He approached and sat at his feet.

> The Lord asked him in a pleasant and friendly
> way who he was, where he came from and what he
> wanted.   He replied to the questions as best
> he could. Then, at God's command, the whitest
> of bread was brought him by the steward, and
> he refreshed himself with it in God's pres-
> ence. The next day therefore, when he re-
> called to his mind's eye all that he had seen,
> like a simple and innocent boy he believed
> that he had been in heaven and that he had
> been fed with the bread of God, and he asser-
> ted as much to others in public.2

In this particular dream, what will become two of Anselm's lifetime preoccupations are clearly expressed:
the journey to God and the eucharist as the transforming
bread of heaven.   Eadmer's introduction to the dream
provides the context for understanding the dream
symbols.   As a small boy Anselm listened carefully to
his mother who transmitted to him the Christian world
view.   From the vantage point of that world view the
main elements of this dream seem to make sense. The
world his mother describes is one that has contact with
divine realities and where God participates as the mind
that rules the order of the universe.

    The mountains in the dream appear to be the
mountains of Aosta, Italy, but in the young Anselm's
mind they are also the mountains that lead to heaven.
As we enter the dream, we see that Anselm is moved to
make a journey to the court of God.   Here his life is
symbolically portrayed as a journey to the Divine, an
image that guides the course of his entire life. When
Anselm begins his dream journey he notices some women
who are serfs of the king.   It is interesting that this
minor aspect of the dream is preserved.   It shows the
women reaping the corn in a careless manner. Without
more information it is difficult to tell whether this
dream image refers to Anselm's early impressions of
women in his society or to certain "female" aspects of
his own soul.   In either case, Anselm is disturbed by
this part of the dream.   Although he intends to report
the idle workers to the king we hear no more about them
after he begins his ascent.

    The ascent of the mountain is not described in any
detail.   We have only the brief words of Eadmer that he
climbed the mountain, but we can imagine that the mountain to heaven in this dream was inspired by Anselm's
local Becca Di Nona, a towering mountain whose summit
often extends into the clouds. The image of Anselm's

journey to God is that of scaling a mountain. The
adventure and danger of climbing such a large mountain
provides a vivid image of Anselm's inner view of the
meaning of life. We see here something that is confirmed by his statements regarding the attractiveness of
the monastic life: for Anselm the only life that cap-
tures his complete interest is a life filled with the
purpose of being with and seeing God.3

Now we come to the image of God in this dream.
Anselm finds God alone with only a steward present.
Anselm reasons that the rest of the household has gone
to harvest the corn. The God Anselm finds in this dream
is not a God ministered to by countless angels and
saints, but rather he is alone and waiting for the
harvest. We might also reflect further on the harvest
image. The occasion when Anselm sees God is harvestime,
autumn. In the dream there is a close connection between the visio Dei and the fruit of the harvest. The
images of the harvest and of autumn both suggest that
the vision of God comes toward the end of the process of
life just as the harvest comes at the end of the growing
season and autumn arrives near the end of the year.

Anselm enters the court and is called by the
Lord. These dream images are rich in intimations concerning the relation of the person to God. Anselm is
invited to the court of heaven, but he himself must make
the climb. There is much that the individual must do to
further the movement toward God. Anselm's negative
attitude toward the lazy serfs who are reaping the
harvest also emphasizes his view of the work and effort
necessary to serve God. But the relation between the
individual and God is not characterized solely by a
person's initiative. In the dream God summons Anselm
and brings him to the direct vision of God in a "plea-
sant and friendly" (jocunda affabilitate) way. God is
approachable and draws man toward him.4 So there is a
certain mutuality that characterizes the relationship
between man and God in this dream. God asks Anselm
questions, wanting to know more about him. This can
also be viewed as a symbol of God's interest in the
individual. More generally, this interaction can be
seen to symbolize the way God approaches man, i.e., with
questions. God asks Anselm what he wants. There is no
answer to this question as Eadmer reports the dream. We
may speculate about what this means, for there are a
number of possibilities. Does it mean that the answer
is not given in the dream itself? Does it mean that the
answer is too obvious to require any comment? (Everyone
knows why man strives to reach God). Or is the question

answered in the next sequence in the dream? If we
contemplate the dream carefully it appears that this
last possibility is the likely one.

    In the scene that follows God's questioning of
Anselm there is a clue to what Anselm wanted. We do not
know whether Anselm's dream actually produced the answer
"the bread of heaven" in his reply to God's question.
But we do have the record of the dream itself to indicate the meaning and end of Anselm's journey to heaven:
to receive the radiant bread of heaven. According to
Eadmer: "Then, at God's command, the whitest of bread
was brought him by the steward, and he refreshed himself
with it in God's presence." This phrase, the whitest,
or most shining, of bread (panis nitidissimus) also
appears in another passage in Eadmer's Life of Anselm
and that context may further clarify this reference. In
that case Anselm as a young man had set out on a journey
from home and was crossing the mountains with a small
group of people. Their provisions were gone and it
appeared that they might starve to death. At the point
of death, one member of Anselm's group miraculously
discovers this "whitest of bread" and it provides the
nourishment necessary to sustain them on the journey.
In this instance, the radiant bread is a miraculous food
that preserves life when death appears inevitable.

    We might also look to Anselm's own thought and
life to shed further light on the heavenly bread
symbol. As already noted in the second chapter, Anselm
lived and wrote in the century when the question
concerning the nature of the divine presence in the
eucharist was vigorously debated. Anselm's intellectual
master, Lanfranc, was chiefly responsible for establishing the orthodox view that God is actually present in
the transformed eucharistic bread. Already in this
childhood dream there appears the theme of eating the
bread of heaven in the presence of God. Regardless how
we interpret the radiant bread of heaven symbol in this
dream, the overall symbolism certainly calls attention
to his future goal of journeying to God. Anselm sees
himself able to climb the mountain of life to heaven and
to see God face to face. This shows a great deal of
optimism about man's relation to God. This childhood
dream highlights a crucial theme that underlies all of
Anselm's life and theology, the transformation of the
human being.

    Thus far in this chapter we have examined human
transformation, a crucial but generally neglected aspect
of Anselm's theology. This theme lies at the heart of

Anselm's theological system and is even symbolically
portrayed in a dream from his earliest years. The
essence of Anselm's transformation motif can be summarized in this way: Human beings are transformed by a
sacramental and meditative process that changes the
human will at the most basic level of "attitude" or
disposition of the will. This change occurs as a result
of being incorporated into the flesh and will of Christ
in the eucharist. Even from the brief overview of
Anselm's theology provided in this chapter, it can be
seen that flesh is central to his understanding of human
transformation in that it initiates the individual into
a transpersonal, spiritual drama. And, if this theme of
the flesh is central to Anselm's view of transformation
and the monastic character of his theology, we might
expect that it has been dealt with thoroughly in Anselm
scholarship. But this is not the case. The role of the
flesh and the transformation theme associated with it
have generally been neglected. Let us determine exactly
how and to what extent this theme has been dealt with in
the Anselm literature to date.

State of the Question

In the past, Anselm's view of the flesh had been
discussed only as a secondary issue within the larger
framework of other doctrines, e.g., will, original sin,
atonement, and the eucharist. Two works published
during the first period of twentieth-century Anselm
scholarship have some bearing on the concept of flesh
in Anselm's theology. Both P. Toner and E. Lohmeyer see
the possibility of Anselm's positive view of the flesh
in their examininations of Anselm's doctrines of will
and of original sin. For example, in the article, "St.
Anselm's Definition of Original Sin," Toner clarifies
the theological background that supports Anselm's view
of the neutrality of the flesh.[5] Toner argues that
Anselm refutes the Augustinian theory of original sin
which held that concupiscence constitutes the principal
element in the essence of original sin.[6] He points out
that Anselm replaced this definition of original sin
with one stressing the negative condition of will rather
than the negative condition of flesh. Toner then shows
how Anselm's definition of original sin as the "lack of
required justice" is in keeping with Anselm's view that
all sin is essentially in the human will. But Toner
fails to draw the corresponding conclusion that, for
Anselm, the flesh need not be considered as a simply
negative concept since it is not irrevocably tied to the
definition of original sin. While Toner does not ex-

plore the significance of Anselm's original sin doctrine for the concept of flesh, he does emphasize that the theological framework in which Anselm considers the flesh is essentially neutral.

Lohmeyer deals primarily with Anselm's doctrine of will from a philosophical point of view.7 Although Lohmeyer did not directly consider the concept of flesh in Anselm's thought, he makes important observations about the metaphysics of human will which throw light on the notion of flesh. What he sees with particular clarity is that Anselm's teaching about the affections of the will is fundamental to understanding the condition of good or evil in the will. He builds on this insight to show that, for Anselm, the material side of man is capable of becoming good, and that man's natural desire for well-being (affectio ad volendum commodum) is good when joined to the desire for justice (affectio ad volendum iustitiam). While Lohmeyer does not draw strict conclusions about the nature of the flesh, he does clarify the metaphysical foundation Anselm established for his positive view of flesh. This first stage of the secondary source material on Anselm's concept of flesh is really only background to an understanding of that concept.

The second stage in the literature begins to deal with that aspect of flesh which makes it so important to Anselm's theology, namely, the participatory character of flesh. The studies of H. Rondet and M. Nédoncelle, written for the Anselm Congress held in Normandy in 1959, represent this stage.

Rondet only touches upon the participatory aspect of flesh in contrasting Anselm's view of original sin with that of St. Augustine.8 He also observes that Anselm emphasized the essential role of the will in original sin while Augustine focused on concupiscence as the mode of transmitting original sin (reiterating the point made by Toner some fifty years earlier). Rondet notes that Anselm's perspective on original sin opened the way for the acceptance of the immaculate conception of Mary since Anselm did not think of the transmission of original sin primarily in terms of concupiscence. Although Rondet believes that, for Anselm, the flesh itself was not the cause of original sin, he does not examine what role the flesh did play in transmitting original sin.

Nédoncelle also deals briefly with the participatory character of the flesh.9 He points out that the distinction between personal and seminal (material or causal) existence was the way Anselm explained the influence of Adam on all men of the human race. Whereas all men were in themselves "personally," they were in Adam "seminally." While Nédoncelle notes that the common origin of their flesh is for Adam's descendants the principle of participation in Adam, he is concerned only with the philosophical implications of this for the definition of the human person.

Nédoncelle also observes that this communication between nature and person makes little sense from the perspective of Aristotelian thought; rather it should be seen in relationship to Neoplatonic thought. Although he goes on to indicate how Anselm added to this doctrine of participation through heredity by using the metaphors of family and serfdom to describe this human solidarity, he does not examine further the character of this participation or specify its interior relationship to the human will. This last point is especially regrettable since Nédoncelle sees Anselm's specific contribution to the notion of person as being the ideas of liberty and rectitude, both of which are the foundation of Anselm's doctrine of will. Although he recognizes the controlling function of rectitude in Anselm's definition of will, he does not relate this rectitude to his previous observations about the participatory character of the human race. Had he done so, he might have made important observations about the relationship between persona and the flesh.

Besides the articles by Rondet and Nédoncelle, there is another work that belongs to this second stage of twentieth-century literature. The basis of G. H. Williams's volume, Communion and Atonement, was actually prepared in 1956, although it was published some four years later. This work is characteristic of the second period in that it is deeply concerned with the Church life and practices that inspired Anselm's redemptive theory. Williams argues that Anselm's doctrine of redemption depends on the realist-eucharistic theory of the eleventh century. This hypothesis emphasizes the importance of the concept of flesh since Anselm's redemptive theory is then seen as the theological explanation of an ecclesiastical fact: in the redemption, Christ provides sinful men with his saving body, concretely presented by the Church in the eucharist. Yet Williams does not investigate the systematic implications of his hypothesis. Thus, the second stage in the literature referring to Anselm's view of the flesh is valuable because of its concern with the participa-

tory character of the flesh and because of its attention
to the life of faith as the inspiration for Anselm's
theology.

We have already observed that the third stage in
Anselm scholarship is marked by attention to the nature
of Anselm's theological system. The major works that
take up that primary question make only passing reference to Anselm's view of the flesh. As we look briefly
at the three major systematic works in this period
(those of Pouchet, Kohlenberger, and Hopkins), we find
that they make observations about Anselm's view of the
flesh that support the contributions of the previous two
periods of Anselm scholarship.

R. Pouchet, for example, is primarily concerned
with the notion of rectitude in Anselm's thought; he
also makes valuable observations about the flesh in
relation to rectitude.10 Drawing largely from Anselm's
De Conceptu Virginali, he shows that the flesh as the
human body cannot be considered negative in itself
because sin lies only in the will. Consequently, the
transmission of original sin must be seen in terms of
the vicissitudes of the human will, not in terms of the
corrupted concupiscence that generates the infant. Here
Pouchet correctly stresses the neutrality of the flesh
by showing that original sin is a lack of rectitude in
the will, and that through sin Adam lost the power to
transmit original rectitude by means of the flesh.
According to Anselm, man's flesh did undergo a permanent
corruption, but this corruption must be seen as the loss
of Adam's original power to transmit rectitude through
propagation. This points to an important aspect of the
concept of flesh which Pouchet did not investigate, the
flesh as the instrument by which men participate in the
"natural will."

In Similitudo und Ratio, H. Kohlenberger suggests
that the physical side of man is not given much weight
in Anselm's thought. Kohlenberger compares the fleshly
dimension of man's being to the aspect of sound in human
speech. He states that Anselm attends primarily to the
spiritual aspects of man's being and his speech.11 The
true essence of man, according to Kohlenberger's interpretation of Cur Deus Homo II/VII, is the spirit. Although Anselm does not devote a separate work to the
flesh, it is not the case that Anselm fails to deal
seriously with the physical dimension of man, as Kohlenberger suggests. On the contrary, that concept is given
proper weight and is crucial to an understanding of his
theological system, as we shall see.

Kohlenberger also notes that Anselm follows the general thrust of medieval thought in viewing rationality as the defining characteristic of man's being.12 Kohlenberger quotes Anselm's <u>Cur Deus Homo</u>, pointing out that Anselm follows Boethius's definition of man as a rational nature. It is without question that Anselm holds such a view of man.13 But in <u>Monologion</u>, <u>Cur Deus Homo</u>, and <u>De Grammatico</u>, another aspect of the definition of man is brought out, mortality, since man is "<u>animal rationale mortale</u>." Kohlenberger correctly observes that in the context of <u>Cur Deus Homo</u>, Anselm wonders whether this latter definition of man is accurate since mortality does not belong to the essence of man according to the Christian doctrine of creation. For Anselm, mortality belongs only to man's corrupted nature. Unfortunately Kohlenberger does not consider the connection between flesh and mortality, a consideration that might have led him to see the important place of flesh in the definition of man as "<u>ein endliches Vernunftwesen</u>."14

J. Hopkins's volume on Anselm also includes some valuable observations about the flesh.15 Hopkins correctly observes that Anselm's view of the body-soul relationship is not Platonistic; for Anselm, the whole man includes his material as well as his rational nature. He underscores Anselm's distinction between the state of man before and after the Fall: before the Fall, Adam had both an immortal body and an immortal soul; after the Fall, the body became subject to death and exerted a corrupting influence on the soul. Thus, Hopkins recognizes that, for Anselm, the body is an integral part of the definition of man and that <u>veritas humanae naturae</u> (true human nature) includes an immortal and incorrupt body. Hopkins notes that the body's original immortality differed from the soul's immortality. Commenting on <u>Monologion</u> 69, he says that the soul had to remain immortal so that it could fulfill its <u>raison d'être</u>, to love God forever, even beyond the death of the body. The most important aspect of Hopkins's discussion of the flesh is his stress on the essential value of the body, recognizing that for Anselm the intermediate bodiless existence between physical death and resurrection is neither the person (<u>persona</u>) nor the human being (<u>homo, humana natura</u>).

From this brief account we can see that the works of Pouchet, Kohlenberger, and Hopkins actually devote little time to Anselm's view of the flesh. Pouchet recognizes the essential neutrality of the flesh; Kohlenberger suggests that Anselm's theological system

spares little attention to the flesh; Hopkins stresses
that, for Anselm, the flesh is an integral part of the
definition of man.   But besides these major systematic
studies there are some articles that deserve mention.

        R. Roques's study of the prayers and meditations
within the Anselm corpus touched upon a very important
element of the concept of flesh, its reference to the
affections and desires of the heart.16 The particular
value of this work lies in its awareness of the positive
role of the concept of flesh in Anselm's prayers.
Roques notes correctly that the flesh is closely related
to the heart as the center of affection and that both
flesh and heart operate in a way that is quite different
from the activity of reason. Roques argues that the
heart involves itself in the body more directly than
does reason, but both the heart and reason imprint
themselves in the body and are spontaneously expressed
by it. Roques further notes that the flesh provides
metaphors for expressing the longings and desires of the
heart in prayer. While Roques has a positive appreciation of the use of the concept of flesh in Anselm's
prayers, he does not apply this insight to any of the
other writings in Anselm's complete works, nor does he
systematically explore the implications of this "language of the flesh" in regard to Anselm's psychology of
the human will.   Yet Roques's observations about the
language of the flesh are very important to an understanding of Anselm's system as we shall see in a consideration of the motif level of Anselm's theological
system.

        G. R. Evans discusses briefly an aspect of the
flesh that is central to Anselm's understanding of
redemption.17   He notes how Anselm uses the close
resemblance between mankind and angels to develop a
deeper understanding of the workings of the human will.
Evans points out that Anselm assumes in De Casu Diaboli
that the will is essentially the same in man and in
angels so the primary concern of that work is not really
the fall of Satan so much as the fall of man. Despite
this basic similarity between man and angels, Evans
correctly observes that there is also an essential
difference between them--humans are generated through
the flesh while angels are directly created by God as
individuals and not as part of a race. Evans identifies
this difference in mode of generation as the reason why
angels could not be redeemed as humans could--because no
one being could stand for all of them as was the case
for mankind. This is indeed a key to understanding the
positive role of flesh in human redemption but Evans

does not develop this insight further, nor does he
relate it to other works in Anselm's entire theological
system.

In a more recent article, G. Heyer, Jr. reiterates
some of the observations made by Williams on the role of
the flesh in Anselm's view of the eucharist.18 Heyer
states that the eucharist is the means by which believers are incorporated into the justice of Christ. He
relates the justice contained in the flesh of Christ to
the restoration of the fallen human will. Perhaps more
clearly than Williams, he connects the eucharist with
the justice that is missing in the human will after
original sin, but he does not specify the general relationship between the flesh and the dispostions of the
will. In other words, he does not explore the role of
flesh in Anselm's overall theological system.

One final article should be mentioned in this
literature survey. In an article on Martin Luther, L.
Murphy explains the lasting impact of Anselm's explanation of the transmission of original sin.19 Thir-
teenth-century theology followed Anselm in considering
the transmission of original sin as the privation of
original justice in those propagated from Adam. Later,
Luther also shared this view, rejecting the Augustinian
notion that lustful concupiscence is the essential factor in transmitting original sin. Murphy highlights
what Toner had already noted many years before: there
is no vice necessarily associated with the flesh. Evil
is essentially a lack of justice in the will, not a
defect in the flesh. And, like Toner, Murphy does not
draw any further conclusions regarding the significance
of the original sin doctrine for understanding the role
of flesh in Anselm's theological system.

There is agreement that Anselm utilizes flesh as a
neutral term. It is clear from the body of secondary
literature that flesh can indicate evil, as in "the
flesh warring against the spirit." But this literature
also perceives that flesh can refer to virtue as in "the
flesh of Christ." This scholarship sees that, in
Anselm's doctrine of original sin, the flesh plays a
role in transmitting original sin, but the relationship
of its role in the original sin doctrine to its role in
other of Anselm's doctrines is yet to be specified.
Within this secondary literature there has also been
some interest in the participatory character of the
flesh, in the relationship of Anselm's concept of flesh
to the eucharist, and in the flesh as a source of
metaphorical language in Anselm's prayers. But none of

these points has been related to the overall meaning of the concept of flesh within the context of Anselm's total theological system.

While these valuable insights can be found in the secondary source material, the works just reviewed have not focused on Anselm's concept of flesh as such, nor have they explored systematically the relation of his concept of flesh to other controlling ideas in his theology. This study will attempt to fill this lacuna in Anselm scholarship by devoting itself directly to the concept of flesh in Anselm's theology. This study will also try to show the character of Anselm's theological system in light of this illuminated concept of flesh because flesh, for Anselm, is not just a single doctrine but a concept that operates as a common and unifying term in all of the major loci of his theology and a motif symbol that evokes the meaning of his entire theological system. In this chapter we have attempted to show how central the transformation motif is to the thrust of Anselm's theology. As we attend to the role of the concept of flesh in this analysis, we shall also be drawn to see more clearly how transformation is a vital concern of Anselm's theology. Because these two motifs are inextricably bound together, the term "transformation complex" is used to designate the complex of ideas associated with flesh in Anselm's work.

NOTES

1.   C. Jung, The Symbolic Life (Princeton, 1976), pp. 229-37.

2. VSA, pp. 4-5. Church's comment re this text: Saint Anselm (London, 1905), p. 14.

3.   Dreams of climbing a mountain are rather frequent and the mountain image is also used clinically and experimentally in projective tests to determine a person's level of aspiration regarding whatever the visualized mountain symbolizes to him or to her. The obstacles that an individual finds impeding the climb are diagnostic in symbolic terms of the psychological hindrances that impede growth (see R. Assagioli, Psychosynthesis [New York, 1982], p. 295). In this dream the mountain represents in Anselm's own terms, the "way to God."

4.   In chapter 2 we mentioned that this view of God as a friend also influenced what has been called the Anselmian revolution in prayer. In this movement of Christian piety, there is a new element of love and understanding.   In the older Christus victor piety, the act of salvation is more remote and the divinity of the God-man is stressed. Anselm's prayers as well as his redemptive theology stress the human elements of the God-man.

5.   P. Toner, Irish Theological Quarterly, 3 (1908), pp. 425-36.

6. Ibid., pp. 425-26.

7.   E. Lohmeyer, Die Lehre vom Willen bei Anselm von Canterbury (Lucka, 1914).

8. H. Rondet, "Grâce et péché: L'Augustinisme de saint Anselme," SB, pp. 155-69.

9. M. Nédoncelle, "La notion de personne dans l'oeuvre de saint Anselme," SB, pp. 31-43.

10.   R. Pouchet, La rectitudo chez saint Anselme (Paris, 1964).

11. "Der Mensch als sprachliches Wesen wird bei Anselm hauptsaechlich in seiner Geistigkeit   betrachtet,

der philosophiehistorischen Tradition gemaess.   Die Leiblichkeit des Menschen, die mit dem sprachlichen Laut als einer sinnenfaelligen Aeusserung des Gedankens verglichen werden koennte, wird nicht beachtet.   Die Leiblichkeit wird ueberhaupt nur nebenbei zur Erlaeuterung des Menschseins in der hypostatischen Union ausgesagt: 'quemadmodum corpus et anima rationalis conveniunt in unum hominem' (CDH II/VII)" (H. Kohlenberger, _Similitudo und Ratio_ [Bonn, 1972], p. 119).

12.   Ibid., pp. 117-18.

13.   CDH II, 1; S II, 98, 4: Homo ergo qui rationalis natura est, factus est."   DG XII; S I, 156, 34-35: "Homo habens rationalitatem."

14.   Perhaps more important than the passages that Kohlenberger cites to describe Anselm's definition of man as _animal rationale_ are the passages that he does not consider in the chapter "Der Mensch als _animal rationale_" (pp. 117-20) namely, those references to man as both physical and rational (_Mon._ XVII, _DCV_ II). Attention to the passages joining the rational and material sides of man would have given a more complete understanding of man as _animal rationale_ in Kohlenberger's study.

15.   J. Hopkins, "Doctrine of Man, Freedom and Evil," in _A Companion to the Study of St. Anselm_ (Minneapolis, 1972), pp. 122-86.

16.   R. Roques, "Structure et caractères de la prière Anselmienne," SR, pp. 119-87.

17.   G. R. Evans, "Why the Fall of Satan?" _Recherches de Théologie Ancienne et Médiévale_, 45 (1978), pp. 130-46.

18.   G. Heyer, Jr., "Anselm Concerning the Human Role in Salvation" in _Texts and Testaments_, ed. W. March (San Antonio, 1980), pp. 163-72.

19.   L. Murphy, "Martin Luther's Marginal Notes to the Sentences of Peter Lombard on the Transmission of Original Sin," _Science et Esprit_, 33 (1981) pp. 55-71.

4

QUESTIONS OF METHOD

Anselm's System

Before entering into this systematic study, some questions demand to be answered. Anselm's writings span a thirty-year period. Over such a long time, most creative thinkers would change their ideas. St. Augustine, for instance, felt obliged to write a book of retractions toward the end of his life, restating and modifying earlier views. What right do we have to assume that Anselm intended his works to fit together into some kind of systematic unity? The answer to this question comes at least in part from Anselm's own statements.

Anselm prefaced three of his works with instructions that were meant to aid the reader in following the systematic logic of those works: in the preface to <u>Cur Deus Homo</u>, Anselm demanded that every transcription of his treatise be integral and complete, with its proper preface and table of contents located at the very beginning. He desired the full list of chapters according to their correct order and title so that the reader might be able to judge the demonstrative value of the treatise from the outset. At the beginning of this preface, he complained about people transcribing only parts of the treatise, indicating how strongly he felt that the work should be read and understood in its entirety.

> There are certain men who without my knowledge
> copied for themselves the first parts of the
> enclosed work before it was completed and
> perfected. Because of these individuals I
> have been forced to finish this treatise as
> best I could and more hastily than suited me,
> and hence in a more abbreviated form than I
> had intended. . . . I ask all those who wish
> to copy this volume to affix this preface,
> together with all the chapter titles, before
> the beginning of the text. This way anyone
> into whose hands the volume comes will see on

its countenance, so to speak, whether the
whole body of the text contains anything which
he may deem important.1

Anselm was upset by the premature copying of his
book because he felt that no single section could be
understood apart from its place within the total context
of the work. The completion and revision, which Anselm
spoke of, includes the logical ordering of the early
material in relation to the total argument of the dialogue. This explains the significance of Anselm's
request that the outline of the entire work be placed at
the very beginning. Only in this way could the systematic relationship of the various parts of the dialogue
be fully appreciated.

In the preface to Monologion, Anselm expresses a
similar wish, saying that the reader will be greatly
aided in understanding the material contained in the
body of the work if he observes at the outset of the
book the intention and method that have guided its
writing. He also hoped in this way to prevent any rash
judgments since one who observes the total systematic
unity of the work will be less likely to misunderstand
individual sections within it.2

Anselm also showed his concern for the systematic
ordering of a number of treatises in the preface to De
Veritate. Here he felt that the full demonstrative
force of these treatises becomes apparent only if they
are read in their proper order and as part of his
intended systematic unity. According to Anselm, one
ought to first read De Veritate, then De Libertate
Arbitrii, and finally, De Casu Diaboli. While he
indicated that these treatises are not related by
continuity of composition, they are so related in style
and content that they should be considered in correct
sequence:

At different times in the past I wrote three
treatises pertaining to the study of Sacred
Scripture. They are similar in having been
written in dialogue form; the person inquiring
is designated "the Student," and the person
answering, "the Teacher.". . . Although these
three treatises are not connected through any
continuation of text, their subject-matter and

similarity of discussion require that they be placed together in the order in which I have mentioned them. Thus, although certain rash individuals have transcribed them in another order before they were completed, I want them ordered as I have listed them here.3

Anselm wanted these treatises ordered and complete because their relationship to each other is itself part of their content. It is here that the systematic character of Anselm's work is understood.

Most contemporary scholars tend to agree that Anselm's thought is systematic, but there has been considerable debate over what the word system means when it is applied to Anselm's writing. For example, J. McIntyre applies the word systematic to the writings of Anselm in two senses, referring to the thematic relatedness of the various works and the uniform method which he finds throughout them. At the Anselm Congress held in Normandy in 1959, McIntyre pointed out a third sense in which Anselm's writings should be seen as systematic: they outline a conceptual system, a complete dogmatic theology. McIntyre stressed this point against those who see Anselm as basically an apologist (e.g., F. S. Schmitt), precisely because apologists are not, to his mind, renowned for their systematic presentations. With regard to the method that unifies Anselm's system, McIntyre sees a mainly discursive argument moving logically from premises to conclusions--the conclusions of one of Anselm's treatises frequently serve as the premises of another.4

J. Hopkins agrees with McIntyre on the discursive character of Anselm's system, though Hopkins describes the system in terms of the consistency of definitions, the logical connectedness of ideas, and the employment of a basic set of examples that reappears in various treatises. Hopkins even speaks of the "almost total internal consistency" of Anselm's works.5 Because of this consistency, Hopkins states that it is not necessary to distinguish between the meaning of terms used in Anselm's early works and the meaning of these same terms in his late writing.6

The best illustration of this consistent terminology, which Hopkins describes, can be seen in two of the fundamental organization principles in the Anselm corpus, namely Anselm's preoccupation with justice and freedom. These terms are defined in Anselm's early dialogues: in De Veritate, Anselm defines justice as "rectitude of will kept for its own sake," and in De Libertate Arbitrii, he speaks of freedom as "the ability to retain rectitude of will for its own sake."7   Through the many years following the writing of these dialogues, Anselm maintains these same definitions so that his final complete work, De Concordia, refers back to the definitions contained in these early works.8   Thus, Anselm is seen to build his lifelong theology around certain key concepts in such a way that he is not forced to withdraw the early foundations for the sake of later developments in his thought.

Stressing the systematic character of Anselm's works in terms of the connectedness of ideas, Hopkins speaks of Anselm's genius for dealing intensively with a certain problem without losing sight of the direction in which his proposed solution would lead. In this regard, he refers to Anselm's handling of the problem of free choice in De Libertate Arbitrii where Anselm shows his awareness of the related question of grace even though he will not take up that question for many years. Hopkins sees another example of this interrelatedness of the Anselm corpus in the question of original sin. Although the immediate aim of Cur Deus Homo is to demonstrate the necessity of the Godman, Anselm realizes that he must at some later time devote himself more extensively to the question of original sin and infant baptism, an issue which is supplementary to the main arguments of Cur Deus Homo.   De Conceptu Virginali provides this necessary treatment.

Another way in which Anselm's writings attain systematic unity is through Anselm's use of standard examples that reappear again and again in his various treatises. For example, Hopkins points out that Anselm uses the same example in two treatises to explain how evil is an absence of required justice and not "something" that exists in a man. Thus, in De Casu Diaboli we find this paragraph:

> Indeed, many things are said according to form [secundum formam] which are not the case according to fact [secundum rem].   For example, timere [to be afraid] is called active according to the form of the word, although it is passive according to fact.   So too, blindness is called something according to a form of speaking, although it is not something according to fact.   For just as we say of someone that he has sight and that sight is in him, so we say that he has blindness and that

blindness is in him, although blindness is not
something but rather is not-something. Moreover, to have blindness is not to have something but is rather to be deprived of that
which is something. For blindness is nothing
other than not-seeing, or the absence of sight
where sight ought to be. But not-seeing, or
the absence of sight, is not anything more
where sight ought to be than where it ought
not to be. Therefore, blindness is not
anything more in the eye because sight ought
to be there than not-seeing, or the absence of
sight, is in a stone, where sight ought not to
be. Also, many other things which are not
something are likewise called something
according to a form of speaking, since we
speak about them as if about existing things.9

This explanation of why we speak of evil as if it were
"something" also occurs in De Conceptu Virginali, and
again we see how Anselm draws upon the example of blindness to illustrate his point: "Injustice, however, is
nothing at all, even as is blindness. For blindness is
nothing other than the absence of sight where sight
ought to be; and it is no more the case that this
absence is something in an eye, where sight ought to be,
than it is in a piece of wood, where sight ought not to
be."10   In both passages Anselm attempts to clarify the
problem of evil by examining the language used to
express the problem.   In both cases he draws upon the
same example from everyday experience to show how
deceptive ordinary language can be.

This case is but one of a number that Hopkins
calls attention to in making his point about Anselm's
use of standard examples to bind together similar
discussions in various treatises and dialogues.11 The
use of these standard examples in treatises dealing with
different topics has the effect of relating them all to
the same world picture and, in this way, reinforcing the
systematic quality of Anselm's thought.

To respond to the question concerning the pro-
priety of interpreting Anselm's writings systematically,
we have considered three arguments: Anselm's own clear
indications of his systematic intentions and the interrelationship of his treatises, McIntyre's emphasis on
Anselm's development of a systematic method and conceptual system, and Hopkins's demonstration that Anselm
utilizes a consistent set of definitions and standard
examples. These considerations tend to reject any

interpretation of Anselm that would deny the systematic
quality of his thought by overstressing the lengthy
period of time in which these works were composed.

Motif Research

     Whereas McIntyre and Hopkins deal with Anselm's
system in terms of the relation of his various concepts
and the discursive character of his argumentation, an
alternative approach has been developed by R. Pouchet
and H. Kohlenberger. Pouchet and Kohlenberger do "motif
research." Basically, they attempt to translate the
unity of Anselm's theological system in light of a
dominating principle that organizes all of the other
concepts in the system. They see the meaning of
Anselm's concepts in their relation to this orientative
principle rather than, as Hopkins contends, in their
relation to one another.

     Pouchet proposes that the basic motif of Anselm's
thought is rectitudo. In his study of Anselm, Pouchet
traces this concept through various works of the cor-
pus.12 He argues convincingly that rectitudo is one of
the fundamental notions inspiring the entire system of
Anselm's thought, recognizing that it is the basis of
the other dominant concepts in Anselm's system: truth,
justice, and freedom. Even sin, both original and
personal, is defined as an absence of required rectitude, and consequently, the satisfaction necessary for
the reparation of sin will be the gift of rectitude
given by the God-man. Pouchet also observes that the
grace possessed by Adam before the Fall as well as the
grace that Christ provides for spiritual rebirth is the
"rectitude of the human will." He further observed that
rectitude is not only the key term in Anselm's theological speculation, but it is also an idea that influenced his personal life as can be seen from various
letters, prayers, and meditations.

     Pouchet's analysis of rectitudo is especially
valuable in that it interprets the systematic character
of Anselm's writings as the fundamental motif that
inspired and unified Anselm's various works.13 Pouchet
interprets rectitudo as a term that refers to God (the
supreme recitude and the source and measure of all other
rectitude), to the world (things as they conform to what
they ought to be), and to the human will (the just man
who possesses uprightness of will).

In the article, "Existe - t-il une 'synthèse' Anselmienne?", Pouchet suggests that Anselm's famous
definition of God as "id quo nihil maius cogitari
potest" represents another important systematic current
in Anselm's thought.14   He notes that this idea of God,
which originates in Proslogion, is also found several
times in Cur Deus Homo.   In book 1, chapter 3 of Cur
Deus Homo, Pouchet sees united the two principal themes
he has identified: the idea of God as sovereign rectitude and the idea of God formulated in Proslogion.
He also notes other phrases that are reminiscent
of the Proslogion's God-concept, arguing that these
various references show that this God-concept is
a unifying theme in Anselm's thought because the
references deal with theodicy, Christian anthropology,
and soteriology (doctrinal areas also dominated and
unified by the notion of rectitudo).

Pouchet observes that these two concepts are
united at the center of Anselm's own thought. But how
are they united?   Are they logically derivable, or is
their ordering more a rhetorical coordination of
relatively autonomous themes?   Pouchet's view is more
the latter. He sees the God-concept as belonging to the
logical-ontological order while rectitudo is considered
to be in the moral-spiritual order. Although he views
fides quaerens rectitudinem as parallel to and the
spiritual foundation of fides quaerens intellectum, he
holds that their respective ontological and moral roots
keep them distinct. Therefore, Pouchet believes that
their unity does not derive from a single concept but
from Anselm's ability to spontaneously coordinate
various themes into an aesthetic unity.

This relationship between the motif symbols
Pouchet has identified can be depicted in this way:

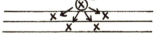

Here ⊗ is the motif and the various x's are the motif
symbols that express the motif at various levels of
thought. The various symbols are not related to each
other directly but through the central motif that they
symbolize. This is in contrast to the more discursive
system described by McIntyre and Hopkins which we have
already seen, where terms are operating on the same
level of thought and connected directly through a
logical link. The system described by McIntyre and
Hopkins would look something like this:

- x - y - z -

Here x, y, and z are various terms joined on the same
level through logical connections. More will be said
later about the different levels at which these two
types of system operate. It is enough to note that the
analysis of Pouchet takes place on quite a different
level from that of McIntyre and Hopkins.

When Pouchet sees Anselm's theology unified by the
fundamental intuitions of De Veritate and Proslogion, he
exposes another aspect of Anselm's conception of
system: this is a system in the sense of a spiritual,
aesthetic, and spontaneous coordination of a relatively
autonomous concept; it is not a strictly rational,
deductive unity.15 This notion of system which Pouchet
identifies also helps to explain why the concept of
flesh plays such an important role in Anselm's system:
Flesh has a wide range of meanings; it possesses the
flexibility to operate as a motif symbol and thereby to
coordinate a number of levels of language and thought.
The extent of this expressive range of the concept of
flesh will be made clear from the word study in chapter
5.

Kohlenberger's Similitudo und Ratio represents a
second attempt to describe Anselm's entire theology in
terms of a single motif. His study examines the relationship between thought and speech in Anselm's writings. He places Anselm's writings within the general
context of medieval thought, saying that the leitmotiv
of this period is the difference between God (the
Infinite) and the world (the finite). He stresses that
while this difference is awesome, it is bridged to a
certain degree by the Christian view that this finite
world is created according to the image of God, and this
similitudo character of the finite world is especially
focused on the human ratio so that the very mode of
operation of human ratio is on the basis of its likeness
to the divine Word. Kohlenberger perceives as a conse-
quence of this position that the world and human thought
both have their foundation in the creative Word of God.

On the basis of this view, Kohlenberger holds
that, for Anselm, rational method is never autonomous
but rather always follows the ontological foundation of
ratio as imago Dei; therefore, Anselm's sola ratione
method cannot mean anything like a purely rational
method in the sense of Descartes's use of a strictly
rational method. For Anselm, ratio is always considered
to be imago Dei and so always refers to God. In this
respect, ratio is never independent of the divine, which
is intimately present as the ontological ground of

ratio.   Kohlenberger   sees human thought and speech
connected   because   they   are   created after God's image,
the God whose thought is his Word.16

     When Kohlenberger describes   Anselm's   entire
theology as a purification of speech, it must be seen
against this divine-likeness character of speech.   Once
the ontological foundation of ratio and verbum are
appreciated, Kohlenberger's description is seen as apt,
for he is merely reflecting Anselm's view that it is
man's task to express the impression of God in him.   And
in his study of ratio and verbum, he is stressing the
linguistic character of that divine impression.

     Kohlenberger sees that Anselm is concerned with
speech as the model of thought (thought as inner speech)
and even the model of man's ethical demands (man's moral
life as based on God's truth and his commands);17 thus,
he argues that verbum is at the center of all Anselm's
concerns, those of knowledge and those of action or
willing. He holds that, for Anselm, the Verbum Dei is
the source of the debere of the created universe, as the
source and measure of human thought and human action.
In this regard, he notes the degrees of reality in Anselm's thought: God's Verbum is the most real, as the
Urbild of all being and knowing, while reality and human
knowledge of reality are the second and third degrees of
reality, both being regulated by the debere of the
Verbum Dei.   In this Verbum, Anselm locates the tension
between God-in-himself and God-as-the-ground-of-other-
being.

     Thus, Kohlenberger's mode of argument is basically
linguistic. The term verbum has a linguistic richness
and complexity that allow it to serve as the foundation
of Anselm's theological method. For Anselm, the Word of
God is the creative force that calls the world into
being as well as the principle that orders reality and
thought.   As such, verbum is one of the cornerstones of
Anselm's system.

     Previously, we considered diagrams that illus-
trated the differences between the spontaneous system
described by Pouchet and the more discursive system
described by McIntyre and Hopkins.   Kohlenberger's
analysis of the motif symbol verbum further specifies
the relationship between these two systems.   His
linguistic approach to the motif of Anselm's theology
shows that these two systems are complementary, not
contradictory. Kohlenberger's study of verbum as "word"
or "language" in all its richness actually is consistent
with and reinforces Hopkins's points about language.

When Hopkins examines Anselm's methods of argumentation, he stresses Anselm's considerations of the various ways in which language is used. He describes the basic principles of syllogistic argumentation which Anselm employed, showing this preoccupation with language to be central to Anselm's discursive system. For example, Hopkins calls attention to Anselm's treatment of contrary-to-fact conditionals in Cur Deus Homo I/XII, showing how logic serves to clarify the use of language:

> Therefore, when we say 'If God wills to lie,' this means 'If God is of such a nature as to will to lie. . . .' And so 'Lying is just' is not inferable therefrom--unless we interpret the if-then statement as an example of our saying about two impossibilities 'If this is true, then that is true,' although neither the one nor the other is true. For example, someone might say, 'If water is dry, then fire is wet,' neither of which component statements is true.18

Hopkins explains that the point made in this case is as much linguistic as it is logical, saying: "Anselm is stressing that we do sometimes say such things as 'If A, then B' where B is known to be contrary to fact and where A is also known, or at least believed, to be contrary to fact. In such cases we are emphasizing the utter preposterousness of asserting A."19 This example gives some indication of Hopkins's concern with Anselm's use of language. Anselm's constant use of such logical and linguistic arguments unifies his theological system. While Hopkins interprets Anselm's linguistic concern primarily in terms of logical clarification and argumentation, he considers Anselm's concern with language as central to his theology. And although he does not deal with language as a motif symbol, his discussion of it is perfectly consistent with Kohlenberger's view of verbum. Kohlenberger is aware of the more discursive use of language which Anselm employs where verbum is considered as logos, the principle of order, but he goes beyond this level to where verbum is the point of contact between divine and human thought. Here, verbum is not only a principle of order, but it is also the source of creation and the divine ground of human thought.

From this brief comparison of the two ways Kohlenberger and Hopkins treat language in Anselm's theology, we can see that there is a complementary

relationship between their different approaches. Recalling the diagram used earlier to describe the relationship between these two approaches to Anselm's system, we
see that they operate on different levels and utilize
different principles of organization. Where Hopkins
sees Anselm's system at one level of language, organized
through logical connections, Kohlenberger sees that
system operating on more than a single level of
language; yet, both of these types of system can be seen
in Anselm's writing, and they coexist in the Anselm
corpus. A diagram might relate these two types of
system in this way:

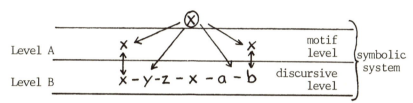

From this diagram, we see that the more discursive
system described by Hopkins operates at a single level,
B. All of the logical connections take place at that
level. But we notice that the symbolic system organized
around the motif of Anselm's total theology, x,
operates at both levels, A and B. This helps to
illustrate why there is no contradiction between these
different notions of system. The motif symbols, the
x's, which serve at level B, are able to be connected
logically in the discursive arguments that operate at
that level. But they also serve to symbolize the motif
of the total system, and in this capacity they also
operate at level A. Here it might also be observed that
the bond linking x to y, z, a and b is of a different
type from the bond linking x to the motif, x. The
former bond is rather tight and logical while the latter
is a looser bond of intuition and feeling. More will be
said later in distinguishing these links within the two
types of system and between them, for this distinction
will serve as a methodological premise in this study
itself. We shall, in separate chapters, analyze
Anselm's writings in these two different ways. For the
moment, however, it is enough to appreciate that these
two notions of system are closely coordinated and
intimately related.

Participation in Anselm's Thought

We have seen that Anselm's system can be
considered from the point of view of a discursive,
linguistic connectedness as well as from the point of
view of a more spontaneous, symbolic coordination. This
study will show how the concept of flesh operates at
both of these levels of Anselm's system. At the more
discursive level, flesh will be considered as a concept
that unifies Anselm's system by its central relationship
to a number of important terms and doctrines; at the
symbolic level, flesh will be seen to symbolize the
motif of Anselm's entire theology. This study will
argue that at the level at which Anselm's system is seen
to be unified by a central motif, the flesh takes a
place alongside those other important symbols studied by
Pouchet and Kohlenberger, rectitudo and verbum. In
fact, it will be shown that at this symbolic level,
rectitudo, verbum, and flesh are intimately related.

These statements raise some questions about the
motif symbols in Anselm's theology: How many motif
symbols are there in Anselm's theological system? Can
any concept function as a motif symbol? How does one
determine which concepts are motif symbols? The answer
to these questions is that only those concepts that are
understood not discursively but by "participation" can
be motif symbols--for knowledge by participation is
orientational. This is why it always expresses a motif
through which all other concepts in the theological
system are related.

This understanding of knowledge through participation that belongs to a special group of signs, i.e.,
motif symbols and sacraments, is worked out in contemporary theology by P. Tillich and by M. Heidegger.
Tillich's distinction between sign and symbol is,
epistemologically a distinction between denotative-dis-
cursive and orientational-participational ways of
knowing.20 Heidegger's distinction between the language
of metaphysics and the language of theology also calls
attention to these two ways of knowing.21

But what these men are discussing here is also
explicitly formulated by Anselm in his own theological
program. Anselm understood that certain terms have a
special symbolic power, that they function sacramentally
and as motif symbols of the whole. These symbols,
according to Anselm, orient all our thinking because
they actually present and participate in the whole of
thought and reality. They structure it or express its

structure. _Rectitudo_, for example, governs all things--
just as does the _similitudo Dei_. Each of these symbols
is the whole because it symbolically stands for (by
participating in) the entire reality it symbolizes;
therefore, when one encounters such a symbol, one experiences the reality it participates in, and this experience of that reality is itself a kind of participation
in the reality. One does not simply "stand apart" from
the reality and understand it objectively or discursively, one actually "takes part in" the reality through
feeling.

H. Richardson, drawing on Anselm's example, describes very succinctly how this participatory causality
operates, and how motif symbols operate differently from
concepts that merely signify an object:

> Feeling perceives by participation. Just as
> feeling is a perception of a whole, so a whole
> is that which is perceived through participa-
> tion. In the perception of a whole, the self
> takes up a position within the whole. In this
> respect, therefore, the perception of wholes
> differs from the perception of individuals,
> for individuals can be observed and denoted
> from "outside." In observation, the perceiver
> and that which is perceived are not one (that
> is, the former does not take up a position as
> "part" of the latter). Rather, they stand in
> opposition to each other. But in feeling, the
> perceiver is one with the thing perceived.22

Here Richardson uses "feeling" to mean that operation by
which we discern the structure of a whole and through which
we judge that things are "fitting" in their relation to one
another. Though Anselm does not speak of feeling in this
way, he does speak constantly of the fittingness of
things--and offers this as one kind of argumentation.
Motif symbols are especially important in communicating
this structure of the whole which is crucial to "fitting
arguments." And it is owing to their participation in the
"whole" that motif symbols are capable of communicating
this "whole."

These considerations help us to understand why every
concept cannot function as a motif symbol, for symbols
function at the level of participation alone. They also
make us aware that Anselm himself intentionally employs
certain terms in this symbolic way to establish a fundamental motif in his theology. He also works out the epis-

temological presupposition of this way of using language,
namely his doctrine of participation.

We see, therefore, that Anselm consciously develops
his theological system on at least two levels: first, on
the discursive level where he operates much like a modern
linguistic analyst in constructing a set of terms which he
circumscribes and links together in a "logical net";
second, on the archetypal-symbolic level where he establishes a basic gestalt, or orientation, for the thinker
himself. Anselm's doctrine of participation is the foundation for this second, or symbolic level of his system, in
the sense that it is the consciously elaborated framework
that establishes the possibility in principle of his motif
symbols and his doctrine of the sacraments. We shall utilize this principle of participation to determine which of
Anselm's concepts are used symbolically, i.e., only those
concepts that are known through participation can be true
motif symbols within the theology of Anselm.

Recent scholarship on Anselm's doctrine of participation has helped clarify the essentially epistemological
interests behind his view, and it has shown how he quali-
fies his position to maintain a metaphysical distinction
between God and creation. First, it should be observed
that Anselm actually uses the word <u>participation</u> infre-
quently. According to F. S. Schmitt's index to his Latin
edition of Anselm's works, there are only six instances of
its occurrence; yet, these six are found in important
passages of three major writings, <u>Monologion, De Veritate</u>,
and <u>Cur Deus Homo</u>. For example, in <u>Monologion</u> XVI we have
the following:

> Hence, it seems that the supremely good Sub-
> stance is called just by participation in the
> quality of justice. But if so (i.e., if the
> Supreme Substance were just in this way), then
> the Supreme Substance would be just through
> another and not through itself. But this view
> is contrary to the truth which we have already
> seen, viz., that whether good or great or
> existing--what (the Supreme Nature) is, it is
> completely through itself and not through
> another. So if it is just only through jus-
> tice, and if it can only be just through
> itself, what is more clear and more necessary
> than that this Nature is itself justice? And
> when it is said to be just through justice, is
> not this the same as (being just) through
> itself? And when it is said to be just
> through itself, what else is meant except that

(it is just) through justice? Therefore, if
someone asks "What is this Supreme Nature
which you are investigating?" is there a truer
answer than "It is justice"?23

This passage is important because it gives Anselm's view of participation, and also because it introduces us to a synonym for participation that Anselm
frequently uses, per aliud. When one thing is what it
is by participation in another, it is so per aliud. As
K. Flasch points out, the distinction between per aliud
and per se is Anselm's basic way of stating the participation doctrine. According to Flasch, Anselm often
substitutes the phrase per aliud for the word participatio, and consequently the argument that the word
participatio rarely occurs in Anselm's writing is in
itself not a convincing point against the significance
of the participation doctrine in Anselm's thought.24
These considerations help us to realize that Anselm's
doctrine of participation is located throughout his
works, and it is not restricted to the word participatio.

It is insufficient merely to say that Anselm has a
doctrine of participation and that it pervades the whole
body of his writing. We must ask more specifically,
what is this doctrine? There is a general, though not
unchallenged, scholarly consensus on how Anselm's doctrine of participation operates. Hopkins and Richardson
represent this general interpretation of Anselm's
doctrine of participation in the introduction to Truth,
Freedom, and Evil. There they state that, for Anselm,
the truth in all things is one eternal being, God or
Truth, and that created things possess their truth by
participation in this divine Truth.25 This appears to
be an unobjectionable description of Anselm's view.

In his review of the Hopkins-Richardson volume,
Schmitt takes exception to their interpretation of Anselm's notion of participation.26 Schmitt objects to
their view, arguing that Anselm's summa veritas is not a
universal in which created things participate; rather it
is a spiritus individuus which creates all things. For
Schmitt, Anselm refers all things back to creation not
to their participation in a divine Exemplar. Schmitt
judges that every doctrine of participation is incom-
patible with the Christian doctrine of creation--and is
eager to preserve Anselm's orthodoxy. In his article,
"Anselm und der (Neu-) Platonismus," Schmitt objects to
the general assumption that Anselm was strongly influenced by Augustine's Neoplatonism.27 He contends that

Anselm has no doctrine of an exemplary cause even though
he acknowledges that Anselm knew about such a doctrine
from Boethius's commentary on Aristotle's causes.
Schmitt is interested in showing that Anselm does affirm
the relative independence of individuals and their
finite relationship--things he sees threatened by a
strong stress on the doctrine of participation.28

What Schmitt appears to be contending for can be
granted, however, without accepting his whole argument
for it. Schmitt is arguing that, for Anselm, there is a
nonparticipational way of knowing independent beings.
But this does not mean that there is not also a special
participational knowing. Rather, for Anselm, there is
both a nonparticipational and a participational
knowing--and the dispute between Hopkins and Richardson
and Schmitt draws attention to this.

Moreover, Schmitt's further specification of the
uniqueness of Anselm's view of participation helps us
understand the special epistemological (as opposed to
metaphysical) interests behind it. Schmitt says that
Anselm has no doctrine of "substantial participation,"
but he acknowledges that Anselm does have a doctrine of
"accidental participation." That is, Anselm affirms
that creatures possess their qualities, though not their
being, by participation (e.g., a man is wise and just
through the qualities of wisdom and justice.) Schmitt
considers this view to be very different from the
Neoplatonic notion of a substance participating in a
substance. Schmitt is eager to disassociate Anselm from
"substantial participation" because he holds that such a
doctrine contradicts the Christian view of *creatio ex
nihilo*.

Yet, in pointing out Anselm's doctrine of "accidental participation," Schmitt is making it clear that
the qualities by which we know things (as opposed to the
substance by which we understand and know them) are
present by participation. That is, he is drawing attention to the fact that the epistemological function of
the doctrine of participation, rather than the metaphysical, is what is truly important for Anselm. He is
suggesting, albeit indirectly, that to the extent that
Anselm has a doctrine of participation, he uses it to
clarify the act of knowing rather than the fact of
being. This point is an important clarification of
Anselm's views on this matter. Still, Schmitt over-
states his case; his distinction between a participation
in substance and a participation in qualities does not
operate at the most important point in Anselm's thought,

namely, with respect to the qualities of divine truth and justice.

Suppose we grant Schmitt's point that it is important to distinguish quality and substance in man; yet neither he nor Anselm would allow such a distinction to be made with regard to God. For Anselm, God is Rectitude, Truth, and Justice. These are not qualities of God. They are his very essence. So, writes Anselm, "therefore, whatever is predicated truly of its essence applies to what it is, not to what kind it is [qualis] or to how great it is [quanta]. For whatever is (subject to) quality or quantity is something else with respect to what it is (i.e., with respect to its essence), and thus is not simple but composite."29 Here, Anselm stresses that God's justice is his essence, that God's qualities are not distinguishable from his very being; thus, it would seem that Anselm's own statements about the unity of divine substance and divine qualities render Schmitt's distinction between substantial and accidental participation inapplicable to the question of knowing things by participation, i.e., per aliud or through God. Hence, in De Veritate, Anselm has the student say: "Nothing is true except by its participation in Truth."30 This is the key sentence that Hopkins calls upon to support his view. Hopkins says, concerning the student's comment, that if Anselm had been averse to Augustine's theory of participation he would either not have introduced the student's remark concerning participation or he would have objected to that remark having introduced it; thus, Hopkins sees in this sentence a positive confirmation of Anselm's own position regarding participation.31 It must be pointed out that Anselm is here still speaking of knowing the truth of a thing not accounting for its "being"--and it is perhaps misleading to call this a "substantial participation" without some further qualifications. While Hopkins seems to give the closer presentation of Anselm's view, Schmitt's objections make us aware of the complexity of Anselm's innovations.

Varieties of Literary Genres

We have considered the question of whether Anselm's writings were composed according to a system or whether they were apologetic and underwent development. If the latter were true, then a systematic analysis would impose onto Anselm's thought categories that would have no place there. Yet, though Anselm wrote in terms of various loci, he frequently drew attention to the

fact that his work is not a series of discrete and unrelated essays. As a sign of Anselm's systematic intent,
we noted how he gave orders that anyone copying Monologion and Cur Deus Homo should reproduce the entire
table of contents at the beginning of the treatise to
show the relationship of the individual parts to the
systematic whole.

We saw that Anselm employed certain basic examples
so that various treatises are related by their uniform
use. With McIntyre, we noted that Anselm related his
works by utilizing the conclusions of one work as the
premise in the argument of another. With Hopkins, we
noted that Anselm further developed a system through his
constant preoccupation with key notions of justice,
truth, and rectitude. All of these considerations make
it clear that Anselm was not a mere apologist and that
he did create a theological system.

The motif research carried out by Pouchet and
Kohlenberger shows how Anselm's thought is organized
around a central motif. Pouchet demonstrated the
significance of rectitudo as one of the most important
symbols which express the motif of Anselm's theology.
He showed how Anselm's preoccupation with rectitudo
dominated his thought and ruled his entire life.
Kohlenberger established that verbum is another motif
symbol. He explained how Anselm's concern with verbum
shaped his theological method and showed the extent to
which verbum is the common ground between human and
divine thought.

The contributions of Pouchet and Kohlenberger went
beyond the illumination of these motif symbols. In
their studies of these symbols, both scholars established the basis of a complex view of Anselm's theological system. This notion of system was found to be a
spontaneous coordination of ideas, organized around the
central motif of Anselm's theology. While we noticed
that this more loosely organized system is in contrast
to the system described by McIntyre and Hopkins, we saw
that these two notions of system are complementary, not
contradictory.

Anselm reorganized the older doctrine of participation to aid his epistemological purposes. We
observed, in the analysis of Schmitt's position, that
Anselm appears to rework the traditional doctrine of
participation in an "epistemological direction" so that
it explains why all truth participates in God, but not
all being. He does so, Schmitt observes, by denying

that there is any participation of substance in God but only participation of accidents, i.e., of those qualities by which we know things. In this way, Anselm protects the doctrine of creation while remaining true to the Christian teaching that God is Truth and all truth is from God. This view of participation was then seen to be the epistemological theory that undergirds Anselm's use of the motif symbols that organize his more complex notion of system.

Now while the project of a systematic analysis of Anselm's theology has been legitimated, there is another series of questions that must be considered before taking up this analysis: Are all of Anselm's writings part of his system or only a few? In approaching Anselm's system, do we confine ourselves to his explicitly philosophical and rational treatises, or do we also study his dogmatic, pastoral, and devotional writings as well?

Our previous attempt to delineate the complex nature of Anselm's system can be of help here. On the motif level, one must discover guiding metaphors and orientating "feelings." Considering this reason alone, We cannot agree that for the study of Anselm's system, his philosophical and speculative writings are more important than his sacramental or meditative writings. Actually, one cannot understand Anselm's system on its motif, or deep, level unless these more devotional writings are handled. But these are the very works which some would eliminate.

M. Charlesworth provides an example of those who would clearly give priority to Anselm's more discursive writings. Charlesworth considers Anselm's thought as separated into two inconsistent parts, one represented by an assent to Scriptural truths without any prior rational justification and the other represented by an independent function of reason prior to faith.32 He sees here a discontinuity between Scriptural faith and rational argument in Anselm's theology. Because he discerns this dichotomy within the Anselm corpus when he considers Anselm's system, he gives priority to certain treatises, Proslogion, Cur Deus Homo, and Monologion. Anselm's dogmatic and devotional works are then relegated by Charlesworth to a secondary place apart from the works that constitute Anselm's rational system. But does such a dichotomizing of Anselm's corpus into contrary literary genres really make sense?

The question about the literary genres is really the question of how one is to approach the various writings within the Anselm corpus. The entire corpus, it will be remembered, is not restricted to the five dialogues and six treatises that are the best known of Anselm's writings. It also contains three meditations, nineteen prayers, and nearly four hundred letters. We have already observed that Charlesworth attended to that first group of writings, the treatises and the dialogues, locating Anselm's system strictly within the boundaries of those works. The other writings of the corpus have been much less noticed, but Anselm's system, in the broadest sense, depends just as much on these devotional and practical writings as it does on the logical and speculative works.

Another instructive attempt to characterize that part of the Anselm corpus represented by the prayers and meditations has been carried out by R. Roques. He accomplishes this task by noting the contrast between Anselm's prayers and his treatises or dialogues. Roques's study of Anselm's prayers also includes the three meditations since Anselm himself gave the title Orationes sive Meditationes to the whole collection. His observations will be considered at some length because of their importance to the notion of system as it applies to the entire corpus.

Roques discusses these differences between Anselm's prayers and his dialogues or treatises in "Structure et caractères de la prière anselmienne."33 There he maintains that the prayers and meditations together constitute a homogeneous literary genre that is specifically spiritual, and this spiritual character distinguishes them from the didactic and logical nature of Anselm's treatises. For Roques, this difference can be described in terms of the purpose of those two types of literature: the prayers and meditations are designed to stimulate humility, piety, and love, while the theological treatises and dialogues are meant to demonstrate a truth by means of necessary reasons.

Roques feels that these radically different types of literature have important consequences for the way each type is to be read. For example, where the major theological treatises must be read in their entirety, following the logical steps of the argument developed in the treatises, the prayers may be read with the freedom to begin and end where the reader wishes, with the only criterion for judging how to read them being the spiritual profit of the reader. In this respect, Roques

argues for a radical difference of intention and method
between Anselm's treatises and his prayers.34 Roques's
position here raises serious questions about the character of Anselm's theological system: Does Anselm
employ two radically different methods within his theological system as Roques maintains? If so, is one
method reserved for the dialogues and treatises, the
other for the prayers and meditations?35

     For example, although Proslogion is a rational
argument, Anselm here develops his famous notion of God
as "id quo nihil maius cogitari potest" within the
context of prayer. Because Anselm's argument is set in
this devotional context, even the more rational elements
can be appreciated fully only within an atmosphere of
prayerful reflection. This is the very point McIntyre
makes when he warns against the characterization of
Proslogion as a strictly rational argument. And to
support his point, McIntyre calls attention to the fact
that C. Webb places his translation of Proslogion in the
category of "the devotions of St. Anselm."36 Also there
is a more recent translation of Proslogion in a book
entitled The Prayers and Meditations of Saint Anselm.(36a) When scholars disagree as to whether Proslogion is speculative philosophy (Charlesworth) or
devotional oratory (Webb), we see that the attempt to
classify the Anselm corpus into writings of various
sharply delimited types is dubious. Not only does one
find this devotional atmosphere in a supposedly rational
treatise, but one also discovers rational argument in
Anselm's prayers. The Meditatio Redemptionis Humanae is
an excellent example--almost one-half of this meditation
summarizes the doctrinal arguments developed in Cur Deus
Homo.

     Therefore, while the general suggestion that one
must be sensitive to the different types of thought
within the Anselm corpus is helpful, it should not lead
one to overlook the strong mixture of logic and
affectivity that often appears within a single work.
For Anselm, there is no sharp separation of the logical
and the affective. Anselm considers the rational to be
affective, and in the ideal case of the righteous man,
the affections are rational. This is the psychological
basis of Anselm's theory of the human will where the
upright will accomplishes its task of willing according
to the dictates of reason through the affection for
justice, and, correspondingly, the affections do not
accomplish their purpose (to aid man in his quest for
happiness and justice) unless they are ordered to the
demands of reason.37 It is in accordance with such a

unified psychology that Anselm's _Meditatio Redemptionis_
Humanae can be understood.   Take the exaggerated language of this meditation, for instance, where Anselm
speaks of chewing and swallowing the words that proclaim
human redemption.   Should one simply take this as
rhetorical exaggeration?   That would be possible only if
one imposed onto Anselm's psychology an artificial
dichotomy.   Actually, Anselm uses this imagery in a
consistent way, stressing that rational truth is meant
to be affectively incorporated, just as the object of
affections is meant to be the rational.   Thus Anselm can
say in this meditation: "Chew by thinking, suck by
understanding, swallow by loving and rejoicing. Rejoice
in chewing, be glad in sucking, delight in swallow-
ing.38 This kind of language can be properly understood only if one appreciates the unity of the affective
and the rational in Anselm's theology.   Then, and only
then, can one see the consistency and systematic quality
of the entire Anselm _corpus_.

        In commenting on Anselm's prayers, Roques himself
observes that certain passages combine the logical and
the affective types of writing.   For example, Roques
describes aspects of Anselm's "Oratio episcopi vel
abbatis ad sanctum sub cuius nomine regit ecclesiam" as
"logico-affectif."39   In another description of the same
prayer, Roques characterizes the style as proceeding
with "affectueuse logique," and in yet another place he
calls the concluding segment of the prayer "supplication-argumentation."40   And when he summarizes the
essential elements of the prayer-type exemplified by
this prayer, he lists "argumentation de type
'logico-affectif' devant Dieu et devant le saint patron"
among those elements.41   In observing these things,
Roques is himself qualifying his own theory, for the
terms "logico-affectif," "affectueuse logique," and
"supplication-argumentation" are apt not only for
Anselm's prayers, as Roques says, but also for his more
expressly logical works (which Roques denies).

        These considerations lead us to say that while
there are two general types of thought in the Anselm
corpus--one being a conceptual, mediated, discursive
type, the other an affective, direct, intuitive type--
these two types of thought are not opposed to each
other. Rather they simply follow the two general movements of the soul toward God, the ratiocinative and the
affective.   According to Anselm's unified psychology,
each type of thought enriches the other and they work
together in the one program of Anselm's theology: _fides_
quarens intellectum. This single theological program is

operative at every point in the Anselm corpus, whether
it be in the more speculative or in the more devo-
tional-pastoral writings. Thus, in order to study
Anselm's theological system, one cannot set aside
certain of his writings as irrelevant.

Methodological Approaches
Within the Anselm Corpus

The preceding discussion of the two general
movements within the Anselm corpus moves from the
question of the literary genres of his writings (the
affective and the logical) to the methodological genres
(the dogmatic and the apologetic). These questions are
very closely related, for the caveats expressed about a
too radical distinction between literary genres also
applies to any attempt to separate Anselm's writings
into two groups, where one group is controlled by faith
and the other is controlled by reason. This question of
the methodological genres is often raised as the
question about which works are theological and which are
philosophical. Or it is raised as the question about
the relationship between fitting and necessary reasons
in Anselm's writings. These are the questions to be
dealt with in this section.

We shall begin by recalling Charlesworth's insistence on a radical distinction between Anselm's arguments from authority and his argumentation by reason
alone. According to Charlesworth, Anselm's position
regarding faith and reason can be seen most clearly in
Cur Deus Homo since this is the best example of his
theological method. Charlesworth argues that Anselm
wants to reserve a place for reason independent of faith
in the data of Scripture, based on the view that Anselm
intended his Cur Deus Homo argument to convince those
who do not accept any supernatural revelation.42 To
support this view, Charlesworth stresses the remoto
Christo and rationes necessariae which are fundamental
to Anselm's method in Cur Deus Homo.

Yet, an appeal to the remoto Christo and rationes
necessariae does not in itself settle the issue since
both of these elements of Anselm's method do themselves
require interpretation; therefore, the argument that
reason is independent of faith on the basis of rationes
necessariae is a circular argument. One might question,
for example, what Charlesworth means by "purely rational
method of investigation of the Cur Deus Homo." If it
were the case that "necessary reasons" automatically
implied a purely rational method in the sense of auto-

nomous reason, then Charlesworth would be quite correct
in seeing an implicit division between scriptural faith
and logical reason in Anselm's system.43   But when he
concludes that Anselm's thought is separated into two
inconsistent parts, we see that he has failed to consider the common root of both faith and reason in the
divine truth of God.44 That is, he has failed to see
what Kohlenberger explicated, namely, that both human
reason and Scripture participate in the same divine
Verbum and hence are consistent in principle (and
complementary in part).   When Charlesworth begins by
separating faith and reason from their common source to
analyze them, it is not surprising that he would conclude that they are contrary.45

     But suppose for a moment that we accept Charles-
worth's view that Anselm works with two separate methods
and has two separate sources of meanings and understanding.   Would we then say that every time a concept
appears in a rational argument that it means one thing,
and every time the same concept appears in a dogmatic
argument that it means another?   Such a view simply does
not work. Take the concept of flesh, for example. The
term flesh, which is an integral part of Anselm's
reasoning about the necessity of the God-man in Cur Deus
Homo, has the same meaning in Anselm's meditation on
redemption and in his prayer to the sacred Cross--a
point for which full evidence will soon be provided.
The meaning of terms in these various kinds of arguments
does not vary but remains the same.   There is a
linguistic method that underlies and unites all the
various kinds of arguments that Anselm makes. And it is
on this linguistic level that Anselm's conceptual system
is worked out.

     But the difference in methods, Charlesworth might
object, does not pertain to the meaning of terms but to
the kinds of arguments employed. Some are "from reason"
and some "from authority, or the testimony of Scripture." However, this proposal also does not fit the
facts, for within the structure of one and the same
argument, Anselm often links propositions whose truth is
from reason with propositions whose truth is from authority.   His arguments cannot be classified as either
entirely rational or entirely dogmatic--for most of his
arguments are both "rational" and "dogmatic." Anselm is
constantly linking Scriptural teachings with teachings
from philosophy or ordinary experience to construct
arguments. This is, in fact, the characteristic form of
his constructive theological thinking.

How, then, does Anselm link ideas from Scripture and from experience? What is the logic of such mixed arguments? Since a scriptural proposition cannot follow from a rational proposition by necessity, it must follow for some other reason. Such other reasons, according to Anselm, are "common consent" and "fittingness." Some things are true by necessity, some are true by experience and common consent, some are true by authority, and some are true because they "fit" with other true things in a harmonious way. He links these different grounds of truth so that his arguments tend always to be a mixture of truths of different types. Such a mixed procedure is different from the modern tendency to separate rigorously rational from, say, aesthetic or scriptural arguments. For this reason, the attempt of Anselm's interpreters to categorize his arguments as exclusively rational or scriptural betrays the modern prejudice and misrepresents his method.

For example, what are we to do with those arguments that proceed in the manner "a--b--c--d," where a is a "necessary reason," but b is an argument from Scripture, and c is a "fitting reason"? For example, in Anselm's argument for the virgin birth, one finds that these different kinds of reasons are linked. It is necessary, says Anselm, that the God-man receive his humanity in one of four ways: (a) from a man and a woman, as in normal procreation, or (b) from neither a man nor a woman, as in Adam's case, or (c) from a man only, as in the case of Eve, or (d) from a woman only. But Scripture is the authority from which we learn that Adam was from neither a man nor a woman, and that Eve was from a man alone. And Anselm concludes from this combination of necessary reasons and Scriptural authority that it is fitting that the God-man be born of a woman alone since that would complete all of the logical possibilities of becoming a man. This single argument then utilizes necessary reasons, scriptural authority, and fitting reasons to arrive at the conclusion that the God-man must be born from a virgin.

Certain scholars would oppose this concentration on the mixed character of Anselm's arguments, criticizing it because it seems to weaken even Anselm's necessary reasons by suggesting they have the same status as fitting reasons. Schmitt makes this point, for example, and stresses the scientific, demanding

character of Anselm's necessary reasons.46   In "Die
wissenschaftliche Methode in Cur Deus Homo," Schmitt
presents his case for this distinction. He speaks of
these necessary reasons as compelling the mind to accept
that a certain truth must be this way and that it could
not be any other way. He observes that these reasons
are applied in a uniform manner throughout Anselm's
various works, from Monologion to Cur Deus Homo, and
that these compelling reasons are even applied to the
question of whether grammaticus is a substance or a
quality. It is because of the rationes necessariae that
Schmitt attributes a genuinely scientific quality to
Anselm's thought.

According to Schmitt, the union of ratio and
necessitas is the foundation of a science's univer-
sality. The ratio, which Schmitt refers to here, is the
objective reason for a thing's being the way it is. He
disagrees with the Anselm commentators who speak of
ratio's connection with amor, gaudium, and pulchritudo.
For Schmitt, ratio is a simple and unmixed concept. He
maintains that while love, joy, and beauty can be produced by the insight (intellectus) into the ratio of a
matter, they do not belong to the essence of the ratio
itself.47 It is this objective ground of ratio, permit-
ting no influence by the affections or emotions, which
leads Schmitt to term Anselm's method "scientific."

When Schmitt distinguishes so sharply between
ratio necessaria and convenientia, he directly contradicts Roques's explanation of the relationship between
rationes necessariae and convenientia.48   Roques states
that, for Anselm, reason and fittingness are not two
different levels of argument within a proof. Rather, he
insists that they share the same degree of necessity
since the highest intelligible perfection corresponds
necessarily to the highest fittingness. Thus, when
Anselm employs ratio, to prayerfully consider the divine
reasons for the mysteries of faith, Anselm finds the
least unfittingness to be no more acceptable than the
smallest lack of reason.

In both types of argument, says Roques, there is a
compelling force that has its source in the nature and
dignity of God. Roques does however allow this much of
a distinction between these two forms of argument:
convenientia refers to the order of God's wisdom and
honor while rationes necessariae refer to divine
intelligence and justice. Yet, since all of God's
attributes are absolutely inseparable, the efficacy of
both types of reasoning are related in God himself.49

Because of this intimate relationship between _necessitas_ and _convenientia_, Roques concludes that the two are practically interchangeable, and so it would be wrong to view the substitution of one for the other as lack of precision.50 If one accepts Roques's argument then one can reply to Schmitt that the insistence upon the mixed character of Anselm's arguments does not intend to reduce necessary reasons to the status of fitting reasons but tends to raise fitting reasons to like status with the necessary.

Moreover, any resolution to the questions raised by the relationship between _rationes necessariae_ and _convenientia_ must consider the larger structures in which both of these types of reasoning operate, namely the divine Truth that is the basis for their efficacy. Roques's approach to the _rationes necessariae_ appears to move in the direction of seeing this broader foundation of necessary reasons. In his introduction to _Cur Deus Homo_, Roques discusses the rationality of Anselm's method more in relation to a higher truth than in relation to its proof characteristics.51 He states that Anselm's rational consistency is in no way an end in itself, and it is in every case subordinate to the truth of Scripture. The _rationes_ are not themselves the truth for Anselm, and they receive their value only insofar as they testify to the truth. The same can be said for the fitting reasons. Their power rests in their relationship to the dignity and nature of God revealed in Scripture.

In this setting, both types of argument are referred to the mind and nature of God. Here it is extremely important to remember McIntyre's observation about what is involved in Anselm's use of the word _ratio_: in Anselm's atmosphere of prayerful reflection, _ratio_ does not in the first instance refer to ratiocination but rather to _ratio Dei_; consequently, Anselm's method does not impose logical principles upon the activities of God, but rather it strives to trace the mind, will, and purpose of God in prayerful thought.52

This point establishes the proper perspective from which to appreciate the relationship between _necessitas_ and _convenientia_. To build further on this foundation, it is important to see that the human _ratio_ is capable of entering into the mind, will, and purpose of God, i.e., the _ratio Dei_ because it is created according to the image of God. It is this understanding that is at the heart of Anselm's necessary reasons. If the _rationes necessariae_ are compelling, they are so because

they express the activity of _ratio_ in its proper correspondence to the rectitude of the divine Word. This
proper activity of _ratio_ is governed by a rectitude
implanted in it, a rectitude that is itself a participation in divine rectitude. This divine rectitude is
the basis of all truth and is perceived only by the
correctly functioning, divinely guided mind. For this
reason, Anselm defines truth as _rectitudo_ _mente_ _sola_
perceptibilis and can speak of the objective reference
of the _rationes_ _necessariae_. The objectivity of the
ratio's functioning is not based on its ability to
compel others who are outside of faith, but on its
immediate access to divine rectitude, which is the
foundation of truth and of _ratio_. In this respect the
rationes _necessariae_ are similar to _convenientia_, since
the latter is also compelling to the extent that it
corresponds to the Rectitude which is God. The source
of all appropriateness is God's rectitude, his nature,
and his dignity. This is the same source of the truth
which grounds necessary reasons and makes them compelling.

It is in terms of the relationship of both these
types of argument to the nature of God that Anselm
himself gives the clearest answer about the question of
their role in his theological system. In _Cur Deus Homo_
I/4, Boso wishes to distinguish sharply between fitting
and necessary reasons, saying that necessary reasons are
the only solid arguments that can convince infidels that
God wished to redeem men by suffering; he also suggests
that fitting reasons are only illustrations and not
convincing arguments. Anselm takes issue with this
viewpoint, insisting that it is convincing to demonstrate something like God's purpose for men by utilizing
fitting reasons:

> _Boso_. All of these things [the fittingness of
> redemption] must be acknowledged to be beauti-
> ful and to be pictures, as it were. However,
> if there is not a solid foundation upon which
> they rest, they do not seem to unbelievers to
> suffice for showing why we ought to believe
> that God was willing to suffer these things of
> which we are speaking. . . . Therefore, first
> of all we must exhibit the truth's firm ra-
> tional foundation, i.e., the cogent reasoning
> which proves that God should or could have
> humbled Himself to (undergo) those things
> which we proclaim. Next, so that this body-
> of-truth, so to speak, may shine even more
> splendidly, these considerations of fitting-

ness must be set forth as pictures of this
body-of-truth.

Anselm. Do not the following considerations
seem to constitute a very cogent argument for
why God ought to have done those things about
which we are speaking?: viz., that the human
race--His very precious work--had utterly
perished; and it was not fitting that God's
plan for man should be completely thwarted;
and this plan of God's could not be carried
out unless the human race was set free by its
very Creator.53

Thus, Anselm maintains that the fittingness of redemption is a sufficiently necessary reason for its actual
occurrence. Included in this appropriateness of redemption are such points as these: that redemption
should occur by a man's obedience since damnation
occurred through a man's disobedience; that the author
of righteousness should be born of a woman since sin and
condemnation had their origin from a woman; and that
redemption should be effected by man in suffering on the
tree (cross) since condemnation occurred by the fruit of
a tree.

For Anselm, such arguments are set alongside the
more logically demonstrated points concerning the virgin
birth and the need for man of Adam's race to redeem that
race. All of these arguments are linked in a totally
coherent structure. The systematic analysis of this
study rests on this type of free interplay of necessary
and fitting reasons. And that juxtaposition should not
be considered an inconsistency but rather an intrinsic
characteristic of Anselm's spontaneously coordinated
system.

The Gilson-Barth Debate

In the history of Anselm studies, two figures and
their great debate have shaped a background to which all
discussion of Anselm's methodology must finally relate.
While the Gilson-Barth writings are not central to our
own methodological concerns, it will be useful to state
briefly the relation of this discussion to theirs.

To the extent that the Gilson-Barth debate establishes those poles of interpretation which characterize
Anselm's method as either purely rational or strictly
dogmatic, it is relevant to the aspect of the question

of Anselm's method being considered in this chapter. My
main concern has been to describe the unified character
of the Anselm corpus, a unity that defies strict division of the corpus into either clear literary or clear
methodological genres. Both E. Gilson and K. Barth are
also arguing for a unified interpretation of Anselm's
method, but they choose to describe this unity in terms
of either the uniformly rational or the uniformly dogmatic.

Gilson presents his views on the rational character of Anselm's method and criticizes Barth's interpretation of Anselm's methodology in an article that is the
focal point of the debate. In this article, "Sens et
nature de l'argument de Saint Anselme," 54 Gilson describes the process of Anselm's thinking as a movement
from faith toward the beatific vision, but he questions
whether this type of thought should be termed theological of purely rational. Gilson's inquiry into Anselm's
method or argument in Proslogion ends with his refusal
to characterize this method as either theological or
philosophical. In describing the method by which Anselm's argument proceeds, Gilson concludes that the
words "purement rationnelle" are quite appropriate, but
because of the nature of the object to which Anselm
applies his rational method, viz., the truths of faith,
Gilson withholds the word philosophical from his
description of Anselm's thought.

Now if one appreciates Kohlenberger's arguments
about Anselm's view of the single source of all truth as
being located in the divine verbum, which is the ground
of all rationality, both human and divine, one can agree
with Gilson's characterization of Anselm's method as
purely rational. And it appears that Gilson himself
would agree with Kohlenberger's view since he argues
that for Anselm all rationality is grounded in faith.
Gilson's position can be interpreted to mean that, for
Anselm, there is sufficient consistency between the
human thought and divine thought that the truth that
the human mind knows is in complete accord with the
truth revealed by Scripture. In this way, faith becomes
the necessary point of departure for all rational investigation because the truth sought after in rational
investigation is the Truth that is God and revealed by
God alone.

This appears to be the rationale behind Gilson's
view that, for Anselm, even a relative understanding of
faith is possible only with the aid of grace. For this
reason, Gilson argues that even the works that would be

considered philosophical in modern terms are, for Anselm, still based on a faith-stance. In fact, he goes
so far as to say that to the extent that philosophy
indicates to us an investigation that starts from rational premises to reach rational conclusions, Anselm
did not write a single work of philosophy.55

Considering these qualifications of his description of Anselm's method as being purely rational, we can
see that Gilson is not holding an extreme, rationalistic
interpretation of Anselm's method, rather, he is arguing
that Anselm employs a pervasive rationality that has
faith as its starting point and that is consistent with
the truth of faith. So long as we presuppose this dogmatic character of Anselm's use of reason, we have no
difficulty accepting Gilson's interpretation of Anselm's
method. Gilson's interpretation is then seen as consistent with Kohlenberger's insight that Anselm's method is
linguistic, which is seen as correct when one appreciates that for Anselm the ground of human language is
the divine Word. In the same way, one can say with
Gilson that Anselm's method is purely rational when one
understands that human reason is made according to the
image of divine reason, and so the purely rational is
not set over against faith but rather is consistent with
faith and has faith as its source.

When this central point of Gilson's characterization of Anselm's method is understood in this way, is it
really that far from K. Barth's position? It is true
that Barth chooses to describe Anselm's method in terms
that differ from those of Gilson. He also selects the
word theological to describe this method, a word that
Gilson feels to be inaccurate. But does Barth understand the word theological as a description of Anselm's
method in the same way Gilson does? In Fides Quaerens
Intellectum, he argues that theology is the concern of
all Anselm's writings, and he maintains that the only
intelligere that Anselm cares about is that desired by
faith.56 Barth maintains that for Anselm, faith does
not require rational proof in the sense of the "existence of faith"; yet, the "nature of faith" does desire
knowledge.57 This distinction is very important because
it recognizes that even if the desire of faith is not
fulfilled in the joy of understanding this Truth, the
believer still remains in relationship to that Truth.
According to Barth's interpretation, even if the joy of
understanding the Truth is not achieved, the relationship of the believer to God still remains, though it is
then characterized primarily as reverence before the
Truth.58

Barth's description of faith as relationship to the Truth, which is God, is a helpful way of viewing the unity of faith and knowledge. Constructed on Anselm's statement that the Christian believes God is Truth,59 Barth's interpretation recognizes that God is related to all that is called truth, not only as _summa_ _veritas_, but also as _causa_ _veritatis_. Barth argues that because God is himself the unity of _intelligentia_ and _veritas_, we cannot believe in him without his becoming the author of a true knowledge of him.60

Here Barth is expressing a view that is close to Kohlenberger's, namely that God's Word, as the source of all truth, cannot be known without there occurring a corresponding human knowledge and truth. While Barth does not speak of this unity in exactly the same terms as Kohlenberger, Barth does see the central role of God's Word in Scripture as the single source of truth.

It is in this light that Barth's interpretation of Anselm's method can be understood and appreciated. Without completely adopting Barth's view, one can appreciate his point that the only _intelligere_ that Anselm cares about is that desired by faith. When one places Barth's point in the context of Kohlenberger's statements about _verbum_ as the key to Anselm's method, it is possible to understand how the Word of God is indeed Anselm's sole concern. Precisely because the _Verbum_ _Dei_ is the source of all human thought as well as the expression of God's thought in Scripture, there is no way for Anselm to avoid God's Word. When he meditates on Scripture, he is in contact with it. When he writes a prayer, he is in the presence of this Word. When he speculates about the incarnation or the nature of God, he remains in touch with God's Word, i.e., God's intimate presence among men.

Thus, Anselm's _sola_ _ratione_ method must be understood in this light. For Anselm, there is perfect continuity between the metaphysical and the historical, and that continuity resides in God's Word, the author of both those realms; therefore, if Anselm argues _remoto_ _Christo_, and if the historical fact of incarnation is temporarily set aside, the metaphysical impact of this fact still remains. The Word of God continues to express this same truth to man, whether it be in Scripture or in the prayerful depths of the human _ratio_. The important fact for Anselm is that God's Word is never separate from the scriptural Word wherever it is expressed so that even when truth is known with no direct, explicit reference to Scripture, it is still the scrip-

tural truth that is known. In Anselm's world of truth,
there is only one truth that is God's Word, and all
other truth is only true to the extent that it shares in
this truth. Truth does not cease to be the truth of
God's word even when it is known sola ratione.

This is the point Barth makes when he speaks of
faith as a relationship to the Truth that is God. In
this light, Barth's position can be appreciated as an
attempt to perceive the unity of Anselm's method under
the "category" of faith, precisely because faith has a
rational foundation that is the Truth of God. When the
positions of both Gilson and Barth are placed against
the background of Kohlenberger's view of the central
role of verbum in Anselm's theology, they are seen to be
emphasizing the unity of Anselm's method from different
viewpoints. Gilson appears to be stressing the rationality of faith while Barth stresses the dogmatic character of reason. The reason that both scholars have
found evidence to support their particular views is
because Anselm does indeed have a unified method, one
which is, so to speak, "dogmatically rational" (Barth's
point) or "rationally dogmatic" (Gilson's point). Their
two positions tend, therefore, to converge. While Barth
and Gilson begin at different places, they come through
their textual analyses to end in much the same place.

While this consideration of the Barth-Gilson
debate is not in any way intended to be a complete
presentation of either scholar's interpretation of
Anselm's method, it does hope to show at what point
their important debate has a bearing on the methodological concerns of this chapter. The contributions of
both these scholars can be appreciated when they are
viewed against the proper background, Anselm's vision of
the divine Word as the single source of all truth. This
we have seen in Kohlenberger's study Similitudo und
Ratio. We saw how this important insight about the
centrality of verbum is at the heart of Anselm's theological system, both on the motif, or deep, level and on
the discursive, or rational, level of his system. On
the deep level, verbum unifies Anselm's system as a
motif symbol, while on the rational level, verbum expresses Anselm's linguistic concern with the relatedness
of the concepts, standard terms, and ideas.

In this section, we have seen how important verbum
is in shaping a proper perspective from which to view
Gilson's and Barth's interpretations of Anselm's
method. In this last regard, verbum is particularly
useful because it is the locus of the unity of divine

and human thought. As such, it ensures the unity of
Anselm's method, because in the divine verbum, rationality and affectivity are joined. Here it is not simply
a matter of the divine substance not allowing any separation of intellectual operations, i.e., the rational
being separated from the affective. While that is
partly the point, we suggest an even more specific
reason for the unity of Anselm's method, namely, that
the one divine Word of God is both the principle of
rationality and order (as logos), and it is also the
principle of creativity, faith, and love (as the Word
that created the world, and the Word made flesh, which
expresses divine love in person). The importance of
this unity of the rational and the affective in the
divine Word is precisely that this Word is, as Kohlenberger has shown, the model of the operation of human
thought for Anselm; therefore, when Anselm sees this
unity of the rational and the affective as the divine
Word, he also recognizes that this is an ideal for the
intellectual operations of man. This is what Kohlenberger means when he speaks of the "similitudo character" of the human ratio in Anselm's thought. Consequently, for Anselm, the unity of theological method and
the unity of psychological operations is founded on the
unity of reason and love in the divine Word.

This unified view of Anselm's method will serve as
the foundation for the systematic analysis of this study
in two ways. First, it determines that the entire
corpus is relevant to a study of Anselm's theological
system. The entire corpus will be dealt with because
Anselm's method permits no division of his works into
separate and unrelated parts. This was the point made
in rejecting Charlesworth's restrictions on the parts of
the corpus which are important for an understanding of
Anselm's system. Such a division of the Anselm corpus
was rejected because his method utilizes the more affective approach to matters under investigation as well as
the more rational approach. His unified psychology
permits him to see how the affective and the logical fit
together in a harmonious way. Especially at the motif
level of Anselm's system, there can be no question that
the rational writings have priority over the devotional-
pastoral works.

The second way in which Anselm's unified method is
the basis for the systematic analysis of this study
deals with the actual approach to the Anselm materials.
The concept of flesh will be studied in a way that
follows as closely as possible the actual argumentation
employed by Anselm himself. In this respect, it is an

attempt to "put on the mind of Anselm" to make explicit how he uses the concept of flesh to shape his theological system at both of the levels that we have discussed--the discursive and the motif.

1.   "Opus subditum propter quosdam qui, antequam perfectum et exquisitum esset, primas partes eius me nesciente sibi transcribebant, festinantius quam mihi opportunum esset, ac ideo brevius quam vellem sum coactus, ut potui, consummare. . . . Hanc praefatiunculam cum capitulis totius operis omnes qui librum hunc transcribere volent, ante eius principium ut praefigant postulo: quatenus in cuiuscumque manus venerit, quasi in eius fronte aspiciat, si quid in toto corpore sit quod non despiciat" (CDH preface; S II, 42, 2-43, 7; AC III, 43).

2.   "Precor autem et obsecro vehementer, si quis hoc opusculum voluerit transcribere, ut hanc praefationem in capite libelli ante ipsa capitula studeat praeponere. Multum enim prodesse puto ad intelligenda ea quae ibi legerit, si quis prius, qua intentione quove modo disputata sint, cognoverit. Puto etiam quod, si quis hanc ipsam praefationem prius viderit, non temere iudicabit, si quid contra suam opinionem prolatum invenerit" (Mon. preface; S I, 8, 21-26).

3.   "Tres tractatus pertinentes ad studium sacrae scripturae quondam feci diversis temporibus, consimiles in hoc quia facti sunt per interrogationem et responsionem, et persona interrogantis nomine notatur 'discipuli,' respondentis vero nomine 'magistri.'. . . Quod videlicet tractatus quamvis nulla continuatione dictaminis cohaereant, materia tamen eorum et similitudo disputationis exigit, ut simul eo quo illos commemoravi ordine conscribantur. Licet itaque a quibusdam festinantibus alio sint ordine transcripti, antequam perfecti essent: sic tamen eos ut hic posui volo ordinari" (DV. preface; S I, 173, 2-174, 7; AC II, 73-74).

4.   McIntyre illustrates his point by saying that two of the premises of Cur Deus Homo were conclusions of Monologion and Proslogion, namely, the existence and triunity of God. He also cites these examples: the conclusion of Epistola de Incarnatione Verbi, (that the Second Person of the Trinity became incarnate) is a premise of Cur Deus Homo; and the conclusions of Monologion and Proslogion (God's three-in-oneness and the coessentiality of the Persons of the Trinity) and of Epistola de Incarnatione Verbi (that the Son is begotten by the Father) are premises of De Processione (see

"Premises and Conclusions in the System of St. Anselm's Theology," _SB_, pp. 95-101).

   5. Both J. Hopkins and M. Charlesworth attribute this unusual consistency over the course of a lifetime's work to the fact that Anselm's thought had already matured before he began to write his important works: "Anselm did not begin writing his formal treatises until he was forty-three, and the main lines of his thought seem to have been well and truly laid by then and to have remained constant" (Charlesworth, _St. Anselm's Proslogion_ [Oxford, 1965], pp. 30-31). See also, Hopkins _A Companion to the Study of St. Anselm_ (Minneapolis, 1972), p. 4.

   6. "Although a distinction between the early and the later Plato, for example, is crucial to discussing his theory of Forms, no such distinction, we have said, helps to understand a single one of Anselm's doctrines. In overlapping works Anselm reaffirms rather than changes his views" (Hopkins, _A Companion_, p. 5).

   7. "De rectitudine mente sola perceptibili loquimur" (_DV_, XII; S I, 192, 7). "Quod 'potestas servandi rectitudinem voluntatis propter ipsam rectitudinem' sit perfecta definitio libertatis arbitrii" (_DLA_ XIII; S I, 225, 2-3).

   8. "Est quidem iustitia quaelibet—magna vel parva: rectitudo voluntatis propter se servata. Libertas autem ista est: potestas servandi rectitudinem voluntatis propter ipsam rectitudinem. Quas definitiones puto me apertis rationibus monstrasse, priorem quidem in tractatu quem feci De Veritate, alteram vero in eo quem edidi De hac ipsa Libertate" (_DCP_ I/VI; S II, 14-18).

   9. "Multa quippe dicuntur secundum formam, quae non sunt secundum rem. Ut 'timere' secundum formam vocis dicitur activum, cum sit passivum secundum rem. Ita quoque 'caecitas' dicitur aliquid secundum formam loquendi, cum non sit aliquid secundum rem. Sicut enim de aliquo dicimus quia habet visum et visus est in eo: ita dicimus quia habet caecitatem et caecitas est in eo, cum haec non sit aliquid sed potius non-aliquid; et hanc habere non sit habere aliquid, immo eo carere quod est aliquid. Caecitas namque non est aliud quam non-visus aut absentia visus, ubi visus debet esse. Non-visus vero vel absentia visus non magis est aliquid ubi debet esse visus, quam ubi non debet esse. Quare caecitas non magis est aliquid in oculo quia ibi debet esse visus, quam non-visus vel absentia visus in lapide ubi visus

non debet esse. Multa quoque alia similiter dicuntur aliquid secundum formam loquendi, quae non sunt aliquid, quoniam sic loquimur de illis sicut de rebus existentibus" (DCD, XI; S I, 250, 21-251, 2; AC II, 149-50).

10. "Iniustitia autem omnino nihil est, sicut caecitas. Non enim est aliud caecitas quam absentia visus ubi debet esse, quae non magis est aliquid in oculo ubi debet esse visus, quam in ligno ubi non debet esse" (DCV, V; S II, 146, 3-5; AC III, 150).

11. The other examples that Hopkins notes are: The rich man in relation to the poor man (Mon. VIII, DLA II); the master-servant (Mon. III, DPS II); the various illustrations of the role of ought and can (DV VIII, CDH II/XVII); and the case of delivering a beating (DV VIII, CDH I/VII) (A Study of St. Anselm, p. 4).

12. R. Pouchet, La rectitudo chez saint Anselme (Paris, 1964).

13. "La rectitudo nous paraît être chez Anselme le centre vital où se nouent la pensée et l'action; pour user d'une autre image, c'est l'itinéraire qu'a suivi son âme de chercheur et de saint, pour aller à Dieu. Souligner la valeur synthétique de la rectitudo anselmienne, voilà toute l'ambition de cette monographie" (ibid., p. 15).

It should be noted that P. Rousseau calls attention to the importance of rectitude for the unity of Anselm's thought in his introduction to Oeuvres Philosophiques de Saint Anselme (Paris, 1947), pp. 29-37. He observes that the notion of rectitude dominates Anselm's two principal approaches to God, namely, rational investigation and moral purification.

14. AA I, pp. 3-10.

15. It should be noted that Anselm himself does not use the word system to characterize his writings. He really has no word to describe this novel type of spontaneous organization; he is in this sense an originator.

16. H. Kohlenberger, Similitudo und Ratio (Bonn, 1972), p. 24.

17. Ibid., p. 119.

18. "Cum ergo dicitur: si deus vult mentiri, non est aliud quam: si deus est talis natura quae velit mentiri; et idcirco non sequitur iustum esse mendacium. Nisi ita intelligatur, sicut cum de duobus impossibilibus dicimus: si hoc est, illud est; quia nec hoc nec illud est. Ut si quis dicat: si aqua est sicca, et ignis est humidus; neutrum enim verum est" (CDH I/XII; S II, 70, 20-24; AC III, 70).

19. Hopkins, A Companion, p. 248.

20. P. Tillich, The Dynamics of Faith (New York, 1957), pp. 41-43.

21. This reading of Heidegger's distinction follows Ott's interpretation of Heidegger in "What is Systematic Theology?" in The Later Heidegger and Theology, ed. J. Robinson and J. Cobb (New York, 1963), pp. 77-111.

22. H. Richardson, Toward An American Theology (New York, 1967), p. 57.

23. "Videtur igitur participatione qualitatis, iustitiae scilicet, iusta dici summe bona substantia. Quod si ita est, per aliud est iusta, non per se.

Ad hoc contrarium est veritati perspectae, quia bona vel magna vel subsistens quod est, omnino per se est, non per aliud. Si igitur non est iusta nisi per iustitiam, nec iusta potest esse nisi per se: quid magis conspicuum, quid magis necessarium, quam quod eadem natura est ipsa iustitia; et cum dicitur esse iusta per iustitiam, idem est quod per se: et cum iusta per se dicitur esse, non aliud intelligitur quam per iustitiam? Quapropter si quaeratur auid sit ipsa summa natura de qua agitur: quid verius respondetur, quam: iustitia?" Mon, XVI; S I, 30, 8-31; AC I, 25.

24. Schmitt argues from the infrequency of usage of the word participatio in the Anselm corpus to the relative unimportance of the concept. Flasch argues against this view.

25. J. Hopkins and H. Richardson, Truth, Freedom, and Evil (New York, 1967), p. 22. They also account for Anselm's particular form of the participation theory by saying that Anselm combined the Platonic notion of participation with the Aristotelian concept of correspondence to conclude the following: "When a proposition has truth of reference, (correct correspondence), it

participates in the Rightness of all things" (pp. 25-26).

26. F. S. Schmitt, AA I, p. 287.

27. Ibid., pp. 39-71.

28. But Flasch maintains that Anselm's notion of participation, elaborated through Anselm's distinction between per se and per aliud, does not endanger the traditional Christian doctrine of creation, as Schmitt has argued. Rather, Flasch argues that there is no danger of pantheism in Anselm's notion of participation because there is no super-ordained unity of the source of participation and the participant. Flasch also disagrees with Schmitt's judgment that Anselm employed only three types of causality in describing the Creator's relationship to the world, efficient, instrumental, and material causality. According to Flasch, when Anselm locates creation in the Verbum Dei, he recognizes that the exemplar cause is at the same time the efficient cause of the world. Flasch sees that the divine Word, which is the source of creation, is the source of truth and justice, and that the relationship between the Creator and creature can be characterized by the notion of participation.

29. "Nihil igitur quod de eius essentia vere dicitur, in eo quod qualis vel quanta, sed in eo quod quid sit accipitur. Quidquid enim est quale vel quantum, est etiam aliud in eo quod quid est; unde non simplex, sed compositum est." Mon., XVII, S I, 32, 1-4; AC I, 27.

30. "Nihil est verum nisi participando veritatem" (DV II, S I, 177, 16).

31. Hopkins, A Companion, p. 133. Hopkins sees that this notion of participation extends to the qualities of justice and goodness: "So then, in the opinion of both Augustine and Anselm, because God exists per se He does not participate in another, whereas other things have justice or goodness or truth as qualities, and so are thought to possess these per deum and thus in a reduced (and nonpantheistic) sense to participate in God, from whom they have their existence" (p. 132).

32. Charlesworth, St. Anselm's Proslogion, p. 34.

33. R. Roques, SR, pp. 119-87.

34. Roques makes this radical distinction with
great clarity in a passage that merits reflection: "Le
point de vue des traités est avant tout logique, intellectuel, objectif: ils s'efforcent d'établir par des
'raisons nécessaires' et par des raisonnements rigoureusement enchaînés (concatenatio, connexio) une vérité
ou un ensemble de vérités cohérent qui, de soi, ne
dépendent pas de l'affectivité du lecteur.   En consé-
quence, c'est d'abord une attitude de rigueur intellec-
tuelle qui s'imposera ici: on devra suivre, du début à
la fin et dans l'ordre même où ils sont proposés, les
arguments et démonstrations developpés par Anselme. Les
oraisons ou meditations, sont au contraire destinées
avant tout à toucher le coeur, à le convertir plus
parfaitement et à le remplir d'amour pour Dieu et pour
les réalités saintes.   Elles ne veulent aucunement
démontrer des vérités de raison ou de foi, même si elle
les rappellent et en font état: le lecteur est censé y
adhérer déjà dans son intelligence, et il s'agit seulement d'y fixer très fortement le coeur, par des 'raisons' qui touchent le coeur.   Or le cheminement de
telles 'raisons' n'est pas essentiellement ni d'abord un
cheminement logique   ou un raisonnement déductif.
L'intuition, la spontanéité, l'affectivité, le 'goût'
réglent ici la démarche de l'âme, et un texte, si
parfait soit-il, ne doit pas empêcher ou retarder cette
démarche dont les fruits très précieux sont l'humilité,
la componction, la piété, l'amour.   D'où la souplesse
extrême et l'extrême liberté qu'Anselme veut laisser à
son lecteur: qui'il lise ce qui lui plaît, qu'il commence et finisse où il lui plaît, qu'il lise lentement,
par petites 'doses,' en méditant lui-même avec l'intensité dont il est capable et en prenant le temps qui lui
convient" ("Structure et caractères de la prière Anselmienne" SR, pp. 122-23).

35. Another way of characterizing the two styles
or types of thought in the Anselm corpus was discussed
at the Anselm Congress in Normandy.   There the discussion centered around P. Evdokimov's article, "L'aspect
apophatique de l'argument de saint Anselme," in which he
argued that Anselm represented an important attempt to
use apophatic theology (SB, pp. 233-58).   Evdokimov
argued that Anselm represented a last attempt in the
Occident to use apophatic theology before Scholasticism
separated itself from the general movement of Oriental
apophatic theology. He characterized the method of the
Proslogion argument as attempting to pass beyond words
into silent contemplation, the very movement of the
apophatic method. In this regard, Evdokimov related the

"id quo nihil maius cogitari potest" to the hesychastic prayer which goes beyond discursive thought to the single word, _Jesus_. The next step after this reductive movement is the awareness of God's presence in silent contemplation (_AA_ III, p. 5).

However, in answer to a question by M. Chenu, Evdokimov balanced his original statements about Anselm's apophatic method by calling attention to the more discursive type of thought found in _Cur Deus Homo_. During the course of this discussion on the apophatic method in Anselm's writings, Dom Vagaggini expanded on Evdokimov's distinction between the two methods, apophatic and cataphatic, saying that the apophatic method corresponds to direct mystical knowledge of God while the cataphatic method primarily employs conceptual knowledge: "L'apophatisme serait ce que nous appelons la connaissance mystique de Dieu, tandis que le cata-phatisme correspondrait à la connaissance conceptuelle dans ce qu'elle a de positif. En effet même la con-naissance conceptuelle de Dieu a quelque chose de néga-tif, comme le prouve la doctrine thomiste de l'analogie qui inclut toujours une négation" (ibid., p. 7).

Dom Vagaggini's insistence that the apophatic and cataphatic methods are not rigorously opposed to each other, but that for Anselm the one moves into the other, is consistent with what we shall say about the affective and logical styles of thought.

Although this study does not propose to deal with the question of mysticism in Anselm's works, two per-tinent articles should be mentioned: P. Evdokimov, "L'aspect apophatique de l'argument de saint Anselme" in _SB_, pp. 233-58, and E. Gilson, "Sens et nature de l'argument de Saint Anselme," _Archives d'histoire doc-trinale et littéraire du moyen âge_, 9 (1934), pp. 5-51. Gilson's general distinction between mystical tonality and mystical experience would suggest a helpful approach to an understanding of this aspect of Anselm's works: "Ainsi qu'on le voit, je ne conteste pas ce que l'on pourrait appeler, en un sens très vague, la tonalité mystique du Proslogion. Il s'agit de savior si c'est une oeuvre de théologie mystique au sens propre, c'est-à-dire 'connaissance de Dieu obtenue par un procédé mystique, lequel doit etre lui-même une expérience de Dieu.'. . . Celui-ci (théologie mystique au sens propre) ne commence que là où Dieu est experimenté' par la connaissance ou par l'amour" (p. 31).

36.   J. McIntyre, "Cur Deus Homo: The Axis of the Argument," SR, p. 112.

36a.   B. Ward, The Prayers and Meditations of Saint Anselm, Middlesex, 1973.

37.   This foundation of human willing is explained in De Libertate Arbitrii and De Concordia.

38.   "Mande cogitando, suge intelligendo, gluti amando et gaudendo. Laetare mandendo, gratulare sugendo, incundare glutiendo" (Med. III; S III, 84, 10-12; AC I, 137).

39.   "Sur un mode logico-affectif, le suppliant argumente à la fois au nom de sa propre incapacité et de sa condition pécheresse, et au nom de la responsabilité constante et permanente du protecteur à l'endroit de l'abbaye ou de l'église qui lui est confiée" (Roques, SR, p. 127.

40.   Ibid.

41.   Ibid.

42.   This is a considerably disputed position that Charlesworth assumes in his interpretation of the purpose of Cur Deus Homo. Roques, for example, maintains quite to the contrary that Anselm's chief purpose in writing Cur Deus Homo is to justify the faith of the believer, and only secondarily does he persuade the unbeliever by showing the internal coherence of his faith. "Méthode du Cur Deus Homo: sa Portée," in Anselm de Cantorbery; Pourquot Dieu s'est fait homme (Paris, 1963), pp. 94-99.

43.   More will be said later about the interpretation of Anselm's rationes necessariae.

44.   "Here, then, we have the two sides to St. Anselm's thought. On the one hand, reason is allowed an independent function prior to faith, and, in some sense, reason can bring us to assent to the truths of faith. On the other hand, St. Anselm clearly acknowledges that faith is possible without any kind of prior rational preparation or justification, and that for the believer the only function of reason is to understand what is already believed. Clearly, as they stand, these two sides to St. Anselm's thought are not consistent, and some kind of distinction between the function of reason which brings us to faith and the function of reason

which operates within faith would have to be made to make them consistent" (Charlesworth, St. Anselm's Proslogion, p. 34).

45. M. Schmaus might question with Charlesworth the viewpoint adopted in this study, since he tends to see Anselm's sola ratione method as supporting an independent value of reason separate from the witness of biblical faith. Schmaus argues that Anselm intended to show that to a great extent one could know the truths of faith through reason without the authority of the Bible, and he sees the rationes necessariae as "zwingende Gruende" which would lead to those truths. Schmaus holds "dass Anselm ueberzeugt ist, man koenne die Wahrheiten des Glaubens zum grossen Teil (magna ex parte) auch durch die Vernunft allein (sola ratione) ohne die Autoritaet der Heiligen Schrift erkennen, wenn auch nicht durchdringen. Er ist sogar ueberzeugt, dass man 'zwingende Gruende' (rationes necessariae) fuer solche Wahrheiten anfuehren koenne." ("Die metaphysisch-psychologische Lehre ueber den Heiligen Geist im Monologion Anselms von Canterbury," SR, p. 189). Schmaus claims to find support for this interpretation of Anselm's method in Epistola de Incarnatione Verbi. He quotes from chapter 6 of this letter, where Anselm speaks of demonstrating by necessary reasons what is held in faith. But even here, when Anselm speaks of proving things about the divine nature and persons apart from Scriptural authority, he does not in any sense see that the truth considered by reason is separate from the truth expressed in the Bible. For Anselm, truth is never separate from the Word of God, even when there is no direct appeal to the testimony of this Word in the Bible.

46. "Trotz der Bestimmtheit, mit der sich Anselm ausdrueckt, hat man viel ueber die rationes necessariae diskutiert. Man hat vor allem versucht, ihren Begriff im Sinne blosser Konvenienzgruende zu mildern. Das ist aber nicht zulaessig, denn Anselm unterscheidet scharf zwischen convenientiae und rationes necessariae. . . . Es geht also nicht an, diese beiden Begriffe bei Anselm zu vermengen. Eine ratio necessaria ist und bleibt eine ratio necessaria--oder Worte haben nichts mehr zu bedeuten" (F. S. Schmitt, SB, pp. 363-64.

47. Schmitt bases this distinction between ratio and intellectus on the following definitions: ratio is the objective reason for a thing, while intellectus is the insight into this reason (cf. ibid., p. 359). In this same article on Anselm's scientific method, Schmitt

suggested that there are three meanings for the word
ratio in Anselm's writing: "Ratio kommt in dreifacher
Bedeutung vor. (1) Einige wenige Male, mit qua oder
quanta (ratione), heisst es: wie; auf welche Art und
Weise. (2) Die zweite Bedeutung ist Vernunft, als
Faehigkeit. Instrument zum ratiocinari (DCP III/11).
(3) Die Hauptbedeutung ist Grund; und zwar objektiver
Grund fuer eine Sache; und zwar mit der Vernunft erfass-
barer Grund; oder das Warum einer Tatsache" (ibid., pp.
358-59. Thus Schmitt's distinction between ratio and
intellectus refers to the third of these definitions of
ratio.

The view that Schmitt expressed in "Die wissenschaftliche Methode in Cur Deus Homo" appears to have
been modified during the course of the discussions at
the Anselm Congress, for there he speaks not only of
rationes as objective reasons, but also as subjective
reasons, and indeed he observes that the two are intimately related: "Il y a deux sens principaux: l'un est
celui de la faculté, l'entendement, l'autre est celui de
fondement (Grund), et en une double acception: fondement
objectif (e.g., huius rei ratio), fondement en quelque
sorte subjectif, en tant que perceptible à l'entendement. Ce qui fait la difficulté, c'est que ces deux
derniers sens, fondement objectif et fondement subjectif, sont intimement mélés de sort qu'il est à peu
près impossible de discerner entre eux" (AA III, p. 74).

48. Roques, Pourquoi Dieu s'est fait homme,
pp. 78-83.

49. "Entre les deux notions (convenance et
raison), le parallélisme est donc absolument rigoureux:
ce qui les distingue, c'est seulement que la notion de
convenance s'inscrit plutôt dans l'ordre de la sagesse
et de l'honneur divins, alors que l'intelligence et la
justice divines seraient plutôt les régulatrices de la
raison. Mais nous tenons d'Anselme lui-même que les
divers attributs de Dieu sont inséparables et qu'ils
sont nécessairement respectés ou violés ensemble"
(ibid., p. 81).

50. "Il serait injuste de voir dans ce croisement
ou dans cette substitution des notions une inconsciente
imprécision de langage: les principes méthodologiques
explicitement formulés par Anselme l'autorisent, quand
il s'agit de Dieu, à considérer comme chargés de la même
valeur logique et démonstrative les convenientiae et les
rationes bien que les unes et les autres correspondent à
deux points de vue distincts" (ibid., p. 82).

51.   Roques makes a very interesting observation
in regard to the notion of proof, saying that the proof
of the heart is a step toward assimilating the mysteries
of faith at a level even deeper than that touched by the
mind's reasoning: "Symétriquement ou corrélativement,
cette loque de la sensibilité spirituelle ou de la
loyauté doit s'imposer au comportement de l'homme. Il
doit faire passer au plus profond de son coeur ce que
son intelligence lui montre comme objectivement vrai et
bienfaisant, et d'abord le mystère de la rédemption.
C'est là, d'une certaine manière, authentifier ce
mystère, lui apporter une sorte de 'preuve' nouvelle, par
la ratification et la reconnaissance du coeur: Fac
precor, domine, me gustare per amorem quod gusto per
cognitionem. Sentiam per affectum quod sentio per
intellectum' (Med. III" "Structure et caractères de la
prière anselmienne," SR, p. 167).

52.   McIntyre, "Premises and Conclusions" p. 100.

53.   "Boso. Omnia haec pulchra et quasi quaedam
picturae suscipienda sunt. Sed si non est aliquid
solidum super quod sedeant, non videntur infidelibus
sufficere, cur deum ea quae dicimus pati voluisse
credere debeamus. . . . Monstranda ergo prius est veritatis soliditas rationabilis, id est necessitas quae
probet deum ad ea quae praedicamus debuisse aut potuisse
humiliari; deinde ut ipsum quasi corpus veritatis plus
niteat, istae convenientiae quasi picturae, corporis
sunt exponendae.

"Anselm. Nonne satis necessaria ratio videtur,
cur deus ea quae dicimus facere debuerit: quia genus
humanum, tam scilicet pretiosum opus eius, omnino
perierat, nec decebat ut, quod deus de homine propo-
suerat, penitus annihilaretur, nec idem eius propositum
ad effectum duci poterat, nisi genus hominum ab ipso
creatore suo liberaretur?"   CDH I/4; S II, 51, 16–52,
11; AC III, 53).

54.   This article appeared in Archives d'histoire
doctrinale et littéraire du moyen âge, 9 (1934), pp. 5–
51.

55.   "Nous savons d'ailleurs que l'intelligence,
même relative, de la foi, ne va pas sans l'aide de la
grâce, et Dieu ne cesse de combler perpétuellement son
Eglise de nouveaux dons. La foi cherchera donc toujour
l'intelligence. Mais il est également vrai que l'intelligence n'a pas d'autre objet à poursuivre que celui de
la foi. Et c'est ce que S. Anselme ne manque pas de

nous rappeler au début de ceux de ses ouvrages qui nous
sembleraient contenir le plus de philosophie, au sens
moderne du mot. Dans la mesure où la philosophie correspond pour nous à une recherche qui part de prémisses
rationnelles pour aboutir à des prémisses rationnelles,
on peut dire que S. Anselme n'a pas écrit un seul ouvrage de philosophie" (E. Gilson, Etudes_de_philosophie
médiévale [Strasbourg, 1921], p. 17). Charlesworth,
whose position we considered earlier, is quite far from
Gilson at this point. Charlesworth himself notes that
Gilson's judgment contradicts his own view that "St.
Anselm cannot be interpreted as having denied in principle the possibility of a natural theology, a rational
approach to God, logically prior to and independent of
faith" (St._Anselm's_Proslogion, p. 45).

56. "Anselm geht es in allen seinen Schriften
(mit einer Ausnahme, viz. De__Grammatico) um Theologie,
um den intellectus fidei. Fides quaerens intellectum
sollte der Titel des Proslogion nach der Angabe des Pro-
cemium urspruenglich lauten. Also das und nur das intelligere kommt bei Anselm in Frage, nach dem der Glaube
'verlangt.' Und die Notwendigkeit Kraft derer es zu dem
hier gemeinten intelligere und dann auch zu dessen
Wirkungen, zum probare und zum laetificare kommt, ist
einzig und allein dieses 'Verlangen' des Glaubens" (K.
Barth, Fides_Quaerens_Intellectum [Munich, 1931], p. 6).

57. "Es ist nicht die Existenz, es ist aber--wir
wenden uns nun der anselmischen Position zu--das Wesen
des Glaubens, das nach Erkenntnis verlangt" (ibid.,
p. 8).

58. In a concise statement on the relationship
between faith and reason, Barth relates both to the one
Truth that is God: "Kommt das intelligere nicht zum Ziel
(und es kommt wahrlich weithin nicht zum Ziel) dann
bleibt an Stelle der Freude an der Erkenntnis die Ehr-
furcht vor der Wahrheit selbst, die auch so um nichts
weniger die Wahrheit ist. Denn wie ganz und gar gemessen ist an der geglaubten Sache, so ist diese Sache bzw.
der Glaube an diese Sache ganz und gar nicht gemessen an
der Sachgemaesheit jener menschlichen Saetze" (ibid.).

59. "Deum veritatem esse credimus," (CDH I/1).

60. "Er ist der Gott, in welchem intelligentia
und veritas identisch sind (Mon. 46), der Gott, dessen
Wort an uns nichts anderes ist, als die integra veritas
paternae substantiae (Mon., 46). Er ist sensibilis, d.
h. cognoscibilis (Pros. 6). Dieser Gott kann offenbar

nicht von uns geglaubt werden, ohne Urheber einer vera
cogitatio zu werden, d. h. der Glaube an ihn erfordert
auch seine Erkenntnis" (Barth, Fides Quaerens Intellectum, p. 9).

WORD STUDY

Structures of Meaning
Within Anselm's System

Within St. Anselm's theological system are various levels, or structures, of meaning. An understanding of Anselm's theological system and of the various concepts that shape that system depend on an appreciation of these "semantic structures."

At one level of analysis, or within one of the structures of meaning, the meaning of a concept is determined by its relationship to other concepts and terms around it. The structure that establishes the meaning of a concept at this level is the "language web" formed by the logical connections that join all of the concepts in the surrounding sentences. This level of meaning is what H. Richardson terms the "category or level of relations" since the meaning of terms at this level is determined by their relationship to other words.1

Such a "relational setting" provides the structure of meaning not only for concepts but also for the contextual, or discursive, level of a theological system. This is true in Anselm's case at least. At this relational level, the system is established by the logical connectedness of technical terms where the argument moves forward precisely by means of the relationship of these terms to one another. On the relational level, just as the meaning of concept is established by the relation of terms to one another in a sentence, so the meaning of system is created by the interrelationship of terms. But whereas the meaning of concept at the relational level is discovered in the context of a sentence or of a paragraph, the meaning of system at this same level is created by the logical bonds that link a number of paragraphs (or even whole treatises) in a coherent argument.

Here we might recall the diagram from chapter 4 which illustrates how such a discursive system is formed:

- x - y - z -

The meaning of this type of system is a product of the linear development of the "rational" argumentation represented by the sequence of letters x, y, z. Such argumentation builds to a conclusion, and this conclusion depends on the relationship of x to y and z. The systematic meaning discovered from the logical interrelationship of these terms is much like the conceptual meaning derived from an examination of the interrelationship of words in a sentence. A study of the interrelationship of concept and arguments is the way to arrive at the meaning of a system on the relational level. The point here is that on this relational level of meaning, both concepts and system are determined by the relationship of terms. And the sentence that provides the contextual, or relational, meaning for a word can be considered a miniature relational system since its meaning is determined by the logical relationship of terms in the sentence. Thus, on the relational level of meaning, either a sentence or a system can be represented in the form -x-y-z- since the principle that establishes the meaning of a concept or of a system at this level is the logical relationship between terms.2

The relational level we have described is the level on which J. McIntyre and J. Hopkins have examined Anselm's theological system. When McIntyre studied the relationship of the premises and conclusions of Anselm's works, he called attention to the logical connections that join Anselm's various theological arguments. According to McIntyre, these logically connected arguments move in a linear progression, forming a "relational system." In such a system all of the key ideas and terms are related to one another, which is exactly what Hopkins pointed out when he spoke of the consistent definitions and basic examples employed throughout the Anselm corpus. The full meaning of these terms on the relational level of analysis is established precisely by seeing their relationship to the other important terms in the context of the entire theological system.

Now in this study we shall be examining the flesh complex, (sometimes called flesh or the concept of flesh) in relation to other terms and doctrines that provide the context, or total language web, within which the concept of flesh receives its meaning. It will be at this level of meaning that we shall consider the function of Anselm's concept of flesh within the context of his doctrines of God, creation, angels, incarnation, redemption, original sin, free will, grace, Church, and sacraments. It is also at this level that we shall see how the concept of flesh functions in relation to other important concepts and technical terms within his theological system, such as freedom, justice, and sin. Such an analysis will follow the observations of McIntyre and Hopkins concerning the principles that guide and shape Anselm's theological system at the relational, or discursive, level. In fact, we shall be following their lead when we examine the concept of flesh as one of the important logical bonds that join Anselm's theological arguments and when we consider how the concept of flesh logically joins the major terms of the system.

Now besides this relational level or structure of meaning, there is another level or structure of meaning. At this second level, the meaning of a concept is determined not by its relation to other concepts and terms but by its power to generate a context or whole or to evoke a gestalt. This is the level of meaning which Richardson has called the "category of wholes" because the entire reality, the whole, is present in the symbol that renders present, or evokes, that reality.3 At this level of analysis, a concept receives its meaning not from its context in a sentence or in a relational system as is the case on the contextual level but rather from its participation in the reality it symbolizes. The symbol communicates by rendering present, or evoking, the reality it symbolizes. This points to an important difference between the relational structure of meaning and the symbolic structure of meaning. When a concept acts as a linguistic symbol, it does not depend on a logical context for meaning; it is not grasped by examining the other concepts and terms of the sentence in which it appears. In fact, the symbol need not even appear in a sentence to communicate its meaning. This is totally different from the relational level where the concept receives its meaning from its context in a sentence or a paragraph.

The symbol may appear as an all-embracing metaphor that does not refer to any other particular word because it implies them all.4 Such a symbol operates poetically by causing the perceiver to become one with the thing perceived. Richardson describes this mode of perception as "a simple kind of consciousness," underlining the direct and immediate character of symbolic perception.5

In "What is Systematic Theology," H. Ott attempts to explain the symbolic structure of meaning by using the illustration of a poem, suggesting that the theological system on the symbolic, or motif, level is understood in the same way a poem is understood. Ott gives this description of how a poem communicates its meaning:

> A poem speaks to us, lays claim upon us in a particular way, has us encounter a certain meaning. In the process, every stanza, every verse, perhaps even many a word speaks distinctively, lays a claim upon us that is all its own. An allusion, a single figure of speech, an evocation lets us meet a whole world, opens up a horizon. A sentence, a few brief words, confront us perhaps with a definitive attitude and answer. And yet the poem speaks as a unity; it is experienced as a single connection of meaning. And thus we have again the situation of the complex structures and the indivisible meaning. A good interpretation of a poem will seek to direct one to the poem's (unspoken) totality of meaning, by carefully touching upon and pointing out the structure.6

Here Ott expresses the very points we attempted to emphasize in the diagram of the symbolic, or motif, system.

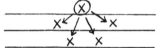

Ott's "totality of meaning" is what we have described as the central motif, or ⊗ in the diagram. This motif is the "whole world" which we meet through the motif symbols, the x's, which correspond to the "figure[s] of speech" and "evocation" of a poem which Ott describes. And here we also see Ott using the language that Richardson describes as being appropriate to wholes: The poem speaks as a "unity" and is experienced as "a single connection of meaning," according to Ott. Ott claims that the poem communicates its meaning by direct evocation, using that mode of perception which Richardson called "feeling." Moreover, Ott recommends that a good interpretation of a poem should "direct one to the poem's (unspoken) totality of meaning."

A word, then, within the symbolic structure of meaning is understood quite differently than the same word within the relational structure of meaning. And just as the relational structure, or level, of meaning is applied to and determines the interpretation of both individual words and entire systems, so the symbolic level of meaning also extends beyond an interpretation of individual words to provide a meaning-structure for a whole system. Whether one considers the system in its symbolic dimension or the concept as symbol, the principles of understanding their meaning remain the same, namely, the participation of symbols in a motif and the evocation of this motif by these motif symbols.

The theological system at the symbolic level is more complex and more difficult to describe than the theological system at the relational level. The diagram we used to compare both types of system provides some help in seeing how the symbolic, or motif, system operates differently from the relational, or discursive, system:

Level A

Level B

In this diagram, ⊗ is the motif that inspires, shapes, and controls the entire system, but it does not do this through the logical relationship of the various terms x, y, z, a, and b, which is the way the relational system receives its form. Rather the symbolic, or motif, system achieves its shape from what R. Pouchet has called a "spontaneous coordination." This spontaneous coordination is achieved through the power of the motif symbols, the x's in the diagram, which evoke the central motif of the entire system; these symbols evoke the motif at more than one level. Consequently, the concept x, which is a motif symbol, may operate as a technical term within the relational, or discursive, system at level B at the same time it evokes the central motif of the theological system at level A, the symbolic level of meaning.

We should note that the unspoken character of the actual motif is represented in the diagram by placing the actual motif ⊗ outside of the motif system itself since one cannot directly examine or represent the actual motif itself. The actual motif remains unspoken and is merely rendered present through evocation. This is an important aspect of the symbolic system, and it is the reason that one cannot simply explain what the motif of the system is. Precisely because the motif itself is an orientational perspective, a reality that is more than all of those symbols evoking it, it cannot be defined, just as the feeling or attitude created by a poem cannot be explained exhaustively by the power of discursive reason. This unspoken totality can only be rendered present by the evocative power of symbols, a

point that we shall develop in the chapter devoted to
the symbolic, or motif, level of Anselm's system.

It is at this symbolic level of Anselm's system
that the studies of Pouchet and Kohlenberger make their
contributions. Pouchet demonstrates how <u>rectitudo</u>
symbolizes the motif of Anselm's theology. Kohlenberger
provides a similar demonstration for <u>verbum</u>. Both
scholars have described an <u>x</u> in our diagram, even though
the motif itself ⓧ remains unspoken. Moreover, we
observed with Kohlenberger how <u>verbum</u> operates at both
levels of meaning, going beyond Hopkins's examination of
<u>verbum</u> at the discursive level of system, illustrating
concretely how an <u>x</u>, in this case <u>verbum</u>, is operative
at both levels of Anselm's theological system. Or again
we see with Pouchet how <u>rectitudo</u>, another <u>x</u>, evokes the
motif of Anselm's theology going beyond the function of
this concept as a term in the relational, or discursive,
level of system where it logically joins Anselm's
definitions of truth and justice.

At this point a word of clarification might be
helpful with regard to the motif level of Anselm's
theology. The motif is the reality that is evoked by
the motif symbols. We have already described this
reality as a whole connection of meaning, and as an
unspoken totality of meaning. These descriptions point
to both the ontological and the epistemological aspects
of the reality that is met through motif symbols. The
ontological foundation of the motif is the reality, the
whole. The significance of this reality is the single,
unspoken totality of meaning. This significance and
meaning are the epistemological dimensions of the reality. It is in this sense that we speak of the motif as
an orientational perspective, influencing our perception
and knowledge. The experience of the reality, the
motif, through the direct evocation of feeling effects a
change in perception in that the motif becomes a horizon
or a perspective through which we perceive the world.

Motif symbols bring us directly in touch with the
motif that effects this change in perception. Because
the motif is a perspective that organizes perception, it
is more than all the symbols that evoke it. The symbols
are not the motif itself. Thus, different motif symbols
can evoke the very same motif. In this sense <u>rectitudo</u>
and <u>verbum</u> evoke the motif of Anselm's theology in the
same way that flesh does. To the extent that these
symbols participate in the motif of Anselm's theology,
they can evoke the motif in such a way that others
experience as a whole the total meaning of this motif.

In this study, we shall see how the flesh complex functions within Anselm's theological system at the symbolic, or motif, level. On this level of analysis, we shall see how flesh joins <u>rectitudo</u> and <u>verbum</u> as a symbol that evokes the fundamental motif of Anselm's entire theology. This symbolic function of flesh will be seen especially in Anselm's doctrine of the sacrament of the eucharist, the sacrament wherein the flesh of Christ is the efficacious symbol that unites man to God by effecting a change in the disposition of man's will. A separate chapter will be devoted to the power of the flesh to effect this union of man's will and God's will in the central mystery of grace accomplished by the God-man.

We have discussed two structures, or levels, of meaning which determine the way in which Anselm's theological system and the concepts within that system can be understood. At the relational level a concept receives its meaning by its relation to the other words around it. And the theological system at this level is a discursive, logically coherent unit. But at the symbolic level of meaning, a concept acting symbolically evokes a whole reality that transcends the symbol itself. The theological system at this level is a unity based on this evocative power of symbols to render present the motif that inspires, shapes, and controls the whole system. We shall devote separate chapters to each of these levels in the course of the systematic analysis of the concept of flesh.

Now we turn to another structure of meaning, namely, the denotative level. Strictly speaking, this is not a level at which systems arise, but it is one other way in which individual words or concepts receive meanings. They can receive meanings by denoting an object or reality. This denotative structure of meaning provides a simpler way of understanding a word than is the case with the relational or the symbolic structures that we described above. The denotative meaning does not depend on its relation to other words in a sentence as is the case with the relational struc-ture, or level, of meaning. Nor does a word at the denotative level evoke the whole reality that it denotes as is the case with a word at the symbolic level of meaning.

Richardson has called this denotative level of meaning the "category of individuals" as opposed to the categories of relations (the relational, or contextual, level) or the category of wholes (the symbolic, or

motif, level). He has related each of these categories
to common linguistic units in this way: the category of
individuals corresponds to the word; the category of
relations corresponds to the sentence; and the category
of wholes corresponds to the paragraph, or rather, to
the central point or idea of the paragraph.7 This way
of picturing the various structures of meaning in terms
of the word, the sentence, and the point of the paragraph, is helpful because it shows something of the
interrelationship between these various levels. The
word is the building block of the sentence and the
paragraph, but on the relational level of meaning, the
sentence determines the word, and on the level of paragraph or the level of wholes, the word may be used as an
image, or symbol, which evokes a whole, or a total
experience which was the point of the paragraph. From
the interrelationship of these linguistic units, we can
see that the denotative level of meaning, the word (or
Richardson's category of individuals), is a first step
in understanding the meaning of a word or of a concept,
and we also see that the other levels of meaning (the
relational and the symbolic, corresponding to the sentence and the paragraph) affect what the word denotes,
and these other levels are in turn influenced by the
denotative meaning.

From this perspective, we see that the denotative
level of meaning is the point at which we must begin
our analysis of the concept of flesh, i.e., by several
simple "word studies." Before examining how that concept functions within Anselm's theological system (at
both the relational, or discursive, and the symbolic, or
motif, levels of the system), we must first establish
its denotative meaning. Yet, this is not as easy a task
as it might first appear to be. The simple denotative
meaning of flesh is difficult to determine. In the
Christian tradition, it has been used to denote many
things. For example, the word <u>caro</u> may denote the body;
at other times it is seen as polar opposite of the
spirit.

One might consider, for instance, the way St. Augustine employs this word since he provides the direct
background for much of Anselm's thinking about the
flesh. Augustine speaks of the flesh primarily in terms
of <u>concupiscentia</u> <u>carnis,</u> and in such terms it denotes a
tendency of bodily senses to distract man from God.
This denotation of the word <u>caro</u> is especially evident
in the <u>Confessions</u> where Augustine speaks of the temptations associated with the flesh:

To this is added another form of temptation
more manifoldly dangerous. For besides that
concupiscence of the flesh which consisteth in
the   delight   of   all   senses   and   pleasures,
wherein   its   slaves,   who   go   far   from Thee,
waste   and   perish,   the soul hath, through   the
same senses of   the   body,   a   certain vain and
curious   desire,   veiled   under   the   title   of
knowledge   and   learning, not of delighting   in
the flesh, but of   making   experiments   through
the   flesh.   The   seat   whereof   being in the
appetite   of   knowledge,   and   sight being   the
sense chiefly used for attaining   knowledge,   it
is   in Divine   language called the lust   of   the
eyes.8

Here Augustine   speaks   of   the temptations of the flesh,
of "delighting in the flesh,"   or   of "making experiments
through the flesh" where "flesh" denotes   a   disobedience
or   rather a distraction from the higher spiritual   functions.   E.   Hendrix refers to precisely this denotation
of flesh as disobedience   and   a   clouding   of the higher
spiritual   faculties   when he interprets Augustine's   use
of the term flesh as concupiscentia   carnis.9   Augustine
uses   the   word   flesh   to   denote   this disobedience   or
unruliness   of the senses especially in   the   explanation
of the original   sin   doctrine.   In the context of that
doctrine,   as   J. Gross has pointed out,   Augustine   uses
the term concupiscentia   carnis synonomously with libido,
lex   peccati,   and cupiditas.10   Thus,   in   Augustine's
original sin doctrine,   the   primary   denotation   of   the
word   caro   is   a tendency of the bodily senses to oppose
the life of the spirit.

This shows   us   a   common denotation of the concept
of flesh developed by Augustine.   In   our   analysis   of
Anselm's   denotative   meaning   of the word caro,   we shall
see that he partly follows Augustine.   But   Anselm also
uses   flesh   to   denote   other   things.   For example,   in
Monologion,   Anselm   uses   caro   to denote   the   body   in
metaphysical and epistemological terms,   as   a   substance
and   as   the   center   of   sensation and perception;   in
certain   personal   letters,   caro signifies familial origin
while   in other   letters   it   denotes   the   physiological
condition   of   a   person;   in De Conceptu Virginali,   caro
denotes the condition of human   nature   in   terms   of the
Augustinian   denotation;   and   in Epistola de Sacramentis
Ecclesiae, caro denotes the resurrected body   of   Christ
and   the   eucharist.   What is particularly innovative   is
that Anselm   also uses caro to denote the dispositions of
the will, a meaning   that can be seen fully only   from   a

systematic analysis but which is already apparent even at the denotative level of meaning.

The variety of denotations makes it clear that flesh is a rich concept involving many meanings and that the analysis of this concept at the denotative level must consider all of these meanings. It must also take into account the fact that Anselm employed different Latin words to discuss the flesh complex. The principal Latin terms that signify flesh are <u>caro</u>, <u>concupiscentia</u>, and <u>corpus</u>. In <u>De Concordia</u>, Anselm uses <u>caro</u> interchangeably with <u>concupiscentia</u>, and in <u>Epistola de Sacrificio Azimi et Fermentati</u>, he equates <u>caro</u> with <u>corpus</u>. Such examples suggest how closely these Latin words are linked in Anselm's thought, and therefore it is necessary to examine all three of these words in Anselm's various treatises to clarify the full range of meaning of the flesh complex on the denotative level of analysis.

One further note should be added: while the "higher" levels of meaning (the relational and the symbolic levels) occasionally come into play even at the denotative level of analysis, those higher levels will here be mentioned only in passing; we shall defer their full consideration to later chapters dealing specifically with those levels. This duplication cannot be avoided. The radical interrelationship of all of these levels of meaning is more primary than the analytical distinctions we shall make concerning them, and so some overlapping of these analytical levels is inevitable.

Choice of Method

There are two general approaches that can be employed in analyzing words or concepts within a given body of literature. One approach is concerned with a quantitative analysis of words while the other focuses on a qualitative examination of words in their variety of usage. We shall briefly describe these two methodological approaches to indicate which is most suitable for studying the denotative meaning of the flesh concept in Anselm's theology.

Content analysis is a quantitative research technique used in a variety of social sciences. It has been utilized in literary studies to solve questions of disputed authorship and in international politics to analyze decision-making and propaganda.11 In psychology, content analysis has been applied to the results of projective tests and some dream analysts perform a content analysis on dream reports to gain an overall psychological portrait of an individual.12

The basic method behind these various applications of content analysis is this: to make inferences about verbal and written material by systematically studying how frequently certain words or categories are used in a given test. The volume <u>Content Analysis</u> provides a concise description of research design in this kind of study: "First, the research question, theory and hypothesis are formulated. The sample is then selected, and the categories are defined. Next, the documents are read and coded, and the relevant content is condensed into special data sheets. After coding . . . counts in frequency or intensity are made. Finally, interpretation of the findings are made in light of the appropriate theory.13 If such a quantitative method were applied to the flesh concept in Anselm's theology, one would examine this category (flesh) by noting all the occurrences of the words <u>corpus caro</u> and <u>concupiscentia</u> in each of Anselm's writings. One would then try to interpret the meaning of this frequency of usage.

Content analysis may suggest in which writings of the Anselm <u>corpus</u> the concept appears most frequently to determine what treatises or meditations to focus on in exploring the role of flesh in his theology. Yet, as we already saw in chapter 4, the entire Anselm <u>corpus</u> must be dealt with to grasp the overall picture of his theological system. Such a quantitative method might at best suggest certain areas of Anselm's work to emphasize, but even a cursory reading of Anselm's collected works provides clues to which writings shed the most light on his concept of flesh.

In relation to this study of the flesh concept it does not appear that a content analysis would contribute greatly to our understanding of the role of flesh in Anselm's theology. The working hypothesis that guides our research is that the flesh plays a major, though essentially unrecognized, role in Anselm's theology. In his index to Anselm's collected works, F. S. Schmitt listed all the important places where the words that denote flesh occur. This listing indicates that the concept of flesh is prominent in Anselm's writings. Yet word frequency does not address the question of the role this concept plays in Anselm's theological system.

A quantitative analysis does not provide the leverage necessary to lift this concept to a point at

which we can begin to see its various meanings at the
denotative level or its significant function in Anselm's
theology. A more productive line of research for this
word study is a qualitative analysis of the concept of
flesh. At this basic, denotative level of analysis we
need to determine, first, the character of the flesh
concept, that is, the various shades of meaning and the
range of ideas and objects it refers to. Here we might
consider the approach taken in <u>The Oxford English Dic-
tionary</u> as a model. This dictionary method gradually
unfolds the layers of meaning of a word. It establishes
the range of meaning by giving cases that concretely
illustrate exactly how the word appears in sentences
drawn from texts.

To illustrate this method, we cite in a very
abbreviated fashion some elements of <u>The Oxford English
Dictionary</u>'s presentation of the English word flesh.14

1. "As <u>a material substance</u>, the soft substance of
   an animal body. Example: 'I am sure if he
   forfaite, Thou wilt not take his flesh' (Shakespeare, <u>Merchant of Venice</u> III, 1, 54)."

2. "A <u>muscular tissue</u>, or the tissues generally, of
   animals, regarded as an article of food. Example: 'Neither do they eat of fat or flesh'
   (Fosbrooke, <u>British Monachism</u> [1843] 70.)"

3. "That which has <u>corporeal</u> life. Example: 'The
   gods, whose dwelling is not with flesh' (Bible,
   Daniel II,11)."

4. "The <u>physical or material frame of man</u>. Example: 'My frighted flesh trembles to dust'
   (Habington, <u>Castara</u> [Arb.] 133)."

5. "The <u>body</u> (<u>of Christ</u>) regarded as spiritually
   'eaten' by believers; also applied mystically to
   the <u>bread in the sacrament</u> of the Lord's
   Supper. Example: 'true bread He maketh, By His
   Word His Flesh to be' (Hymns A. and M., 'Now my
   tongue IV')."

6. "The <u>animal or physical nature of man; human
   nature</u> as subject to corporeal necessities and
   limitations. Example: 'The Heart-ake, and the
   thousand Naturall shockes that Flesh is heyre
   too' (Shakespeare, <u>Hamlet</u> III, 1, 63)."

7. "In expressions relating to the <u>Incarnation</u>: The days of his flesh: the period of <u>his earthly life</u>. Example: 'Our Lord Jesus himselfe all the daies of his abasement and flesh endured them' (Rogers, <u>Naaman</u>, 2)."

8. The <u>sensual appetites</u> and inclinations as antagonistic to the nobler elements of human nature. Example: 'By . . . conquering penance of the mutinous flesh' (Shelley, <u>Hellas</u> 156)."

From the examples cited above we can see that the word <u>flesh</u> has a multiplicity of meaning on different levels. For example, flesh denotes various material elements in the first four definitions: material substance, muscular tissue, corporeal life, and the physical frame of man. But it can also refer to metaphysical, moral, and spiritual states, as in the last four definitions. Definition 6 denotes the metaphysical condition of human nature as limited by the physical world, while no. 8 refers to the negative moral qualities associated with the sensual appetites. Finally, definitions 5 and 7 denote aspects of Christian doctrine: no. 5 refers to the spiritual body of Christ in the eucharist and no. 7 refers to God's incarnation in a human body. So this qualitative dictionary method well illustrates the variety and levels of meaning of flesh. Already we see meanings that are opposed to each other at different levels, and this characteristic multi-meaning allows flesh to symbolize the transformation process.

This is exactly what we see in Anselm's theological use of flesh: it symbolizes the transformation of the individual and of the human race. This might be called the "transformation potential" of the term <u>flesh</u>. By following a qualitative dictionary method in this word study we shall establish what flesh denotes in Anselm's writing and also show how it can potentially function in his theology. Let us anticipate slightly what will be grounded in depth in the word study. The transformation potential found in the wide range of meaning that is suggested in the Oxford English Dictionary presentation is shown even more clearly in Anselm's theological use of flesh. Table 5.1 will illustrate this point. The range of meaning of the concept of flesh extends from the morally and spiritually negative meanings as "the will of fallen angels" and "unrestrained appetites" to the spiritually positive meaning of the "eucharistic body of Christ."

Table 5.1. Range of Meaning of the Concept of Flesh

        9. Eucharistic body of Christ
        8. Eucharistic bread   +
        7. Earthly flesh of Christ

        6. The immortal body
        5. Dispositions of the will   ±
        4. Source of perception

        3. Life "according to the flesh"
        2. Unrestrained appetites   -
        1. The will of fallen angels

These nine cases bring out the widest range and diversity of meaning of flesh and they highlight the transformation potential of flesh as well. In one sense Anselm's theology can be thought of as a reflection on the transformation of the flesh, i.e., how salvation history leads from the negative states of the flesh referred to in cases 1 through 3 to the positive states represented in cases 7 through 9. The following analysis of these nine basic usages will suggest how Anselm organizes his theology to express the transformation of the flesh from the Fall of Satan and Adam to the restoration in Christ.

Nine Basic Usages

In this part of the chapter we are going to examine nine cases in which Anselm uses the word _flesh_. The cases are arranged so that they move from the more negative denotations, such as "desires of the flesh" to the positive ones, such as "the holy body of Christ." Three negative, three neutral, and three positive cases have been chosen for this study to represent, as far as possible, the full range of meaning. Because the concept of flesh has such varied meanings, some of the cases may also refer to other more positive or more negative denotations. So, for example, one aspect of the word _concupiscentia_ in case no. 1 may also refer to a usage of the flesh concept that might be correctly considered a neutral meaning. This situation makes it clear that this classification is not meant to be absolutely fixed but merely illustrative.

The Latin words examined in these cases are _caro_ (four times), _corpus_ (four times), and _concupiscentia_ (one time). The Latin words were chosen to bring out, so far as possible, the range of meaning of the concept of flesh, not primarily to have an equal distribution of

the words <u>caro</u>, <u>corpus</u>, and <u>concupiscentia</u> in the nine
cases. Case 5, for example, has both <u>caro</u> and <u>corpus</u> in
the same text, illustrating that it is somewhat arbitrary to call that case an example of <u>caro</u> rather than
of <u>corpus</u>. The method in each of the cases will be
uniform. There will be four parts to each case:
(1) The Latin word will be listed along with a brief
"title" describing the usage derived from the above
table, Case 1: <u>concupiscentia</u> as "a will or desire."
(2) The text immediately surrounding the word usage
will be presented. (3) A commentary on the usage,
exploring some of the implications of that particular
usage, will be provided. (4) A sentence summarizing
the meaning of the usage will be given.

Case 1: <u>Concupiscentia</u> as "the fleshly will of fallen
angels."

Text: <u>De Casu Diaboli</u>

> For if his [Satan's] will was good, then he
> fell from such great good into such great evil
> because of a good will. Likewise, if his will
> was good, God gave it to him, because from
> himself he had only nothing. Therefore, if he
> willed what God gave to will, how is it that
> he sinned? Or if he had this will from
> himself, he had something good which he did
> not receive.
> On the other hand, if his will is evil and
> is something, then it is again the case that
> this will is only from God, from whom is
> everything that is something. And we can in
> like manner ask how he sinned in having a will
> which God gave, or how God could have given an
> evil will. But if this evil will was from the
> Devil himself and is something, then (the evil
> angel) had something from himself and it is
> not the case that every being is good. And
> if, indeed, an evil will is a being, then evil
> won't be nothing, as we are accustomed to say
> it is. Or if an evil will is nothing, then
> [the Devil] was so gravely damned for nothing,
> and hence was damned without reason.
> However, what I am saying about the will
> can be said about concupiscence or desire,
> since the will is concupiscence and desire.
> And just as there is a good and an evil will,
> so there is a good and an evil concupiscence
> and a good and an evil desire.15

Commentary:

This case illustrates an especially important meaning of the flesh concept." It is easy to see that flesh can refer to the body and the frequent "Pauline" use of the term (see case 2) shows that the notion of flesh can refer to both body and mind. But here concupiscentia simply denotes the appetitive character of the will.

The context of concupiscentia in De Casu Diaboli shows that there can be no question of body (corpus) involved here since the discussion is about angels. It is precisely the lack of a body that distinguishes angels from men; otherwise, both angels and men are, for Anselm, essentially rational wills. Therefore concupiscentia is in this case an appetitive, bodiless will, and Anselm states that this appetite can be either good or bad, just as the will or desire can be either good or bad.

But in what sense can this appetitive willing be considered flesh? A complete answer to this question requires more than this denotative analysis of the terms caro, corpus, and concupiscentia. If there is a connection between concupiscentia as an appetitive will and caro and corpus as the human body, it must extend beyond a linguistic tie of the type suggested thus far in this analysis: namely,

    (a)   caro=concupiscentia
    (b)   caro=corpus
    (c)   concupiscentia=corpus

Such a conclusion does not necessarily follow, of course, since each of the terms has a range of meaning. And while two of the terms may intersect with a third term, that does not guarantee that they will intersect with each other. A simple diagram illustrates this point:

A B C

Though A intersects with B
And C intersects with B
It does not follow that A intersects with C

It is possible when using the Pauline sense of flesh (as in case 2) to go beyond the meaning of body (some of B is not A).

A   B
corpus   caro

And the phrase "mystical body of Christ" (case 9) goes beyond the meaning of <u>caro</u> (some of A is not B). Thus <u>corpus</u> and <u>caro</u> do not have exactly the same range of meaning even though they usually refer to the same thing.

In this case <u>concupiscentia</u> appears to go beyond the meaning of flesh because it refers to the appetitive willing of angels (some of C is not B).

B caro
C concupiscentia

It is also clear that <u>caro</u>, referring to a strictly neutral sense of body, does not include <u>concupiscentia</u> (some of B is not C).

A more complete diagram of the relationship between <u>concupiscentia</u>, <u>caro</u>, and <u>corpus</u> according to this analysis would be:

corpus
concupiscentia
caro

The extreme instances of both <u>concupiscentia</u> and <u>corpus</u> establish the limits of the flesh concept. At the one extreme is <u>concupiscentia</u> as a disembodied appetitive will. At the other extreme is <u>corpus</u> as a mystical body (the Church). Neither of these extreme cases can be called flesh in the proper sense of the term, but they do emphasize two aspects of flesh as isolated from the complex term itself. Both of these extreme cases have two meanings. They have an immediate contextual meaning, i.e., <u>concupiscentia</u> as an appetitive will of angels and <u>corpus Christi</u> as the mystical body of Christ the Church, but they also point beyond these contexts to suggest transferred meanings. These transferred meanings of the extreme cases are of particular importance to the concept of flesh.

The extreme case of <u>concupiscentia</u> points to the appetitive, volitional aspect of flesh, while the extreme case of <u>corpus</u> points to the participatory aspect of flesh. These two aspects of flesh are not contradictory, but are rather two distinct features that may be singled out for special attention. This analysis has merely focused on these two features; it is for the systematic analysis to study the relationship between these two aspects of flesh and their theological implications.

Conclusion:

In case 1 flesh denotes the appetitive character of will, which, in the fallen angels, is completely negative.

Case 2: Caro as "desires of the flesh" or "unrestrained appetites."

Text: De Concordia

> And Paul says regarding those who against their will experience the flesh, i.e., carnal desires: "There is no condemnation to those who are in Christ Jesus, who do not walk after the flesh"--i.e., who do not freely consent [to the flesh]. When he says this, without question he signifies that those who are not in Christ are followed by condemnation as often as they feel carnal desire, even if they do not walk in accordance with it. For man was made in such a way that he ought not to feel carnal desire, just as I said regarding anger. Therefore, if anyone considers carefully what I have said, he does not at all doubt that those who cannot--by their own fault--receive the word of God are rightly to be blamed.16

Commentary

In this case Anselm calls the human passions and appetites **flesh** (caro and **concupiscentia**) on the authority of St. Paul. Here Anselm characterizes flesh as an independent principle that acts contrary to the human will and is to be considered sinful.17 Anselm continues to draw on Paul when he distinguishes between those who unwillingly feel the desires of the flesh and those who "walk according to the flesh." The difference between these two categories of men lies in the condition of their will. Those "who walk according to the flesh" willingly experience the desires of the flesh and are consequently not of the spirit. Those who experience the flesh but do not walk according to the flesh are those who experience the flesh as an independent power, yet do not consent to follow that power.

One might expect that Anselm introduces this distinction between those who do and do not willingly submit to this power to assert the importance of the

will in determining the morality of an act or condition.   While it is true that for Christians the moral
condition is determined by the will, it does not follow
that evil is only attributed to the personal will that
consents to evil. Anselm interprets Paul's statement
"There is no condemnation to those who are in Christ
Jesus, who do not walk after the flesh," as meaning
there is condemnation for those who experience the
desires of the flesh and who are not in Christ, even if
they do not personally consent to the flesh. On the
surface this appears to contradict the position so
clearly set forth in De Conceptiun Virginali and De
Libertate Arbitrii that sin is only in the will. Anselm
anticipates such an objection when he goes on to explain
that the reason men are condemned for simply experiencing the desires of the flesh without consenting to them
is because those desires of the flesh ought not even to
be experienced.

At this point one must look carefully at the moral
injunction "ought not to feel carnal desire." Generally
the realm of morality, the "ought" of life, is restricted to value judgments involving the rational
will. But here it would seem that Anselm is extending
the ethical sphere to the physical structure of the
human being: it is not simply consent to a physical
experience which is judged to be sinful, but it is the
physical experience itself which is condemned. A point
of view that strictly separates the body from the mind
cannot comprehend Anselm's seemingly undifferentiated
metaphysics on this point. This difficulty arises from
the close association between the body, human nature,
and the desires of the body. A closer look at Anselm's
psychology is necessary at this point.

For Anselm, the human being is composed of body
and soul. Both of these aspects of man possess certain
instruments or powers. The instruments of the body are
the five senses and the bodily members, while the instruments of the soul are memoria, ratio, and voluntas
(Mon. LXVII). When seen in this way, there appears to
be a rather straightforward series of operations that
are performed by each of the faculties: the physical
faculties are to present perceptions to the mind so that
this information can be processed and presented to the
will for decisions. In this light, the physical faculties are morally neutral. The ratio and voluntas seem
to constitute a moral realm where one can clearly talk
about responsibility. Yet this explanation of the
relationship between the body and the mind is only one

side of the body-mind interaction, the side that considers how the human being functions ideally.

Now the other side of the body-mind interaction
concerns itself with how this interaction actually takes
place. The neutrality of the senses just discussed is
not in fact the real condition of man, or at least, it
is not the only condition. The senses have a movement
of their own which is not simply subject to the personal, rational will, as illustrated in case 2). It is
this appetitive quality of the body which Anselm calls
flesh, and to the extent that the body has desires,
passions, or appetites, it cannot be strictly separated
from the will. In this respect the flesh might be said
to have an "unwilling will," that is, a will that is not
immediately subject to the rational will. Nevertheless,
it would be a mistake to consider this will as beyond
the realm of responsibility. While the individual's
personal will is not responsible for the existence of
those desires of the flesh, Man is responsible for this
condition. "Man" here refers both to Adam, the first
man, and to human nature, which was completely contained
in Adam. The precise connection between Adam and human
nature will be explored in a later chapter; here the
primary concern is the relationship between the body and
human nature.

The actual condition of the body (where it does
not simply put man in touch with the outside world
through sensation, but also has passions that desire
independently of the personal, rational will) is
attributable to the corruption of human nature. In
fact, Anselm equates here the corrupted human nature
with the body of flesh. What is corrupted about "corrupt human nature," where human nature is seen as a
composite of body and soul, is the body, the flesh.
This follows from Anselm's view that the instrument of
the rational will remained intact even after the
corruption of human nature.

Because the corrupted body is in a condition in
which it ought not to be, human nature is said to be
responsible for this fallen state. Thus desires of the
flesh, passions of the body, and corrupt human nature
all refer to the same metaphysical condition.

Conclusion:

In case 2 flesh denotes the human passions that
act contrary to the will; this is a negative meaning.

Case 3.   Caro as "life according to the flesh."

Text: Epistola de Incarnatione Verbi

>Putting aside the things of the flesh, let us live according to the Spirit before, I say, we examine and judge the deep things of faith. For he who lives according to the flesh is carnal or natural [animalis]; and of him it is said that "the natural [animalis] man does not perceive the things which are of the Spirit of God." But he who "by the Spirit puts to death the deeds of the flesh" is made spiritual; and it is read of him that "the spiritual man judges all things, but is himself judged by no one." For it is true that the more richly we are fed on those things in Sacred Scripture which nourish us through obedience, the more precisely we are carried on to those things which satisfy through understanding. . . . For he who does not believe will not experience; and he who has not experienced will not know. For the more experiencing-a-thing is superior to merely hearing about it, the more knowledge from experience surpasses knowledge at second hand.18

Commentary:

The setting of this case is a letter that Anselm addressed to Pope Urban II regarding the error which was held by Roscelin, even though he does not mention Roscelin by name. The error Anselm attacked dealt with the mystery of the Incarnation, maintaining that either the unity of God required God the Father and the Holy Spirit to be incarnated with Christ or else it was necessary to admit a plurality of gods. (In 1092 this error was condemned by the Council of Soissons.)

Before Anselm actually begins to deal with the question of the Incarnation, he describes the spiritual condition required for such an investigation. One of the important conditions for understanding this mystery of faith is to put "aside the things of the flesh" (caro) and live according to the Spirit. In this context, flesh refers to the man who does not perceive spiritual things. Anselm quotes from Paul's epistles to the Corinthians and to the Romans where Paul uses the word flesh (sarx) negatively, referring to the "whole man," body and soul, who sets himself against the Spirit. By this use of the term flesh, Paul dis-

tinguishes between those who live with Christ, through
Christ's power, and those who live without Christ,
relying on themselves.19

   Anselm follows Paul in this case, adapting Paul's
broad usage to his own investigation of the Incarnation. Anselm employs the term flesh here to indicate
the whole man, not just the body. Along with Paul,
Anselm sees the fleshly or natural man as the man who is
without Christ. In the immediate context of case 3, the
man who is without Christ is the man who does not
believe in Christ and the mysteries of faith. Thus
Anselm places Paul's concept of flesh in the service of
his own theological method, fides quaerens intellectum.
The man of the flesh is he who attempts to understand
the deep things of faith without first believing.

   This case illustrates a negative use of the flesh
concept which has virtually no connection with the flesh
as body, except insofar as the whole man is composed of
body and soul. It should also be noted that in this
case there is no redemption of flesh since to be con-
verted to the standpoint where one believes is to cease
to be fleshly and to become spiritual. Thus in this
negative case the opposite of flesh is not redeemed
flesh, but rather spirit.

Conclusion

   In case 3 flesh denotes the man who does not
perceive the spiritual; this is a negative meaning.

Case 4. Corpus as "source of perception."

Text: Monologion

      For in ordinary usage we recognize that we can
      speak of a single object in three ways. For
      we may speak of it either (1) by perceptibly
      employing perceptible signs (i.e., signs which
      can be perceived by the bodily senses) or (2)
      by imperceptibly thinking to ourselves these
      same signs, which are perceptible outside us,
      or (3) neither by perceptibly nor by imper-
      ceptibly using these signs, but by inwardly
      and mentally speaking of the objects them-
      selves by imagining them or by understanding
      their respective definitions, depending upon
      the type of object.20

Commentary:

In this case Anselm speaks of the flesh (corpus) in a completely neutral way. The body in this context is simply the physical aspect of man which makes him part of the physical world. But the flesh (corpus) is also the source of sensation and perception. From these two perspectives man can be seen both as a material body that can be an object in the physical world and as such can be perceived or imagined in the mind of another man and as that part of man which senses and perceives objects in the physical world.

This case is located in a discussion about the relationship between the Creator and his creation, between existence in thought and existence in creation. Even though this discussion is about God's mind in relation to the created world, the model that Anselm uses to clarify this relationship is the human artisan. Anselm holds that God had a mental concept of creation before he actually created it, in much the same way that an artisan has an image in mind before he executes his work. This mental existence in the creator's thought is not "nothing," but rather is a special kind of existence. It is this notion of mental existence which is contrasted to the physical existence of the body. In such a context, flesh is neutral because it is contrasted with the mental rather than with the spiritual or the moral dimensions of man.

This section of Monologion gives some perspective on Anselm's view of total human nature. The flesh is considered here in terms of its ontological status rather than in terms of its religious or moral condition. The flesh (corpus) is seen as somewhere in between the mental and physical world, in the same way as it was considered to be between the moral world of the will and the amoral world of brute animals. On the merely physical side, the body is an object that can be placed alongside other physical objects in nature. Regarding its role in perception, however, the body is not simply an object. The senses of the body function as the bridge between the world of objects and world of the mind. The mind utilizes the perceptions of the bodily senses to form images of the physical objects perceived.

Beyond this image-forming power of the mind which can view objects by the vision of conception (Mon. X) there is the faculty of reason which can think of the universal essence of the object presented by percep-

tion.   Case   4   also   shows   another   mental   function,
namely,   the power to create conventional signs.   Anselm
even considers   such   signs   as   two   distinct methods by
which   an object can be expressed, according   to   whether
such signs   are   perceived by the senses or conceived by
the mind.   Thus, for Anselm,   there   is   a   mental   world
made   up   of   conceived   images,   abstract   thoughts, and
word-signs;   this mental world is linked to the   physical
world of objects by the senses of the body.

In   another   context   Anselm   speaks   about   these
senses of the body as   "instruments" of the body (case 2)
which   parallel the "instruments"   of   the   soul,   namely
memoria,   ratio,   and voluntas.   It has already been seen
that the flesh not   only   has senses, but also appetites.
The foregoing observations   about   the unique ontological
status of flesh may prove helpful for   understanding   the
moral   status   of   flesh.   The flesh (corpus) is a unique
entity in the order   of being.   It appears to have a mode
of existence which shares   characteristics   of   the ontological   levels   immediately   above   and   below it.   The
senses   of   the   body   explain   the   body's   unique place
between the mental and the physical.

In a similar way the appetites are responsible   for
their   unique   place   between the moral and amoral realms
of being.   Because the   flesh   is   said   to possess these
mental   and   moral   instruments, it could conceivably   be
hypostatized so that   one   might   speak   about   its being
morally responsible.   The quasi-mental attributes   of the
bodily   senses   do   not   refer   to the mental function of
ratio in the expression "rational   will."   The same can
be   said   about   the   volitional character of the   bodily
appetites.   Yet, just   as   the   senses   contribute   to the
functions   of   ratio proper, so do the appetites contribute to the working of   the   rational   will.   The precise
role   of the bodily appetites in personal   volition   will
be examined   in the next chapter when flesh is considered
more broadly as   humana   natura.   It is under this notion
of human nature as it is exemplified   in   Adam   that   the
clearest   statements   about   the moral character of flesh
will be seen.

Conclusion

In Case 4 flesh denotes   the human body as a physical object in the material world;   this   is   a   neutral
meaning of flesh.

Case 5.   Caro as a "disposition of the will."

Text: De Conceptu Virginali

> But because Adam and Eve sinned personally--
> sinned even though originally they were strong
> and uncorrupted and had the ability always
> easily to keep justice--their whole being
> became weakened and corrupted. Indeed, the
> body [became weakened and corrupted] because
> after their sin it became like the bodies of
> brute animals, viz., subject to corruption and
> to carnal appetites. And the soul [became
> weakened and corrupted] because as a result of
> the bodily corruption and the carnal appe-
> tites, as well as on account of its need for
> the goods which it had lost, it became infec-
> ted with carnal desires. And because the
> whole of human nature was in Adam and Eve, no
> part of it being outside of them, human nature
> as a whole was weakened and corrupted.21

Commentary:

In this case the flesh denotes the human condition, both in its righteous state before man's sin and
in its corrupted state after the Fall. This denotation
helps to explain how human nature was corrupted in
Adam. The flesh (corpus) is seen to be the point on
which Anselm focuses in his explanation of the change
brought about in human nature because of Adam's sin.

Before Adam's sin the flesh (corpus) was not
subject to the bodily appetites or desires. This does
not mean that the flesh did not exhibit desires, but it
does mean that these desires were always in accord with
the rational will. This point is central to Anselm's
theory of the human will which considers the general
desire for happiness to be inseparable from the will; so
long as this desire is coordinated with justice there is
no sin. In the context of this case, Anselm speaks of
this coordination of the general desire for happiness
with the demands of justice in terms of the relationship
between the body, the bodily appetites and the soul.
The soul is said to be infected with carnal feelings for
two reasons: the first is the corruption of the body
and its appetites and the lack of goods in the soul.
These two reasons appear to be two aspects of the same
problem. The corruption of the bodily appetites refers
to the unrestrained condition of the desire for happiness, while the lack of goods in the soul refers to that

part of the will which had restrained the desire for
happiness before Adam sinned. This case illustrates the
importance of the concept of absence in Anselm's
thoughts about the will and evil. When Anselm speaks
about the corruption of human nature in terms of bodily
appetites, it might appear as though evil were in fact
"something." But that same condition can more accurately be spoken of as a lack in the soul. This connection between the moral condition of human nature
described on the one hand in terms of the state of the
flesh and on the other hand in terms of the state of the
soul suggests that the flesh and the soul may be two
ways of describing the same phenomenon. Yet both of
these terms have a wide range of meaning, and so one
must inquire what meaning of flesh is actually
describing the condition of the soul. Furthermore, it
will be necessary to specify what aspect of the soul is
meant by this particular meaning of flesh. Although
this issue cannot be explored fully in this chapter, a
diagram will suggest the general relationship between
this meaning of flesh and the soul:

In case 5 the discussion centers around the moral
condition of human nature, which might be called the
natural will. The corruption of human nature affected
the desire for happiness in the natural will so that
this desire was no longer subject to the rational will.
(This will be demonstrated systematically in chapter
6.) It is in this sense that the desire for happiness
appears to become an independent principle and is
considered flesh in the negative sense. This is seen
when Anselm likens fallen man's body to the bodies of
brute animals. In animals the bodily appetites are also
an independent force, not subject to rational control.
Yet this is no problem for the animal since he ought not
to possess the single coordinated force of appetitive
energy guided by the rational will. According to
Anselm, it is proper to speak of moral culpability only
where the required is lacking. Thus, in this case, the
flesh appears negative insofar as man's bodily appetites
lack the limits placed on them by justice before Adam
sinned.

It would be more correct to say that in this case
the flesh denotes that area of the soul which contains
the dispositions of the will. In this way Anselm speaks

about the same phenomenon from two different perspectives, i.e., from the perspective of man's body and from that of his soul. He describes man's corruption in two ways that show this convergence of body and soul in the denotation of the word flesh: the body becoming subject to carnal appetites and (b) the body becoming infected with carnal feelings. The term "carnal feelings" illustrates how the flesh can refer to an area of the soul, namely, the dispositions of the will. In this light we see how Anselm is describing the same human condition using the vocabulary of the body and of the soul.

Anselm's unified view of man enables him to apply terms of the flesh to man's moral condition, just as he attributes moral qualities to the tendencies of the flesh, whether that be the corrupted flesh of Adam or the righteous flesh of Christ. The remarkable point of case 5 is that flesh can denote the condition of the human will, and more specifically, it denotes the dispositions of the will.

Conclusion

In case 5 flesh denotes the dispositions or affections of the will which make the will either good or evil; in this sense flesh is neutral.

Case No. 6: Corpus as "an immortal body."

Text: Cur Deus Homo

> Anselm. Indeed, if man is to be perfectly restored, he ought to be restored to such a state as he would have been in had he not sinned.
> Boso. It cannot be otherwise.
> Anselm. Therefore, just as had man not sinned he was to have been transformed into incorruptibility with the body he had, so it ought to be the case that when he will be restored he will be restored with the body in which he lives during this present life.22

Commentary.

In this case the flesh (corpus) denotes an immortal body that reflects the moral condition of the life a person has led. Here the flesh is in itself neither positive nor negative. The flesh is seen here as part of the total human nature that is body and soul, and consequently the destiny of the body is the same as that of the soul. This follows the standard Christian teaching about the resurrection of the body, wherein the body exists unendingly; however, it may be transformed through the experience of death.

The general context of this passage is a discussion about the effect of original sin on man. The flesh was subject to neither corruption nor unrestrained bodily appetites before Adam sinned (case 5). The flesh somehow had the capacity to undergo moral change. The original sin doctrine makes much of this negative change in the flesh: the will of Adam decided for all men of the human race what would be the possibilities of the flesh. The flesh that would have been immortal and subject to no unrestrained appetites became mortal and irrationally appetitive. Such a change in the flesh raises the question of whether further changes are possible according to the principle that what happened once can happen again.

If the flesh were open to moral change in the case of Adam, could not another such change be anticipated? The Christian doctrines of incarnation and redemption could conceivably offer an answer to this question. It might be objected that Adam holds a unique place in relation to the human race and so the change that he effected in human flesh is irreversible and unique. While this objection might be sustained regarding the mortality of the flesh, it could be overruled regarding the appetites of the flesh. And the eucharistic flesh of Christ is not only free from unruly appetites, it is also immortal (cases 8 and 9). This is not the place to discuss the mortality of Christ's flesh, since that question is too complex to be discussed within the context of this particular case. The point being made here is simply that the flesh of Christ offers an example of flesh which is both completely human and yet quite different from the flesh after Adam's sin. Because Anselm's theological system is consistent, this condition of Christ's flesh has important implications for all human flesh. The nature of these systematic implications will be demonstrated in chapter 6.

At this point it is enough to say that the original sin doctrine can be understood as a statement about the changes undergone by both the soul and the flesh. The doctrines of incarnation and redemption can also be understood in a similar way: what Anselm maintains about the moral and spiritual changes resulting from Christ's saving work in the world he finds reflected in the human flesh. In this sense the flesh is, for Anselm, a symbol of the spirit or of the will. This concrete symbolization of spirit, or will, in the flesh will be considered in detail later.

Conclusion

In case 6 flesh denotes the immortal body that may be in a good or evil condition; this is a neutral meaning of flesh.

Case 7:   Caro as "the earthly flesh of Christ."

Text: De Veritate

If you also consider something from the standpoint of the nature of things--for example, the driving of iron nails into the body of the Lord--would you say that His frail flesh ought not to have been penetrated, or that, once penetrated by sharp iron, it ought not to have felt pain?23

Commentary

The context of this case is not immediately concerned with the concept of flesh, but it will offer an occasion to consider a denotation of the concept with which we have not yet dealt. Anselm introduces the example of Christ's flesh to illustrate a point of logic: he is attempting to distinguish between different senses of the word ought. Ought can refer to a characteristic of nature, as in Case 7 where the body ought to feel pain when pierced because it is the nature of the body to feel pain when pierced. But ought usually refers to a moral judgment, as can be seen in this same example, where the body of Christ ought not to feel pain when pierced because piercing the flesh of Christ is an unjust act.

In Anselm's thought, ought can apply to either the natural or the moral order. Anselm's use of ought when referring to the natural order sounds strange to modern ears because the scientific world view speaks of natural events as taking place according to regular, predictable laws, even if these laws are based on probability, not absolute certainty. Today there is no sense of a personal agent maintaining the natural laws, only a view of predictable regularity.

While Anselm denotes a difference between the "natural ought" and the "moral ought," he also recognizes their single source, the personal God of the Bible. It is important to perceive the broad metaphysical range covered by ought in Anselm's thought, since it undergirds his entire theological system.

This particular case not only shows the interrelationship between the moral and natural orders, it also focuses on the unique position that flesh holds in both of those realms. Because this case refers both to human flesh and to the flesh of Christ, it assumes a slightly different status than flesh in the other cases already considered. The flesh of Christ is mortal; in this sense it is similar to other human flesh. Yet even here there is a difference between Christ and all other men: other human flesh is mortal owing to Adam's sin; Christ's flesh is mortal through the power of God. In chapter 6 it will be seen how the Second Person of the Trinity assumed mortal flesh precisely for the purpose of redeeming man. This situation furnishes a perfect illustration of the unity of Anselm's universe, where the physical, the moral, and the spiritual are coordinated: the physical characteristic of mortality reflects the moral corruption of Adam's will since it was the result of his sin. The physical characteristic of mortality is also important because Christ uses it for the spiritual purpose of redeeming human nature.

Christ's flesh is also different from other human flesh in that it does not "weigh down the soul." Christ has retained the justice that Adam lost for other men. For this reason, the flesh spoken of in case 7 is not simply neutral, but must be considered positive because of its special relationship to justice. In chapter 6 we will explain how Christ, by virtue of the virgin birth, escaped the fleshly condition of other men.

It might also be noted here that the flesh of Christ considered in this case differs not only from the flesh of other men but also from the eucharistic flesh of Christ (cases 8 and 9). The eucharistic flesh is immortal, while the flesh of the earthly Christ is mortal. We shall see that the eucharistic flesh is spiritually positive in that it is the method of incorporating men into Christ. Now it is seen from case 7 that the earthly flesh of Christ was morally positive in that it did not weigh down Christ's soul. The relationship

between the eucharistic and the earthly flesh of Christ
raises the question of whether the eucharistic flesh
does for other men what Christ's earthly flesh did for
him, namely, assist him in preserving justice. The
systematic analysis of the concept of flesh will throw
light on this possibility.

Conclusion

In case 7 flesh denotes the earthly body of Christ
which did not weigh down his soul; here flesh is just
and positive.

Case 8: Caro as "the unleavened flesh of Christ," or
"eucharistic bread."

Text: Epistola de Sacrificio Azimi et Fermentati

Hence, the Lord is seen to have called Himself
and His flesh bread and to have produced His
Body from bread only for the following reason: [to indicate] that just as common bread,
whether unleavened or leavened, gives transi-
tory life, so His Body gives eternal life,
irrespective of whether [the bread of His
Body] is leavened or unleavened. Nevertheless, in the Law, where nearly every action
bore a symbolic meaning, the eating of unleavened bread at Passover was commanded in
order to indicate that the Messiah whom [the
Jews] were expecting was going to be pure and
sinless, and in order to admonish us who were
to eat of His Body to be likewise free from
all 'leaven of malice and wickedness.' However, now that we have passed from ancient
foreshadowing to a new reality, now that we
eat the unleavened flesh of Christ, we have no
need of this former symbolism in the bread
from which we produce this flesh.24

Commentary

This case (and Case 9) presents the most positive
use of the term flesh. It appears in Anselm's letter on
the symbolism of the eucharistic sacrifice, where he
defends the Latin custom of using unleavened bread for
the eucharist. In this context, flesh refers to the
flesh of Christ in the sacrament that gives men spiritual life.

Anselm insists here that the importance of this sacrament is not to be found in the particular type of bread used for the consecration. Nevertheless he does make the point that there is a symbolic reason for using bread in the consecration. The symbolic significance of the bread lies in its being nourishment for man's body. Just as bread is a basic food of the body, so the eucharistic bread is the primary nourishment of the spirit.

But even though the substance of bread was chosen for its symbolic value in the eucharistic sacrifice, that does not mean that the symbolic aspect of this sacrifice is primary. What is most important is the reality of Christ's flesh, since this is the real mode of incorporating men into the life of Christ. Even though the appearance of the consecrated bread remains as a symbol, this is clearly secondary to the actual flesh that is made present in the consecration of the bread.

To the extent that symbolism plays a significant role after the bread is changed into the flesh of Christ, it is the imagery of "unleavened flesh" (azimam carnem) which Anselm employs. The term "unleavened flesh" signifying sinless flesh may not appear to be very significant as an isolated term, but when considered in the light of Anselm's total theological system, eating the unleavened flesh of Christ explains how the Christian's will and behavior become righteous. This point will be explored in the chapter dealing with Anselm's theological system. Here we might simply observe that Anselm's use of the term "flesh of Christ" is not merely metaphorical, but is also and primarily sacramental. Through the flesh of Christ man is offered not merely the example of Christ's obedience unto death (Christ as exemplum), but most importantly, the instrument that effects an ontological change in man (Christ as instrumentum).

Conclusion

In case 8 flesh denotes the eucharistic bread that becomes the "flesh of Christ," a completely positive denotation.

Case 9: Corpus as "the eucharistic body of Christ".

Text: Oratio III: "Prayer Before Receiving the Body and Blood of Christ"

> This your holy Body and Blood, which I desire
> to receive, as cleansing from sin, and for a
> defence against it.25

Commentary

In this prayer Anselm uses the word <u>corpus</u> flesh
to denote the "eucharistic flesh of Christ." Anselm
prays that the flesh of Christ may incorporate him into
the Church, which is also the body of Christ (<u>corpus</u>
<u>Christi</u>). The body of Christ is now seen to have three
meanings: the earthly body of Christ, the eucharistic
body of Christ, and the mystical body of Christ. The
word <u>body</u> in the term "mystical body" cannot simply be
identified with flesh, since the term "mystical flesh"
is never used to denote the Church.

When the word <u>body</u> denotes the Church, it emphasizes the organic unity that characterizes the Church.
It is important to distinguish this strictly metaphorical use of the term "body of Christ" from the sacramental meaning of the "eucharistic body of Christ."
Anselm can use the word <u>flesh</u> to denote the eucharistic
body of Christ because both flesh and body are used in
this case to denote the physical aspect of man. But
flesh and body do not have the same transferred meanings
and consequently it is not appropriate to speak of the
Church as the "mystical flesh of Christ."

This difference between the sacramental and the
metaphorical meanings of the word <u>flesh</u> is important for
a proper appreciation of the eucharistic body of
Christ. The eucharist is not the body of Christ in a
metaphorical sense; it is the flesh of Christ in a
sacramental sense. And as a sacrament, it renders
present the actual reality of the resurrected body of
the God-man, Jesus, to a body that will not die again.
Only by appreciating the realism of the eucharistic
presence can one understand the significant place that
the flesh holds in Anselm's theological system, a point
that will be made clear in chapter 6. The integral,
systematic role of flesh is especially evident in case 9
because here the eucharistic flesh is placed in the
context of redemption. This is in marked contrast with
case 5, in which attention is focused on the negative
role of flesh in Anselm's treatment of the redemption.
In this case the eucharistic flesh is seen to transmit
the efficacy of Christ's redemptive death to the

believer. How does Anselm reconcile these disparate
notions of flesh within the same redemptive theory?

The answer to this question is not evident from
the observations made thus far in this analysis of the
word flesh on the denotative level. Only a careful look
at Anselm's total theological system can furnish that
answer.

Conclusion.

In case 9 flesh denotes the eucharistic flesh of
Christ which incorporates men into his mystical body;
this is a fully positive usage.

The Spectrum of the Flesh Complex:
Hints of Transformation

Now we have seen the wide range of meaning of the
term flesh as examined under the Latin words caro,
concupiscentia, and corpus. Are we to conclude from
this study that the term flesh is merely equivocal and
that those widely different meanings have nothing to do
with each other? Or might we ask whether there is some
inner relationship between these various meanings.
Merely to ask this question is to move into a higher,
systematic level of analysis. We shall now take up this
question and in doing so indicate how the denotative
analysis moves naturally into a more systematic
analysis. In this way the last section of this chapter
will anticipate some of the considerations of chapter 6,
which will deal specifically with the relational level
of meaning. So at this point we shall review the range
of meaning of the term flesh that has been uncovered in
the preceding analysis and summarize these denotations
in a diagram.

On one end of the spectrum stands the morally
negative sense of the term. The cases that illustrate
this negative sense refer to the flesh as corrupted by
Adam's fall. This is the corrupted concupiscence that
Augustine denotes by the word flesh in his doctrine of
original sin. This morally negative sense denotes the
body with its unrestrained appetites (case 2). Anselm
also uses the word flesh to denote both body and soul
when a person is opposed to the spirit, i.e., when a
person is without or opposed to Christ (case 2). In
this denotation Anselm uses flesh in the Pauline sense
of "walking according to the flesh." He also uses flesh

in this sense to denote those who do not see spiritual things, or those who try to understand the deep truths of faith without believing (case 3). In the rather extraordinary case where flesh denotes an appetitive will in angels (case 1) the flesh concept does not even have reference to a body. While this is a limiting case, it focuses on a very important aspect of flesh, namely, that flesh is an appetitive will, and in the case of the fallen angels, that fleshly will is totally negative.

The word _flesh_ was also seen to have a morally neutral denotation. We examined three cases of the neutral denotations of the concept of flesh. The first was seen in case 4 where the body is considered as the source of sensation and perception. The word _flesh_ also has a morally neutral denotation when it refers to a desire, or will, that is neutral in the sense that it can become either morally negative or morally positive. This point is brought out already in case 1 although this indifferent character of the word _flesh_ was seen primarily in case 5 where flesh denoted a disposition of the will. While the word _flesh_ in this case mainly denoted the carnal feelings in the soul as a result of Adam's sin, it was seen that flesh could also denote the positive feelings or affections that motivate the soul to will righteously, those feelings that Anselm calls the "disposition toward justice." Case 6 similarly denoted the immortal body of man, as it will reflect the condition of the man's spirit after death. Since this immortal condition may be either positive or negative, the flesh is again essentially neutral in its denotation.

Finally, the flesh not only has the negative and neutral denotations that we have seen, but it also denotes a morally positive reality when it signifies the earthly flesh of Christ that did not weigh down his soul (case 7). Such a use of the word _flesh_ denotes a body that is perfectly upright from the very moment of conception. The eucharistic flesh of Christ presents another positive denotation of flesh. The eucharistic bread (case 8) not only is itself the virtuous resurrected body of Christ, it also transforms the flesh of Christians so that they too become virtuous. Case 9 shows that the eucharistic flesh of Christ brings about this positive transformation of the flesh of Christians by incorporating them into the mystical body of Christ, the Church.

This notion of the transformation of the flesh is a striking feature of Anselm's theology for it is the key to understanding the problematic relationship between the positive and negative denotations of the word _flesh_. Because flesh is itself neutral, but capable of becoming moral according to the appetites associated with it, it is capable of being transformed from a positive to a negative condition and vice versa. Precisely how Anselm uses this notion of transformable, or moralizable, flesh will be seen in the systematic analysis of the concept of flesh. But even from the study of the various denotations of the flesh concept, we can already trace the outline of how this transformable quality of flesh is used to shape Anselm's theology in the following way.

Case 5 shows that Adam was originally in a condition in which the appetites of the body did not weigh down the soul. This state of original justice is described as a condition of perfect harmony between body and soul. But this same case also shows that through original sin the flesh became infected with appetites that prevented man from even understanding justice. This move from original justice to original sin provides the first example of a transformation of the flesh, a negative transformation. In this transformation the appetites of the body ceased to be subject to the rule of reason: the flesh that was morally upright, in that it functioned as it was required, no longer acted properly. For Anselm, it is this absence of required uprightness which constitutes injustice.

Anselm also speaks about this negative transformation of human nature as a loss of justice in the will. He characterizes the fall from grace as a lack of obedience on the part of the flesh and a lack of justice on the part of the will (case 5). But what is the relationship between the failure of the fleshly appetites to obey the rational will and the loss of justice in the will? It has already been suggested in case 5 that these two conditions are actually only two aspects of a single condition, or rather two perspectives from which man's condition is viewed. This will be demonstrated in the systematic study of the transformation of the flesh. Precisely what is involved in this first, negative, transformation of the flesh will be seen from a study of Adam's influence on human nature in the doctrine of original sin.

But the study of the denotative meanings of flesh in this chapter also shows that another transformation of the flesh has taken place, and this time it is a positive transformation. Case 7 illustrates that the Incarnation returned the flesh to its original state of justice. The flesh of Christ is seen to be as obedient to his rational will as was the original flesh of Adam. A systematic study of the concept of flesh must also be concerned with this positive change in the flesh. This movement of the flesh to a morally positive state can be studied best in the virgin birth doctrine.

Yet a third transformation of the flesh occurs in the renewal of the corrupted flesh born through Adam. Cases 8 and 9 show that this is not simply a repetition of the positive change brought about in the incarnation of Christ. In Christ's own situation, one cannot properly speak of a renewal of the flesh since the flesh never weighed down the soul in his case. But in the case of other men, the original, negative influence of Adam must be taken into account. This final transformation of the flesh can be understood from a systematic study of the influence of Christ on human nature in the doctrine of the Redemption.

Thus, already in this denotative analysis we get an idea of how Anselm uses the flesh as a central concept around which his systematic theology revolves. The broad range of meaning of the concept of flesh enables it to organize Anselm's theology in such a way as to express the universal history that moves from the good creation of all things through the Fall of Satan and Adam to the restoration in Christ. From figure 5.1 we can summarize this movement of salvation history:

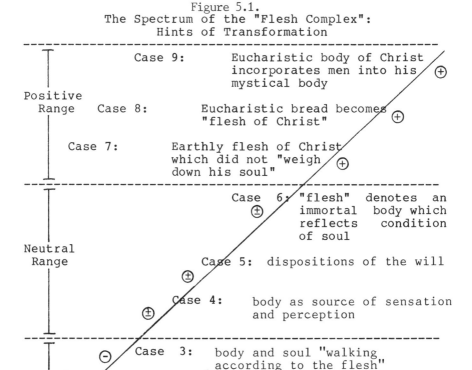

Figure 5.1.
The Spectrum of the "Flesh Complex":
Hints of Transformation

Figure 5.1 furnishes an overview of the richness and complexity of the concept of flesh. It is precisely this richness that enables it to serve on both levels of Anselm's theological system, i.e., as a term on the discursive level and as a symbol on the motif level. This demonstration of the range of meaning open to the concept of flesh also illustrates the relationship of the denotative level of analysis to the more complex levels, the relational and the symbolic levels. What we have called the range of meaning of the concept of flesh refers to the variety of meanings which this concept has. The various objects or realities denoted by flesh determine to a large extent the way in which that concept can be utilized within Anselm's theological system.

This analysis, then, has dealt with the flesh concept on the first, or denotative, level of meaning. This level can now be contrasted with a second level of meaning, the relational, or contextual, level, where flesh is considered in its relation to other concepts and terms, and where the bonds that connect terms are primarily logical bonds, in the linear fashion "x-y-z." The first level of meaning of the concept of flesh can also be contrasted with a third level of meaning, the symbolic level, where flesh acts as a motif symbol. At this symbolic level the concept of flesh evokes feelings that are associated with it. At this level the flesh concept will be examined in terms of its capacity to act as a motif symbol. Here its meaning will not be determined primarily by its denotative meanings, or by its logical context, but rather by its symbolic and sacramental role.

This study will now proceed from this analysis of the concept of flesh at the elementary, denotative level of meaning through the contextual meaning of the concept at the relational level of Anselm's system to the symbolic meaning of flesh at the motif level of his theological system. In the same way that there is one language that can be analyzed at different levels of meaning, so Anselm's single theological system can be examined at levels that correspond to these structures, or levels, of meaning that we have considered in this chapter. We now move on to the relational meaning of the concept of flesh.

NOTES

1.   H. Richardson, <u>Toward an American Theology</u>
(New York, 1967), pp. 95-97.

2.   This present examination of the discursive
level of Anselm's system   should   be   viewed   as only one
analytical   perspective   from which we can consider   this
system.   Our present concern   with the linear and
deductive moments of this system would be   misleading if
one were to view this level of the system in total
isolation from the deeper symbolic, or motif, level. It
must be stressed here that there is really   only one
theological system, and both the   discursive and motif
levels of that system are woven together. Although it
is useful for the purpose of analysis to distinguish the
deductive level from the motif level, they are never
separate from each other in reality.   Thus, when we
describe the "discursive system" as being linear in the
fashion -x-y-z-, we are simplifying the actual dynamics
of the entire system.

Even the elements of this linear discursive level
of Anselm's system are influenced by the symbolic role
that these same elements play in the deeper level of
Anselm's system. There is also an interflow back and
forth among most or all of the elements of the linear
system, and so we might more accurately diagram the
discursive level of Anselm's system in this way:

Therefore, it is merely for the sake of analysis that we
have simplified this diagram of the rational argumentation that appears in Anselm's system. It is precisely
the point of this study that it would be a mistake to
view Anselm's theological system simply as a discursive
system without sensitivity to the way in which the
deeper symbolic dimension of his theology permeates and
enlivens this system at every turn of his argument; for
this reason the final chapter will show by way of an
illustrative case how the different levels of the system
coinhere and enrich each other.

3.   Richardson, <u>Toward an American Theology</u>,
p. 88.

4.   In chapter 7 we shall consider at length the
use of metaphor and   symbol   on   the   motif level of Anselm's theology.   At this point we wish merely to
indicate what is, in this study, the relation between
metaphor and symbol.   Metaphor is, in the first instance, symbolic language. It is in this sense that the
words constituting the flesh complex are metaphorical
and symbolic.   Metaphorical and symbolic describe the
way that the flesh complex as a motif symbol operates,
namely, by means of evoking the reality in which it
participates. Later we shall go beyond this definition
of metaphor as symbolic language to speak more broadly
of enacted metaphor as symbolic actions and symbolic
objects. We shall see this notion of enacted metaphor
when we discuss the role of flesh in the sacrament of
the eucharist. Thus, in this study, we shall extend the
notion of metaphor to mean the same thing as symbol and
symbolic action.   Both metaphor and symbol are then
directly related to sacrament which is an efficacious
symbol or an efficacious, enacted metaphor.

5.   Richardson, Toward an American Theology,
p. 57.

6. H. Ott, "What Is Systematic Theology?" in The
Later Heidegger and Theology, ed. J. Robinson and J.
Cobb, Jr. (New York, 1963), p. 100.

7.   Richardson, Toward an American Theology,
pp. 95-97.

8.   "Huc accedit alia forma tentationis multi-
plicius periculosa, Praeter eam enim concupiscentiam
carnis, quae inest in delectatione omnium sensuum et
voluptatum, cui servientes   depereunt qui longe se
faciunt a te, inest animae per eosdem sensus corporis
quaedam non se oblectandi in carne, sed experiendi per
carnem vana et curiosa cupiditas, nomine cognitionis et
scientiae palliata.   Quae quoniam in appetitu noscendi
est, oculi autem sunt ad cognoscendum in sensibus principes, concupiscentia oculorum eloquio divino appellata
(I Jon. II/XVI)"   (Confessionum X/XXXV. English translation by Edward Pusey in The Confessions of St. Augustine (New York, 1951), pp. 204-5).

9. E. Hendrix concisely states the relationship
between flesh and this disobedience or distraction from
the spiritual: "Die Konkupisczenz ist für Augustin denn
auch nicht der sinnliche Genuss als solcher im physio-
logischen Sinne, von dem man auch einen guten Gebrauch
machen kann, sondern die inobedientia carnis, wodurch

auch bei dem erlaubten und guten Gebrauch des Sinnlichen
sowohl beim Sexuellen, als auch beispielsweise sogar
beim Essen und Trinken, eine Gewisse Verdunkelung oder
sogar Hemmung der hoeheren geistigen Funktionen auf-
tritt" ("Platonisches und biblisches Denken bei Augustinus," Augustinus Magister, I (Paris, 1952), p. 289.

10. Gross's position is developed in his article,
"Das Wesen der Erbsuende nach Augustin," Augustinus
Magister, II, p. 778. In fact, H. Staffner lists a
number of scholars who interpret Augustine as locating
the essence of original sin in this unruliness of the
flesh, especially in the sexual aspect of concupiscentia
carnis. Among those cited are J. Tixeront, J. B. Kors,
N. Merlin and J. Gross. See "Die Lehre des Hl. Augustinus ueber das Wesen der Erbsuende," Zeitschrift fuer
Katholische Theologie, 79 (1957), 386-87.

11. R. North, et al., Content Analysis (Northwestern University, 1963).

12. P. Stone, et al., The General Inquirer: A
Computer Approach to Content Analysis (Cambridge, Mass.,
1966), p. 6; C. Hall, The Meaning of Dreams (New York,
1953).

13. North, Content Analysis, p. 38.

14. The Oxford English Dictionary, vol. IV
(Oxford, 1933), pp. 314-16.

15. "Si enim bona fuit, propter bonam voluntatem
cecidit de tanto bono in tantum malum. Item si bona
fuit, deus eam illi dedit, quia non nisi nihil habuit a
se. Si ergo voluit quod deus dedit velle: quid
peccavit? Aut si a se habuit hanc voluntatem, habuit
aliquod bonum quod non accepit. Quod si mala est et
aliquid est, iterum occurrit quia non nisi a deo est, a
quo est omne quod aliquid est; et similiter quaeri
potest quid peccavit habendo voluntatem quam deus dedit,
aut quomodo potuit deus dare malam voluntatem. Si vero
haec mala voluntas ab ipso diabolo fuit et aliquid est:
habuit a se aliquid, et non est omnis essentia bona, nec
malum erit nihil sicut solemus dicere, siquidem mala
voluntas essentia est. Aut si mala voluntas nihil est,
propter nihil et ideo, sine causa tam graviter damnatus
est. Quod autem dico de voluntate, hoc ipsum dici
potest de concupiscentia sive disiderio, quoniam et concupiscentia et desiderium voluntas est; et sicut est
bona et mala voluntas, ita est bona et mala concupiscen-

tia et bonum et malum desiderium" (DCD VII; S I, 244, 16-245, 3; AC II, 143).

16. "Et cum Paulus de illis qui carnem, id est concupiscentias, sentiunt nolentes, ait: 'nihil damnationis est iis qui sunt in Christo Iesu, qui non secundum carnem ambulant,' hoc est non voluntate consentiunt: sine dubio significat eos qui non sunt in Christo sequi damnationem, quotiens sentiunt carnem, etiam si non secundum illam ambulant, quoniam sic factus est homo ut eam sentire, sicut de ira dixi, non deberet. Si quis igitur quae dixi diligenter considerat, nullatenus eos, qui propter culpam suam verbum dei nequeunt suscipere recte arguendos dubitat" DCP III; S II, 274, 11-18; AC II, 210).

17. According to O. Kuss, St. Paul also sees the flesh as a principle to which man is subjected and a power which is opposed to God's world: "Die Sarx ist wie eine Macht, ein 'Prinzip,' dem der Mensch unterworfen ist, ohne die Moeglichkeit einer wirksamen Gegenwehr zu haben, und diese Macht ist ihrem Wesen nach allem feind, was zu Gottes Welt gehoert. 'Das Sinnen des Fleisches ist Feindschaft gegen Gott (τὸ φρόνημα τῆς σαρκὸς ἔχθρα ἐις θεόν); denn dem Gesetze Gottes unterwirft es sich nicht, es dann das ja auch nicht' (Roem. 8/7), und aus dieser Gottfeindlichkeit ergibt sich das Resultat des 'Sinnens des Fleisches': es ist das absolute Unheil, 'der Tod' schlecthin (Roem.8/6 τὸ γὰρ φρόνημα τῆς σαρκὸς θάνατος) ("Das Fleisch" in Der Roemerbrief [Regensburg, 1959], p. 515.

18. "Prius inquam ea quae carnis sunt postponentes secundum spiritum vivamus, quam profunda fidei diiudicando discutiamus. Nam qui secundum carnem, vivit, carnalis sive animalis est, de quo dicitur: 'animalis homo non percipit ea, quae sunt spiritus dei; qui vero 'spiritu facta carnis mortificat,' spiritualis efficitur, de quo legitur quia 'spiritualis iudicat omnia, et ipse a nemine iudicator.' Verum enim est quia quanto opulentius nutrimur in sacra scriptura ex iis quae per oboedientiam pascunt, tanto subtilius provehimur ad ea quae per intellectum satiant. . . . Nam qui non crediderit, non experietur; et qui expertus non fuerit, non cognoscet. Quantum enim rei auditum superat experientia, tantum vincit audientis cognitionem experientis scientia" (EDIV I, S II, 8,14 - 9,8; AC III, 12-13).

19. Kuss, "Das Fleisch," pp. 514-19.

20. "Frequenti namque usu cognoscitur, quia rem unam tripliciter loqui possumus. Aut enim res loquimur signis sensibilibus, id est quae sensibus corporeis sentiri possunt sensibiliter utendo; aut eadem signa, quae foris sensibilia sunt, intra nos insensibiliter cogitando; aut nec sensibiliter nec insensibiliter his signis utendo, sed res ipsas vel corporum imaginatione vel rationis intellectu pro rerum ipsarum diversitate intus in nostra mente dicendo" (Mon. X; S I, 24, 29 - 25, 2; AC I, 18-19).

21. "Quoniam autem personaliter peccaverunt, cum originaliter fortes et incorrupti haberent potestatem semper servandi sine difficultate iustitiam: totum quod erant infirmatum et corruptum est. Corpus quidem, quia tale post peccatum fuit, qualia sunt brutorum animalium, corruptioni et carnalibus appetitibus subiacentia. Anima vero, quia ex corruptione corporis et eisdem appetitibus atque ex indigentia bonorum quae perdidit, carnalibus affectibus est infecta. Et quia tota humana natura in illis erat et extra ipsos de illa nihil erat, tota infirmata et corrupta est" (DCV II; S II, 141, 9-16; AC III, 145).

22. Anselm. "Quippe si homo perfecte restaurandus est, talis debet restitui, qualis futurus erat, si non peccasset."
    Boso. "Aliter esse non potest."
    Anselm. "Quemadmodum igitur si non peccasset homo, cum eodem quod gerebat corpore in incorruptibilitatem transmutandus erat, ita oportet, ut cum restaurabitur, cum suo in quo vivit in hac vita corpore restauretur" (CDH II/3; S II, 98, 14-20; AC III, 99).

23. "Quid etiam si secundum rerum naturam consideres, ut cum clavi ferrei impressi sunt in corpus domini: an dices fragilem carnem non debuisse penetrari, aut acuto ferro penetratam non debuisse dolere?" (DV VIII; S I, 187, 33-35; AC II, 89).

24. "Propter hoc ergo solum videtur se et carnem suam 'panem' vocasse et de pane corpus suum fecisse, quia sicut iste panis azimus sive fermentatus dat vitam transitoriam, ita corpus eius aeternam, non quia fermentatus est vel azimus; quamvis in lege, ubi fere omnia in figura fiebant, praeceptum sit azimum in Pascha panem comedere, ut ostenderetur quia Christus quem exspectabant sincerus et mundus futurus esset, et nos qui manducaturi eramus corpus eius, similiter (mundi) esse moneremur ab omni 'fermento malitiae et nequitiae.' Iam vero postquam de veteri figura ad novam veritatem

venimus et azimam Christi carnem comedimus, non est
nobis necessaria illa vetus figura in pane, de quo
carnem ipsam conficimus" (EDSA I; S II, 224, 9-225, 6;
AC III, 234).

25."Hoc sanctum corpus tuum et hunc sanctum
sanquinem tuum, quae ad emundationem et defensionem a
peccatis accipere desidero" (Orat. III; S III, 10, 6-8;
PAM, 100).

FLESH IN ANSELM'S THEOLOGICAL SYSTEM

The Structure of Anselm's System

The word study undertaken in chapter 5 established the range of meaning of the concept of flesh as it appears in the St. Anselm corpus. While there was some attempt to see how these various meanings are related in the transformations of the flesh which constitute salvation history, the main object of the preceding analysis was to examine the Latin terms that express the concept of flesh in Anselm's theology. Now a different approach will be taken to determine the role that flesh plays in Anselm's theological system. In this section we shall examine Anselm's relational, or discursive, system to discover how Anselm uses the concept of flesh as one of the important bonds that link that system.1

We shall begin this section by giving an overview of the structure of Anselm's system. First we shall attempt to diagram Anselm's theological system, showing the systematic movement of salvation history and the important place of flesh in that system. Then we shall sketch the principal doctrines that constitute this system, indicating the role of flesh in each of these doctrines.

Figure 6.1 shows the four principal conditions of flesh. The first condition is Adamic flesh as it was created good and just. God created men (creatures of flesh) as well as angels so as to have a perfect number of rational natures in the heavenly city. When Satan and Adam fell they failed to fulfill the plan that God intended for rational natures. The fall of Adam through his act of disobedience is the transition from Adamic flesh to fallen flesh. As we have already seen from the word study, this fallen flesh is both the body that weighs down the soul and the will that lacks the disposition toward justice. Thus, the corruption of the flesh is a corruption of the whole man, body and soul. It is also a corruption that affects all men, that is, it is a corruption of generic humanity in Adam. This corruption of Adam's race is transmitted to the individuals of that race through the physical act of sexual intercourse and that corruption is itself manifested in individual persons as a corrupt concupiscence in the body.

Figure 6.1.   Anselm's Theological System

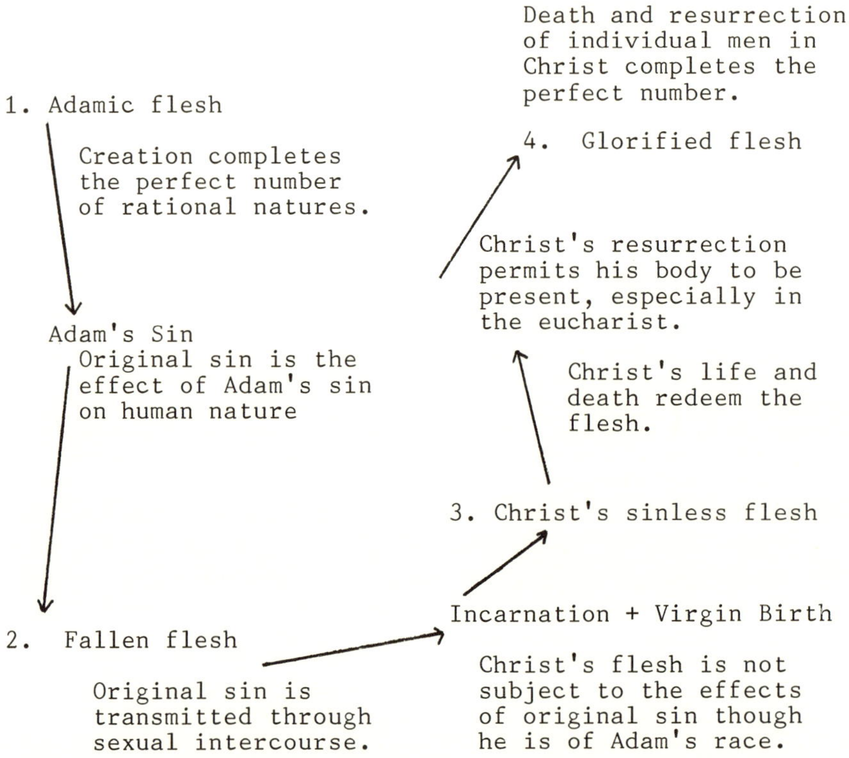

1. Adamic flesh

    Creation completes
    the perfect number
    of rational natures.

    Adam's Sin
    Original sin is the
    effect of Adam's sin
    on human nature

2.   Fallen flesh

    Original sin is
    transmitted through
    sexual intercourse.

Death and resurrection
of individual men in
Christ completes the
perfect number.

4.   Glorified flesh

Christ's resurrection
permits his body to be
present, especially in
the eucharist.

    Christ's life and
    death redeem the
    flesh.

3. Christ's sinless flesh

Incarnation + Virgin Birth

    Christ's flesh is not
    subject to the effects
    of original sin though
    he is of Adam's race.

Because sexual intercourse is the mode of incorporating individuals of Adam's race into the "fallen
flesh," that sexual link must be broken to arrive at the
new condition of the flesh, namely, sinless flesh. The
transition from the fallen flesh to sinless flesh is the
crux of the Cur Deus Homo argument. It is at this point
that Anselm takes special pains to demonstrate that the
God-man is of the flesh of Adam but not through the
flesh of Adam. This means that Christ is truly a man of
Adam's race, that is, he participates in Adam's race or
is from Adam but he is not subject to the corruption of
Adam's will since he was not conceived by means of
Adam's reproductive power. De Conceptu Virginali, a
sequel to Cur Deus Homo, takes up this question and
gives it thorough treatment.

The redemption of the flesh in Christ represents
the transformation of generic humanity that is parallel
to the transformation of generic humanity into fallen
flesh. The redemption of the flesh occurs through
Christ's life, death, and resurrection. But the central
point of redemption in Cur Deus Homo is Christ's cruci-
fied body. We shall see how important to Anselm's
redemptive theory is Christ's offering of his body in
the crucifixion.

The final state of flesh is the glorified flesh.
This state of flesh is seen first in the risen body of
Christ. Directly related to Christ's risen, glorified
flesh is the mystical body of Christ, the Church. Men
are initially incorporated into this body of Christ
through baptism. But more central to Anselm's theological system is the completion of this incorporation
through the eucharist. This mode of incorporation into
the glorified flesh of Christ is strikingly parallel to
the physical incorporation of individual persons into
the fallen flesh of Adam. In the same way that individual persons were incorporated into the fallen flesh of
Adam through the physical act of sexual intercourse, so
individual persons are incorporated into the glorified
flesh of Christ through the physical-sacramental act of
eating the body of Christ in the eucharist. This transmission of glorified flesh is central to Anselm's theological system and it shall be discussed at both the
discursive and motif levels of his system.2 The escha-
tological completion of God's plan is begun through this
incorporation of men into the mystical body of Christ.

It is finally completed with the death and resurrection
of individual men as they take their place in the
heavenly city.

Thus, we see from the figure 6.1 the program of
Anselm's theological system as a circular movement from
creation through the fall and redemption to the glorious
fulfillment of God's plan. It is also clear that the
transformation of the flesh is at the heart of this
system. Now we shall consider in table 6.1 the
principal doctrines that make up the theological system
in figure 6.1. Again we shall note the function of
flesh in each of these doctrines.

Table 6.1 Doctrinal Role of Flesh

Anselm's Doctrine	Role of Flesh
1. God: As supreme Rectitude (Truth and Justice), God governs the way in which his plan may be fulfilled, i.e., there can be no arbitrary act of divine will which would violate the justice of his nature.	The flesh must be just in order for man to be happy.
Creation: There are at the outset no obstacles to the fulfillment of God's plan since all was created good.	Flesh is created with original justice.
2. Angels: Along with men, angels set up the general framework within which human redemption takes place. There is a perfect number of elect natures (angelic and the human nature) that God foreknows.	Angels are not created in one nature as are men; angels are not reproduced by the flesh, and therefore fallen angels cannot be redeemed since flesh is the principle of transformation.
3. Original Sin: Human nature was created perfect in Adam. Adam is the	Adam corrupts the flesh.

archetypal figure
in whom the sin of the
person corrupted the
nature since the
entire human nature
was present in Adam.

Transfer of original sin: The flesh corrupts
Here the order of   the descendants of
person and nature   Adam's race.
is the opposite of
Adam's first sin; here
the nature that
infants receive causes
them to sin personally
as soon as they have a
rational will.

4. Incarnation: (This is the   The Second Person of
single case where the   the Trinity assumes
nature does not corrupt   sinless flesh.
the person.) The Second
Person of the Trinity
assumes a sinless
humanity that is not
influenced by the per-
sonal will of Adam.

Virgin Birth: This doc-   Virgin birth explains
trine explains how   how the God-man es-
the Second Person of   capes the sinfulness
God was able to   of Adam's flesh.
assume the humanity
of Adam's race with-
out inheriting the
original sin normally
carried with that
humanity.

5. Redemption: The God-man re-   The mortality of the
deems human nature   flesh permits the
by offering his obe-   God-man to offer his
dience in life and   death as atonement
death to God. The   for Adam's sin.
humanity that Christ
assumed permitted him
to die since God can-
not die. Yet, because
of the communication
of characteristics,
the God-man's death
has infinite worth and

is the perfect satisfac-
tion for Adam's sin.

6. Free Will: Anselm's complex
   doctrine of willing
   shows how the natural
   will, which was recti-
   fied by the God-man,
   influences the per-
   sonal will of men.

   The flesh represents
   the natural will
   which is at the same
   time a disposition of
   the personal will.

7. Grace: In Anselm's doctrine
   of will, grace is seen
   as Christ's gift of the
   disposition toward
   justice to the will.
   This gift is given in
   baptism and in the
   eucharist.

   The eucharistic
   flesh transmits the
   disposition toward
   justice to the will of
   Christians.

8. Resurrection: The resurrection of Christ's body
   is the archetype of
   bodily resurrection
   into glory for all
   other just men.

   Christ's risen body is
   the eucharistic
   flesh that transforms
   Christians according
   to the likeness of
   Christ's own death and
   resurrection.

This doctrinal summary touches the main points of Anselm's theological system. The column on the right also
highlights the function that flesh plays in this doctrinal structure. Again we see how the transformation
of the flesh is central to Anselm's theological system.
The thread of flesh is woven through the doctrines of
creation, angels, original sin, incarnation, virgin
birth, redemption, free will, grace, and resurrection.
Now I shall focus on those aspects of the flesh which
play a major role in transformation as seen in Anselm's
system.

Flesh as a Participatory Nature

In Cur Deus Homo Anselm discusses redemption in
the context of saving the original plan for rational
nature; he does not stress so much the number of individual men.3 Human beings are not redeemed as individuals. It is precisely their sharing in the race of Adam
that distinguishes men from angels. If God had redeemed
angels, he would have had to do so on an individual
basis, for angels are unique creatures; they were not

created in the same way as human nature was (as a race). Angels were created individually.

This difference between man and angels is very important for the operation of Anselm's redemptive system. Belonging to the human race gives man both advantages and disadvantages. The great advantage of human nature is that it could be saved as a race once sin infected that nature because all men are a part of that one race in the flesh. The disadvantages are that man is weaker than angels and is created of a mortal race.

Even with regard to the perfect number in God's plan for creation, Anselm understands this number not so much in terms of individual beings as in terms of natures.4 This makes it obvious why Anselm seeks a solution to the problem of redemption in terms of natures. It is this concern for the correct number of natures which dictates how the incarnation must take place, at least to the extent that it is human nature that must be saved and not simply a perfect number of beings.5 Yet, it must still be insisted that a perfect number of beings is also necessary for the total order of God's universe since Anselm speaks of a number of men (homines) as completing the intended number of rational natures.6

The first part of Anselm's argument in Cur Deus Homo might be summarized in this way: man has the capacity to be happy, and some men must be happy; yet, in actuality man is not happy. Man must meet the demands of justice, but he cannot. God alone can save man, but man himself ought to make satisfaction for sin. It is to this dilemma that Anselm recommends the solution of the God-man.

The God-man as a solution to the human condition must take into account the fallen state of mankind and how it is possible to correct the natural sin that is the result of Adam's fall. When Anselm analyzes the sin of Adam and Eve, it becomes evident how natural sin is related to personal sin. Since Adam and Eve were originally able to retain uprightness of will for its own sake, their entire humanity was strong; being able to retain uprightness, they were free from both sin and death. But when they committed personal sin, both the body and the soul became weak and corrupt. The body of human beings became like brute animals under the yoke of corruption and carnal appetites. The soul became infec-

ted with carnal feelings because of bodily corruption
and the lack of justice.

In the case of Adam and Eve, it was the person
that corrupted the nature. Because of their personal
sin, all human nature was completely weakened and
corrupted as there was no human nature outside of
them.7 Now that Anselm has shown that human nature was
completely though not essentially corrupted, he must
explain how that corruption of human nature can be
overcome so that the God-man can assume sinless
humanity.

When the personal sin of Adam and Eve became a
part of human nature, that nature could then be
reproduced only in its corrupted form just as human
nature would have reproduced itself in righteousness had
the original humans retained the uprightness with which
they were created.8 For this reason, even infants are
under the obligation to make satisfaction for the first
sin and for the absence of original justice which could
have been retained. But Anselm adds a very important
reservation about original sin in infants: since it is
impossible to speak of a just man unless he has a
rational will, so it is also impossible to speak of an
unjust child unless he has a rational will. Thus,
original sin can be ascribed to infants but only after
they have rational wills.9

When Anselm states that infants do not have sin at
the moment of conception, he appears to contradict the
Bible which says: "I was begotten in iniquity, and in
sin did my mother conceive me" (Psalm 51:5). He
resolves this conflict by saying that the Bible often
asserts that something has already happened when it
really means that it is certain to happen. In the same
way, man is said to be conceived in iniquity and sin,
not because there is already iniquity or sin, but
because the person who comes from the conception will
have sin as soon as he has a rational soul. Sin is said
to be in men at conception because they contract the
necessity of sinning in the seed, even though they will
not sin until they are human beings with rational
wills. Yet, the seed itself that is taken from the
parent has no sin since sin is only in the will.10

Anselm's insistence that sin exists only in the
will opens the way to understanding how the God-man
could be part of Adam's race without participating in
original sin. All other men existed in Adam causally as
if in his seed (natural existence) while they exist in

themselves personally (personal existence). Christ, on
the other hand, only existed in himself personally and
never existed at all in Adam through his reproductive
nature. It is important to note that Anselm is not
denying a natural existence to the God-man, i.e., his
being in Adam. If Anselm were to deny this, the
efficacy of Christ's redemptive death would not extend
to Adam's race. Rather, Anselm is saying that Christ
was indeed in Adam, but he was in Adam in a way quite
different from that of other men. All other men were in
Adam by the power of Adam's reproductive nature. This
means that they were subject to Adam's will since Adam
was in the unique situation in which his will affected
the nature that was in him. Thus, for men to be under
the power of the reproductive nature was also to be
under the power of Adam's will.

In De Conceptu Virginali, Anselm stresses that
Jesus alone was present in Adam by the power of God's
will and not by the power of Adam's nature or will.
Therefore, when Adam sinned, the corruption of his
reproductive nature did not affect Jesus, even though
Jesus was part of human nature.11   Anselm can make such
a statement only because he distinguishes between the
corrupted reproductive nature and human nature, i.e.,
the corrupted flesh and the flesh; this is the
foundation on which De Conceptu Virginali is built.

Human nature itself as the flesh is a
participatory nature, and as such, it separates man from
the angels. This participatory quality was seen to
enable the redemption of man while the redemption of
angels was impossible in Anselm's thought. The term
"reproductive nature" stresses this participatory
quality of the flesh by underlining the solidarity of
human nature in its physical dimension. It also calls
attention to the special relationship that exists
between the first man and the rest of the human race.
Thus, if flesh as a reproductive nature signifies the
unity of human nature, the corrupted flesh or corrupted
reproductive nature signifies the unity of that nature
with Adam.12   In this context, it makes good sense to
distinguish between Jesus's assumption of the flesh,
i.e., his being in Adam, and Jesus's being free from the
power of Adam's reproductive nature. The flesh as a
participatory nature does not necessarily mean that this
nature will forever participate in Adam's will. By
freeing the flesh from identity with the corrupted reproductive power, Anselm opens the way for a rectification of the flesh so that human nature might participate
in a will other than Adam's.

This notion of flesh as a participatory nature is related to certain of the denotative meanings of the flesh complex that we saw in chapter 5. The corrupt concupiscentia that we observed there (case 1) referred to the corruption of that originally upright reproductive nature that God gave to Adam. The bestial pleasure (bestiali voluptate) that became associated with this reproductive nature was not of the essence of that reproductive nature. In this regard we perceive how these bestial pleasures that are the flesh as corrupted concupiscentia are like the carnal appetites that constitute one of the figurative meanings of caro, and that made man's body like the body of brute animals.

But before Adam's sin there was no sin associated with Adam's reproductive nature, and there is still no sin in the body's seed even after Adam's sin. The reproductive nature through which mankind propagates itself is the flesh not only in regard to the corrupted concupiscentia associated with it, but also in regard to the physical means whereby human beings are generated. Propagation makes each man Adam ("Est quidem unusquisque . . . Adam per propagationem" DCV X; S II, 151, 6-7), and the reproductive nature that permits propagation works only through the joining of man and woman ("non accepit naturam propagandi nisi per virum simul et mulierem" DCV XI; S II, 153, 6-7). Thus the reproductive nature that makes us all brothers in Adam operates only through the human body (in the literal sense of corpus). In this respect, that reproductive nature that unites all men as sons of Adam is a meaning of the flesh complex that derives from its function in Anselm's discursive system.

Anselm also emphasizes that the will that accomplished redemption was the divine will, for that man's will was the same as God's will.13 If the will can be considered God's most important contribution to the incarnation, then it is possible to consider mortal flesh as humanity's crucial contribution to the God-man. When the Word assumes human nature, he assumes the mortal flesh;14 this is that characteristic of man after the Fall which sets him apart in the world of rational natures. Anselm even goes so far as to speak of the incarnation as the assumption of "mortality."15 Mortality is assumed because the God-man must be able to die; as a perfect man, the God-man would have the opportunity to offer his death as a gift to God. As God, he cannot die, but as man, he can die. Thus, the ability to die comes from his humanity; the ability to offer his death as a gift to God stems from his perfect humanity; the

infinite value attached to that death derives from his
divine personhood. According to Anselm, one can discuss
Christ's perfect humanity either in terms of the virgin
birth freeing him from all sin or in terms of the "one
person in two natures" doctrine excluding from his
humanity any imperfection not useful to the redemption.
But the feature that comes strictly from his humanity is
mortality while the element that comes strictly from his
divinity is the dignity of his person as God. This
forms the heart of Anselm's argument about the necessity
for the God-man to redeem mankind.

Flesh as a Disposition of the Will

The mortality of the flesh is a necessary condition of the God-man's atoning for Adam's sin. Yet,
payment for Adam's desertion of original justice represents only the first of two debts that human nature
contracted as a result of Adam's fall. The other debt
that human nature owes to God is the perseverance in
justice demanded of every rational creature. How does
Christ's death remove this debt of human nature?16

The actual restoration of justice is necessary to
remove this second debt. It was established in the discussion of the human will that the Fall did not corrupt
the instrument of willing. The result of original sin
was that the disposition of the will toward justice was
lost. But man retained the ability to preserve uprightness of will, even when that uprightness was deserted by
Adam. To see exactly what happened to the human will in
Adam's fall, it is necessary to consider again the relationship between the human person and the human nature
in Adam.

In each man, there is a personal will and a
natural will. For example, Anselm says that Adam's
decision to eat the fruit of the forbidden tree came
from his personal will rather than from his natural
will. Yet, because the human person does not exist
without human nature, there is an interaction between
the personal will and the natural will. When Adam
sinned personally, his nature also sinned.17 Because
Anselm's definition of sin is "the absence of required
justice," the justice Adam lost from his personal will
was also lost from his natural will. And it is the
absence of justice from the natural will which in turn
causes infants to sin personally as soon as they have a
rational will.18 The reason for their personal sin is
this: although the _instrumentum_ is intact in the

infant's rational will, the disposition toward justice is absent. Anselm might have stated this situation another way: Although the infant has the ability to retain justice as soon as he possesses a rational will, he does not have the justice he is able to retain. (Of course, this description of the infant's situation does not apply before he has a rational will.) Here it is important to see the relationship between the will as affectio (disposition) and the natural will.

In De Casu Diaboli, Anselm presents the beginning of his theory on the dispositions of the will.19 The two fundamental dispositions of the will are seen to be the disposition toward happiness and the disposition toward justice. Anselm states that no willing would take place at all if the rational will did not possess that first disposition. Regardless of whether a rational will is just or unjust, it desires to be happy.20 Yet, it has also been seen that in Anselm's world of thought no one can be happy unless he is just. For this reason, it is possible to have a conflict within the rational will: the will may desire happiness, but it may lack the disposition toward justice. In that event, the will is frustrated.

This frustration is possible because these dispositions of the will are not necessarily found together in the same will. While the disposition toward happiness is always present in the will, the disposition toward justice is added to the will and can be removed from the will. Anselm calls the disposition toward happiness the natural will in that it is always found in the rational will and by means of this disposition, the will as instrumentum is moved to operate. It is this fundamental disposition of the will which permits one to speak of the instrumentum as having the ability to will.21

The disposition toward justice was added to the will so that the disposition toward happiness would direct the will only within certain restricted bounds. Thus, the rational will would continue to desire happiness, but only that happiness that it should have. Both dispositions were originally present in created rational wills, and their interaction allowed created rational beings to be both just and happy.22

In De Concordia Praescientiae, Anselm speaks of the basic differences between these two dispositions: (1) the disposition toward justice is separable from the instrument of the will, while the disposition toward happiness is inseparable; (2) the disposition toward happiness is not the object that the _instrumentum_ wills, but the disposition toward justice is the actual object that the _instrumentum_ ought to will. The disposition toward justice is already justice.23 When Adam sinned personally, he lost the disposition toward justice, and the God-man rectifies human nature by restoring to man's will this disposition.

It was seen that Adam's personal will lost the disposition toward justice for the natural will because all men, except the God-man, were in him by the power of his reproductive nature. Thus, it is by the power of the reproductive nature that the lack of the separable disposition of the will (the disposition toward justice) is passed on to all men of Adam's race. If Adam had been confirmed in justice, his reproductive nature would have carried this disposition; because Adam deserted justice, his reproductive nature carries the absence of this disposition. It is the reproductive nature that explains how all men participate in the natural will of Adam. The flesh either carries or does not carry the disposition toward justice. After the Fall, the flesh of Adam carries only the absence of this required disposition of the will.

This explains why the God-man assumed the flesh (a human nature) rather than another individual man. The problem for man after the Fall was a deficient flesh, one that did not possess the disposition toward justice. Individual men all retained intact their personal faculties of reason and will. But without the disposition toward justice, these faculties did not in fact operate correctly. Thus, the God-man assumed flesh so that this disposition toward justice could be restored to it, thereby enabling individual men to retain that justice.24

It is only because Anselm holds that the flesh is essentially neutral that he can effectively use it as the vehicle for redemption. The entire argument of _De Conceptu Virginali_ rests on the distinction between the corrupted reproductive nature and human nature. Though the flesh was, in fact, corrupted by Adam's sin, that corruption did not alter the essential character of the flesh. The flesh remained, even after the Fall, essentially neutral. That is the reason the God-man could assume sinless flesh from Adam's sinful race. Furthermore, it is on the basis of Anselm's complex view of the human will that he can show how the flesh, which carries a disposition of the will, can alter the activity of the will.

It is clear that the participatory character of the flesh enables the personal will of Adam to affect all men. This very same characteristic of the flesh permits redemption to be extended to all men. The God-man is the new Adam in that he personally makes the flesh righteous by the same principle that Adam made the flesh sinful: the archetypal person (be it Adam or Christ) can affect the nature of man. The person of Adam made the flesh sinful because that flesh was in him by the power of his reproductive nature. The person of the God-man makes the flesh righteous because that flesh was assumed into his Person (the Second Person of the Trinity) by the power of the Holy Spirit. The parallel is clear.25

Flesh as the Principle of Transformation

In this chapter we have seen the transformation of the flesh in terms of the various denotations of the flesh and in its relation to other doctrines of his dis-cursive system. In this doctrinal context the flesh serves as one of the important bonds which give coher-ence to this discursive system. We might even say that the various transformations of the flesh help to make a coherent story out of the individual doctrines. This is the story of the failures and triumphs along the road to union with God. The flesh is the term that ties this story together by concretely expressing the human condition and by affording a model for Anselm's theory of human transformation.

The various doctrines of Anselm's system show that the flesh complex is crucial to Anselm's discursive system because it gives the necessary coherence to his argument. We saw that Anselm's doctrine of redemption operates on the level of generic humanity (the flesh) and that in order for the Second Person of the Trinity to redeem human nature, he had to assume the flesh of Adam's race. If he had not assumed that particular flesh, the men of Adam's race could not have been redeemed. This human nature, the flesh of Adam's race, is the single subject that undergoes the metamorphoses from original justice to the corruption of the Fall to redemption (including resurrection) in the God-man. In this way, flesh, in Anselm's theology, expresses the story of human nature so that there is the continuity of a single subject, the flesh of Adam's race rather than a

discontinuous series of events which have no related
meaning.

The flesh is capable of integrating the story of
human transformation because of its participatory character. The flesh as a reproductive nature shows how all
human beings participate in a single nature. Anselm
uses his doctrine of angels effectively to make this
point: what enables mankind to be redeemed as a race is
the fact that it was created as a single reproductive
nature, not as separate natures, which is the case with
the angels. The human method of propagation is the mark
of the flesh, and it shows how intimately all men are
related to each other. In fact, men are so related in
their nature that what happens in one generation affects
other generations.26

The participatory character of the flesh was seen
particularly in relation to the archetypal figure,
Adam. In his doctrine of original sin, Anselm shows how
the person of Adam corrupted all of the men of his race
since all men participate in Adam's will.27 This will
is not a personal but rather a natural will. We saw
that the transformations of the flesh actually refer to
the changes in this natural will. The person of Adam
was responsible for this first change in the will of
man's nature, or the flesh.

Then we saw that the doctrines of incarnation and
virgin birth explained how Christ was able to assume
human nature without inheriting the corrupted will of
that nature. The flesh of Christ was free from the
influence of Adam's will because he was conceived by the
power of the Holy Spirit and not by the power of the
reproductive nature. Consequently, Christ did receive
his humanity from Adam's race (since the Virgin Mary was
of Adam's race) and he was, therefore, in a position by
being part of that race, to rectify the natural will of
the flesh.

In figure 1 we noted four different conditions of
flesh, namely, Adamic flesh, fallen flesh, sinless
flesh, and glorified flesh. In each of these cases the
condition of flesh represents generic humanity. We
emphasized the importance of Adam and Christ, the two
archetypal figures embodying these conditions of generic
humanity. Individual men are related to the generic
humanity embodied in Adam and Christ in such a way that
they participate in them.

In Chapter 8 we shall diagram the parallel between
the physical mode of participation in these archetypal
figures. Here we simply wish to point out the important
interplay between the individual's flesh and generic
flesh in Anselm's theological system. In Adam, generic
flesh was created good and then it was corrupted. The
individual men of his race share in the corrupted condition of Adam's fallen flesh because they are produced by
the power of Adam's reproductive nature. This generic
condition is manifested in individual persons as a corrupt concupiscence of body and will. Thus individual
men bear a physical and spiritual mark of their participation in Adam.

Christ as the second Adam receives his sinless humanity by means of the virgin birth. In the same way
that Adam's generic humanity was confirmed in injustice
through his disobedience, so Christ's generic humanity
was confirmed in justice through his obedient life and
death. Individual men also bear the physical and
spiritual mark of being incorporated into the glorified
flesh of Christ. They eat the eucharistic body of
Christ, and they experience the righteous concupiscence
that Christ gives to the will of those who are incorporated into his mystical body.

This relationship between the genus and the individual is central to Anselm's notion of transformation
through the flesh. As we saw in figure 1, this relationship between generic flesh and individual flesh is
the key to God's plan for a perfect number of rational
natures. Once the God-man restores generic flesh,
individual men can be incorporated into it, and through
their death and resurrection in the likeness of Christ's
death and resurrection they take their place in the
heavenly city, thereby contributing to the perfect
number of rational natures there.

Thus, we have seen in this chapter that the flesh
is the model for human transformation in that it
illustrates the relationship between the individual and
the race, and grace and free will. The participatory
character of flesh shows how man's condition is affected
by the personal will of the first man, Adam. In the
flesh the entire race shares this state of the nature's
corruption. So the individual is intimately related to
all other men in the universal human condition, a condition of corruption. But the flesh also illustrates how
the human condition is rectified by grace. When the
human will is just, the retention of justice is performed by the individual's own personal will. Yet, the

factor that enables his personal will to be just in the first place is the disposition toward justice, that grace that the God-man gives to the will.

Thus, the flesh offers a model for explaining how a man can be said to be just through the activity of his own personal will (since it is his own personal will that retains rectitude of will) and through grace (since his own personal will is able to retain rectitude only if the disposition toward justice is given to it). Anselm's doctrine of the eucharist goes yet another step, explaining how this disposition toward justice is actually extended to the Church by means of the righteous flesh of Christ in the sacrament of the eucharist. Therefore, in the final chapter, we shall look at Anselm's doctrine of the eucharist to see how it completes Anselm's discursive system. But first we shall turn to the other level of Anselm's system, the motif level, since an understanding of this level is essential for a full appreciation of Anselm's doctrine of the eucharist.

NOTES

1.   This   analysis of Anselm's theological system
may be supplemented   by   consulting   James Gollnick, "The
Flesh Complex in St. Anselm's Theology," (Ph.D. thesis,
University of Toronto, 1974).

2.   This   point   will   be dealt with primarily in
chapters 7 and 8 of this study.   Chapter 7 considers the
motif level of Anselm's theology while chapter 8 is
devoted exclusively to Anselm's understanding of the
eucharist.

3.   In the next paragraphs we shall see that, for
Anselm, redemption of both the nature and the individual
is important for the divine plan.   Note 4 illustrates
the point made here regarding Anselm's emphasis on the
nature.

4.   "Sed et si perfectio mundanae creaturae non
tantum est intelligenda in numero individuorum quantum
in numero naturarum, necesse est humanam naturam aut ad
complementum eiusdem perfectionis esse factam, aut illi
superabundare, quod de minimi vermiculi natura dicere
non audemus" (CDH I/XVIII; S II, 77, 20-78, 4).

5.   R. Southern has stated that the damnation of
even a single nature would frustrate the plan of God;
this follows from Anselm's ideal world where the species
is more real than individuals. See Saint Anselm and His
Biographer (Cambridge, 1963), p. 100.

6.   "Quare possumus--ut puto--dicere deum consti-
tuisse 'terminos populorum iuxta numerum' electorum
hominum, quia tam diu erunt populi et erit hominum in
hoc mundo procreatio, donec numerus eorundem electorum
compleatur; et eo completo   cessabit esse hominum
generatio, quae fit in hac vita" (CDH I/XVIII; S II, 83,
12-16).

7.   "Quoniam autem personaliter peccaverunt, cum
originaliter fortes et incorrupti haberent potestatem
semper servandi sine difficultate iustitiam: totum quod
erant infirmatum et corruptum est. . . . Et quia tota
humana natura in illis erat et extra ipsos de illa nihil
erat, tota infirmata et corrupta est" (DCV II; S II,
141, 9-12).

8. "Sicut itaque sinon peccasset, qualis facta est a deo talis propagaretur; ita post peccatum qualem se peccando fecit talis propagatur" (DCV II; S II, 141, 19-21).

9. "Puto nullatenus illud posse asseri esse in infante, antequam habeat animam rationalem, sicut nec in Adam fuisse iustitiam, priusquam fieret homo rationalis. Nam si Adam et Eva generassent sine praecedenti peccato, non tamen esset in semine iustitia nec esse posset, priusquam formaretur in viventem hominem. Si ergo semen hominis non est susceptibile iustitiae, priusquam fiat homo, non potest suscipere originale peccatum, antequam homo sit" (DCV III; S II, 142, 13-19).

10. "Nam et si vitiosa concupiscentia generetur infans, non tamen magis est in semine culpa, quam est in sputo vel sanguine, si quis mala voluntate exspuit aut de sanguine suo aliquid emittit. Non enim sputum aut sanguis, sed mala voluntas arguitur" (DCV VII; S II, 149, 6-9).

11. "Verum quamvis constet eos omnes in illo fuisse, solus tamen filius virginis valde diverso modo ab aliis in illo fuit. Omnes quippe alii sic fuerunt in illo, ut per naturam propagandi, quae potestati et voluntati eius subdita erat, de illo essent; solus vero iste non sic in eo fuit, ut per naturam aut voluntatem eius de illo fieret" (DCV XXIII; S II, 163, 20-24).

12. This notion of flesh as a reproductive nature follows from DCV VII, X, and XI.

13. "Quoniam ergo voluntas dei nulla necessitate facit aliquid, sed sua potestate, et voluntas illius fuit voluntas dei, nulla necessitate mortuus est, sed sola sua potestate" (CDH II/XVI; S II, 121, 28-30).

14. McIntyre notes that the Anselmic form of communicatio idiomatum is not total since it extends to his sinlessness, omnipotence and wisdom, but not to his immortality. See St. Anselm and His Critics, p. 140. McIntyre also observes that the God-man can be thought of as merely a perfect man in his life, while the divine dignity plays a crucial role in his death.

15. "Illa hominis assumptio in unitatem personae dei non nisi sapienter a summa sapientia fiet, et ideo non assumet in homine quod nullo modo utile, sed valde noxium est ad opus quod idem homo facturus est. . . .

Sapienter namque assumet deus mortalitatem, qua sapienter, quia valde utiliter, utetur" (CDH II/XIII [emphasis added]; S II, 112, 22-113, 9).

16. The failure to see this "internal" aspect of Anselm's argument has led many critics to dismiss Anselm's redemptive system as a medieval drama hopelessly pitting compassion against honor and justice. But Anselm's total thought is not so much juridical as it is ontological and spiritual, though all three of these types of thought are involved. The proper payment for the offense of sin is secondary to the rectification of human nature. Critics miss this point by ignoring Anselm's treatises on will and original sin, thereby stressing inordinately the feudal and commercial influences on Anselm's atonement theory.

17. "Est peccatum a natura, ut dixi; et est peccatum a persona. Itaque quod est a persona, potest dici 'personale'; quod autem a natura, 'naturale,' quod dicitur 'originale.' Et sicut personale transit ad naturam, ita naturale ad personam, hoc modo: Quod Adam comedebat, hoc natura exigebat; quia ita ut hoc exigeret creata erat. Quod vero de ligno vetito comedit, non hoc voluntas naturalis, sed personalis, id est propria fecit. Quod tamen egit persona, non fecit sine natura. Persona enim erat quod dicebatur Adam; natura, quod homo. Fecit igitur persona peccatricem naturam, quia cum Adam peccavit, homo peccavit" (DCV XXIII; S II, 165, 5-13).

18. "Similiter fit in infantibus e converso. Nempe quod in illis non est iustitia quam debent habere, non hoc fecit illorum voluntas personalis, sicut in Adam, sed egestas naturalis, quam ipsa natura accepit ab Adam. In Adam namque, extra quem de illa nihil erat, est nudata iustitia quam habebat, et ea semper nisi adiuta caret. Hac ratione quoniam natura subsistit in personis et personae non sint sine natura, facit natura personae infantum peccatrices" (DCV XXIII; S II, 165, 15-21).

19. This theory was not to be fully developed until the writing of De Concordia Praescientiae et Praedestinationis et Gratiae Dei cum Libero Arbitrio at least seventeen years later. The particular value of the earlier treatment is that the created rational will is discussed in terms of an angel. This focuses on the dynamics of the will without yet introducing the further question regarding the distinction between personal and natural will. It can, therefore, be considered a type

of preliminary "thought experiment"; see J. Hopkins and
H. Richardson, Truth, Freedom, and Evil, pp. 44-45.

20. "Beatus autem non potest esse, si non vult
beatitudinem. Dico autem nunc beatitudinem non beatitudinem cum iustitia, sed quam volunt omnes, etiam
iniusti. Omnes quippe volunt bene sibi esse. Excepto
namque hoc quod omnis natura bona dicitur, duo bona et
duo his contraria mala usu dicuntur. Unum bonum est
quod dicitur iustitia, cui contrarium est malum iniustitia. Alterum bonum est quod mihi videtur posse dici
commodum, et huic malum opponitur incommodum" (DCD XII;
S II, 255, 2-8).

21. "Nullus cogitur vel timore vel sensu alicuius
incommodi, nec attrahitur amore commodi alicuius ad
volendum aliquid, nisi qui prius habet naturalem voluntatem vitandi incommodum aut habendi commodum, qua
voluntate se movet ad alias voluntates" (DCD XII; S II,
254, 23-26).
It should be noted that "natural will" is not used
here in the same way as natural will versus personal
will in the discussion of human nature. Since the
discussion here is about angels, "natural" means that
which was created as essential to rational natures in
general, namely, angels and men. In the other context,
"natural" refers to the human will which participates in
the condition of human nature in Adam. That having been
said, however, it can still be maintained that the
disposition toward happiness is "natural will" in both
senses of the term.

22. "Quoniam ergo nec solummodo volendo beatitudinem, nec solummodo volendo quod convenit cum ex
necessitate sic velit, iustus vel iniustus potest
appellari, nec potest nec debet esse beatus nisi velit
et nisi iuste velit: necesse est ut sic faciat deus
utramque voluntatem in illo convenire, ut et beatus esse
velit et iuste velit. Quatenus addita iustitia sic
temperet voluntatem beatitudinis, ut et resecet voluntatis excessum et excedendi non amputet potestatem. Ut
cum per hoc quia volet beatus esse modum possit excedere, per hoc quia iuste volet non velit excedere, et
sic iustam habens beatitudinis voluntatem possit et
debeat esse beatus" (DCD XIV; S II, 258, 18-26).

23. "Quae duae voluntates etiam in hoc differunt,
quia illia quae est ad volendum commodum, inseparabilis
est; illa vero quae est ad volendum rectitudinem, separ-
abilis fuit--ut supra dixi--in principio in angelis et
in primis nostris parentibus, et est adhuc in hac vita

manentibus. In hoc quoque differunt, quia illa quae est
ad volendum commodum, non est hoc quod ipsa vult; illa
vero quae est ad volendum rectitudinem, rectitudo est"
(DCP III/XII; S II, 284, 10-16).

   24. The restoration of the disposition toward
justice is the merit or grace which the God-man won by
his death. Cf. DCP III/XIII; S II, 285, 7-287, 21.

   25. G. H. Williams has called attention to this
parallel in Anselm: Communion and Atonement (St. Louis,
1960). In the next chapter, we shall examine some of
the points which Williams makes in his study.

   26. This notion of generation is important for
Anselm's system because he considers all generations to
be seminally (not personally) present in Adam; therefore, all men are generated from Adam (DVI I, II).
There are no such generations of angels.

   27. In the next chapter follows a more complete
discussion of the significance of the archetypal figures, Adam and Christ, in Anselm's theology.

7

FLESH AT THE MOTIF LEVEL OF ANSELM'S THEOLOGY

The Motif Level

The motif level is one of the three levels operative in St. Anselm's thought. We have already seen how
the concept of flesh functions at two other levels. On
the first, or denotative, level, we have observed the
wide variety of meanings that flesh has, giving us some
idea of the richness of the concept of flesh as Anselm
uses it in his various writings. It ranges from its
practical usage in everyday language (the physical
aspect of man or the appetites of the body) to a rather
technical, philosophical level (a disposition of the
human will). It also varies from negative meanings (the
will of fallen angels, or a way of life opposed to the
spirit) to positive meanings (the flesh of Christ or the
eucharistic bread).

On the second, or relational, level, flesh was
considered in its logical relation to other concepts
within the language web of various theological doctrines. The consistency and richness of the concept of
flesh permit it to play a role in explaining individual
doctrines as well as coordinating various doctrines
within Anselm's entire system. It would appear that it
is precisely the wide range of meaning of this term
which enables it to perform this systematic role so
well. From its obvious connection with propagation it
receives its association with the doctrines of original
sin and redemption. Yet, in its theological-philo-
sophical function, it receives the meaning of a natural
will, derived primarily from the doctrine of original
sin, to explain the corrupted will found in Adam's
descendants. In Anselm's psychological reflection on
the dynamics of personal volition, the flesh concept
refers to the disposition that moves the will to action.

Now, on the third level, the motif level, we are
going to examine the concept of flesh as an orientational metaphor governing Anselm's entire life and
thought. This can be especially discerned within the
devotional context of Anselm's theology. On this level,
we shall observe how flesh is a metaphor for intimacy

and feeling in prayer, and how it is the efficacious symbol of Christ's gracious presence in the eucharist. In relation to Anselm's theological system, prayer and eucharist (the prayer of prayers) are not mere doctrines within his discursive system. While we shall see in chapter 8 how the doctrine of the eucharist functions within Anselm's theological system at the discursive level, it goes far beyond the logical role. At the motif level, one can actually say that eucharist spells out, or evokes, Anselm's entire theological system.

Here we are at the deepest level of Anselm's theological system, the level at which his system is spontaneously coordinated through the power of motif symbols to evoke the meaning of his theology as a whole. On this motif level, Anselm's theology is seen as an indivisible unity that cannot be divided into parts. This is the level of Anselm's theological system to which H. Ott calls attention in "What is Systematic Theology?" He argues that the deepest meaning of a theological system is not at the level of systematizing and arranging doctrines but rather at the level of experiencing the one and indivisible meaning of the theological system.

Ott explains that the point of systematic theology is to illuminate and to express the depths of faith in such a way that the one subject matter of theology becomes perceptible. He maintains that he is following Anselm's lead when he suggests that the goal of the theological system is actually to evoke the subject matter being considered.

> Incidentally, I have no scruples, in this attempt to lay hold of the commission and the correct course for systematic theology, against appropriating positively the motivation that Anselm of Canterbury gives in Cur Deus Homo as characteristic of his own theological thinking. Many had asked him, he writes at the beginning of that tractate, to formulate in writing his thoughts on the question of the incarnation of God. He yields to their request, for they had asked him, "not in order that they might attain to faith through reason, but rather that they might

enjoy in their understanding and contemplation
what they believed, and that they might be
prepared as much as possible always to give
satisfaction to all who ask them the reason
for the hope that is in us." It could not be
better said. Theology has to do with giving
an account to others and to oneself. But at
the same time and in unity with this, there
takes place in theology the joy of faith
beholding itself in the medium of thought.1

Here Ott emphasizes the aspect of joy which is such a
central part of theology at the motif level. By sing-
ling out Anselm's phrase, "that they might enjoy in
their understanding and contemplation what they believed," Ott observes that, at the motif level, theology
has the power to evoke the reality it contemplates, and
in doing so, theology brings with it the joy that comes
from being in the presence of God.

We also see here how close theology comes to
prayer. At their deepest levels both theology and
prayer usher man into the holy presence of God. Both
establish this presence at the most profound levels of
human feeling, enabling man to participate in the
reality to which he addresses himself. In this chapter
we shall observe how Anselm's devotional life is the
context in which his theology arose. We shall discover
how the flesh concept is related to this life of prayer
which is at the heart of Anselm's theological system on
the motif level, and we shall see that this life of
prayer both sustains and gives rise to his speculative
intellectual activity. At base, for Anselm, all
thinking originates in and is a form of prayer. Prayer
is the form of any theological motif, and, as we shall
see, the content of that form in Anselm's theology is
the flesh of Christ.

Metaphorical Language

In chapter 2 we examined the monastic-devotional
context of Anselm's theology. In that life setting, we
noted that prayer is the origin and form of all Anselm's
thinking. We saw that prayer was evident throughout
even his most speculative intellectual work, citing the
creation of his ontological argument for the existence
of God in Proslogion as a prime example of this union of
prayer and profound thought. The life context of
Anselm's theology already brings us in touch with the
deepest level of his theology, namely, the motif level.

But there is also another indication of being at the motif level of Anselm's theology. The more passionate, nondiscursive language that characterizes prayer also alerts us to the fact that we are at the motif level. While we have made the point that prayer is the context of all Anselm's thought, including his more discursive, speculative thought, we shall see that there is an especially direct and even passionate language that is characteristic of Anselm's prayer and that can be distinguished from the more discursive thought that we examined at the relational level of Anselm's system.

In fact, R. Southern argues that the evocative and passionate language of Anselm's prayers constitutes a genuine revolution in medieval piety.2 Southern compares the emotion and passion of Anselm's prayers with the sobriety of the earlier Carolingian piety:

> Anselm's prayers marked the moment of rebound. They introduced into a tradition still Carolingian in temper a new note of personal passion, of elaboration and emotional extravagance, which anticipated some of the chief features of later medieval piety. They owed their power to an unusual combination of intensity of feeling and clarity of thought and expression. They show little sign of the exact and metaphysical mind which was soon to produce some of the classics of Christian theology: but when these later works had been written it was possible to see that they displayed many of the same qualities as the prayers.3

He calls attention to another significant feature of Anselm's prayers in noting that the emotional intensity of his prayers is also combined with clarity of thought. Furthermore, he observes that Anselm's later, more discursive, theological works have many of the same qualities as his prayers, referring primarily to the deep feeling and passion of these works. This last point is especially important because it stresses that there is a unifying tendency in Anselm's theology which constantly merges devotional prayer and reflective thought. Thus, while we may distinguish two types of language in Anselm's theology, one more emotional and passionate, the other more logical and speculative, we should also realize that these two types of language are intended to complement each other and that both types are found in Anselm's treatises as well as in his prayers.

In "Structure et caractères de la prière anselmienne," R. Roques devotes considerable space to the discussion of this difference between the two types of language which Anselm uses.4   Roques points out that where the more discursive type is used to demonstrate certain truths through logically joined arguments, the more affective type is meant to stimulate piety and love.5   We would characterize this difference of language type, or literary form, in a similar way, saying that where Anselm's more discursive thought communicates by laying out linear arguments, prayerful reflection as motif reflection, seeks to gather up in compact form the deepest feelings of the heart that express the unity of the whole. This compactness and directness of prayer, this ability to express the unity of the whole, is achieved through the use of metaphors, because metaphors express a larger reality (e.g., a whole outlook) in a limited symbol.   Therefore, the presence of powerful metaphors offers us additional evidence that we are at the motif level of Anselm's theology.

We might pause here to consider precisely what a metaphor is and how it operates.   The metaphor (derived from the Greek words meta [over] and pherein [to carry]) is a figure of speech which unites one thing to another.   It transfers (carries over) characteristics from one thing to another.   Metaphors are especially helpful when dealing with the experience of the mind or of the spirit, inner experience which we cannot simply describe but which we wish to communicate to some degree.   Metaphor transfers the language of description into a language of evocation.

Many of the metaphors which we shall be looking at operate on the principle of synecdoche, where a part or an individual is used for a whole or a class, e.g., my flesh is me; not that I am only flesh, but flesh is a part of me which represents the whole person. Or we might use another example: When Anselm employs the metaphor of eating to express the intimate union of the soul with Christ, he is not thinking that only the mouth is in touch with the body of Christ, rather he means that the act of eating and the commitment of the total person are one, i.e., they participate in one another. This participation of realities in one another is the metaphysical principle that underlies the linguistic use of metaphor.

The motif level of Anselm's theology must be expressed by metaphors because the motif-level has to do
with wholes. The whole meaning of his theology can only
be evoked symbolically, i.e., by a part. Here we see
that metaphor and symbol come together to evoke a whole
context, not to denote one particular thing.6   Thus,
when we say that we eat the flesh of Christ, we are not
merely eating just his flesh, rather our whole persons
are participating in his death, sharing God's grace,
becoming one Church. The metaphor of eating evokes the
sense of intimacy and union which occur in the physical
act of eating; the flesh of Christ evokes the entire
spiritual reality believed in by the Christian.   Thus,
metaphors evoke whole realities and entire life contexts.   In this way, metaphors are appropriate to the
motif level of Anselm's theological system, that level
which deals precisely with the life context of his
theology.

In chapter 8 we shall pay particular attention to
the role of flesh as sacrament; however, at this point
we shall examine the role of flesh as a source of some
of Anselm's most powerful metaphors expressing his love
for God and his spiritual desire for things divine.   We
shall pay special attention to the way the body and its
various parts serve as metaphors for the deepest feelings of devotion and the most profound acts of love in
his prayers. Already in this study of the flesh concept
as seen in the metaphors of Anselm's prayers, we shall
note the central role of eucharistic imagery in evoking
feelings of desire for and intimacy with God.   But
because we shall treat directly the role of the concept
of flesh in Anselm's theology of the eucharist in a
separate section, the eucharist will be considered here
only insofar as it touches upon the bodily metaphors
employed in his prayers.

In **Oratio** III ("Prayer Before Receiving The Body
and Blood of Christ"), Anselm expresses his devotion to
the passion of Christ, speaking of his desire to perceive this mystery in his mouth and in his heart.7   It
is especially interesting to note the close relationship
between the heart and the mouth expressed in this passage.   The heart and the mouth are closely linked because they both refer to the affections that are kindled
in receiving the body of Christ in the eucharist. The
metaphors of the flesh are important in Anselm's prayers
because the perceptions of the body and the feelings of
the heart both refer to a direct, intuitive experience
of the mysteries of faith.

Oratio III is rich in these physical metaphors of
intimacy, especially as they refer to the reception of
the eucharist. The body that is the eucharist is
received by the mouth and the heart of the Christian.
To anticipate slightly what we shall see in the section
on eucharist, we emphasize here that, for Anselm, the
body of Christ in the eucharist not only is the symbol
of the whole Christ, but it is the real presence of this
Christ, the embodiment of the rectitude which is the
Word of God. The eucharist that effects the presence of
Christ in his justice and truth is brought into immediate contact with the Christian through the mouth. The
mouth that receives the body of Christ symbolizes the
heart that receives the presence of Christ. Both the
mouth and the heart express the direct reception of
Christ by the Christian and the response of the Christian in love. Thus, the mystery of faith that the mind
seeks to understand by reason is appropriated directly
by the body and heart of the Christian who receives the
eucharist. It is the integration of these moments of
approach to God (by understanding and by devotion) that
Anselm underscores at the beginning of "Meditatio
Redemptionis Humanae" as "Chew by reflecting, suck by
understanding, swallow by loving and rejoicing." Moreover, in Oratio X ("Prayer to St. Paul"), he deplores
the disjunction of the activities of reason and of the
heart, where truth shows something to be the case, and
yet the affections do not feel the power of this truth.8

These two approaches to God may be described var-
iously as mediated and direct, the logical and the
intuitive, the rational and the affective, or the mind
and the heart (or flesh). It is important to remember
that Anselm recognized the value of both approaches and
that both shape his theological system as two moments in
the movement of the soul toward God. But it is equally
important to see that the concept of flesh is utilized
by Anselm to describe one of these approaches to God,
the affective approach.9

Other of Anselm's prayers offer further examples
of how he expresses the affections of the heart by the
metaphors of the body: in his "Prayer to St. Nicholas,"
Anselm employs the word viscera to denote the feelings
of the heart.10 And Oratio X uses viscera in the same
sense.11 The very same use of the word viscera, which
can refer to either the flesh of a body, or the internal
organs, is also seen in his third "Prayer to Mary."12
At the same time, it should be observed that viscera has
the same ambiguous usage as the other terms referring to
the flesh which have already been noted. For example,

the prayer to Mary balances the positive sense of viscera as "the heart" with the negative sense which refers
to "the concupiscable desires of the flesh."13

The affections touch the deepest level of the
human being and are, for Anselm, the source of just or
unjust willing. There are various terms that refer to
that inner realm of the human will: caro, corpus, concupiscentia, viscera, affectus, and desiderium. Whether
these terms are positive or negative depends on the
particular context in which they are used.14 But it is
precisely this changeable character of the terms which
signifies the concept of flesh that highlights this
concept in Anselm's theology. The flesh is a central
concept in Anselm's theological system precisely because
it provides a powerful symbol for the changes in the
human will owing to the Fall and to redemption. The
flesh is placed together with the terms affectus and
desiderium because these terms represent the psychological region in which the human will experiences
redemption. Therefore, the flesh is on one level a
metaphor for the dispositions or affections of the will,
expressing the motivation behind human willing, while on
another level it is the symbol which both signifies and
effects the state of any particular human will. It is
necessary to examine both of these aspects of flesh in
more detail to fully appreciate the richness of this
concept in Anselm's theological thought.

As metaphor, the flesh is the appetitive character
of the human will. The flesh and its aspects are a
vocabulary in which to express in bodily terms the
longings and desires that actually move the will to
act.15 Therefore, Anselm employs the vocabulary of the
bodily functions as metaphors to speak about the affections. For example, in the "Prayer to Mary Magdalene,"
he speaks of her thirsting after the mercy of Christ.16
And in his prayer to Christ, Anselm recalls the imagery
of the Psalms where thirsting after the Lord is the
expression of longing for God.17 Anselm also uses the
verb "to hunger after" (esurire) to express his longing
in Oratio XII ("Prayer to St. John the Evangelist").18
In his "Prayer to St. Stephen," Anselm again uses the
verb esurire, asking that his hungering soul might be
satisfied with the bread of charity.19

The metaphors provided by the physical process of
breathing also hold an important place among those words
that express the affections in Anselm's prayer. "To
sigh after," or "long for," and "to pant for" (anhelare)
are present in various prayers as well as in other

affective passages in Anselm's writings. One example of
this breathing metaphor has already been noted in Oratio
II. In Oratio VII, Anselm prays to Mary for mercy,
saying that he is panting for her.20 In another prayer
to Mary, Anselm also uses the same verb anhelare to
express his longing.21 Nor does Anselm restrict these
expressions of longing to his prayers; the word anhelare
is used in this same sense of longing in both Proslogion
and in a letter to Pope Urbain II, recommending Cur Deus
Homo.22

In his "Prayer to Christ," Anselm combines many of
these physical metaphors, saying that he thirsts after
the Lord, hungers after him, desires him, sighs after
him, and longs very much for him.23 This flood of
affection expressed in terms of bodily processes illustrates the directness of the affections that move the
heart and will of the Christian. It appears that the
basis of the most daring expressions of love and commitment are derived from the body. The very same words
that could describe a soul blinded by attachment to the
world are used to express divine attachment. The principal value in the metaphor of the flesh is its directness and its power. No other aspect of human experience
points so well to forces that move the will to action.
It is as though the closer Anselm wishes to get to the
source of human motivation and will, the more he is
drawn to the bold metaphors of the flesh.24

Of all the metaphors associated with the flesh,
the metaphor of eating has the most importance in
relation to the flesh as will, and, as we shall see, is
of crucial importance to Anselm's doctrine of the eucharist. Eating, chewing, and sucking are the images
that express the attraction of the Christian soul to the
sweetness that is God. Apart from Anselm's specifically
eucharistic meditation ("Meditatio Redemptionis Humanae"), there are other prayers that make appeal to
oral images. In the "Prayer to St. Stephen," for
example, Anselm speaks of his love of the words that
Stephen spoke on behalf of his murderers, expressing his
love and contemplation of these words in terms of eating
and sucking.25 Anselm also speaks of the taste that
comes from loving God in Oratio XII.26 There are also
many other references to the taste of holy love, characterizing this taste as full of sweetness and savour.27

The metaphor of taste has a particular power not found
in other images of the physical senses. Regarding this
metaphor, P. Adnes has made some valuable and pertinent
observations. In "Goût Spirituel," he describes the

special place taste has among the physical senses employed as metaphors for the soul's experience of God.28
Adnes recognizes the special directness and intimacy
that set taste apart from sight, hearing, and even
touch: where sight and hearing create a certain distance between the object perceived and the subject, and
touch maintains a certain exteriority, taste produces a
kind of symbiosis between subject and object. He also
states that taste is the most subjective of all the
senses, the least intellectualizable and the most inti-
mate.29 Finally, Adnes also points to that special
relationship between the spiritual sense of taste and
the Word made flesh, present in the eucharist.30

The Motif of Transformation
Through the Flesh of Christ

Now we shall attempt to show how Anselm's
devotional life and his use of metaphor, which we have
seen in a general way operating at the motif level, also
apply specifically to Cur Deus Homo, the work that is at
the heart of Anselm's views of transformation. First,
we shall perceive how the context of Cur Deus Homo is a
devotional context. What we have observed about the
deep personal and spiritual involvement that nourished
the creation of Proslogion (in chapter 2) can also be
found in Cur Deus Homo. At this level of analysis we
shall determine how Anselm's devotional life influenced
the writing of Cur Deus Homo, and how the work can even
be interpreted as a reflection on the liturgical life of
the Church, the arena of transformation for Anselm.
Second, we shall take a closer look at the relation of
Anselm's prayer to Cur Deus Homo by examining Anselm's
"Meditatio Redemptionis Humanae," a work that Southern
has called "a devotional summary of Cur Deus Homo."31

In this remarkable meditation we shall see what
Cur Deus Homo actually looks like when it is cast in the
form of a prayer. Because this meditation summarizes
the doctrine of Cur Deus Homo in the language of prayer,
we shall be able to see how Anselm applies the concept
of flesh to his theological system in a metaphorical
way. This is in direct contrast to the relational use
of the flesh concept at the discursive, or relational,
level of his theological system, a use that we studied
in chapter 6. The prayerful view of Cur Deus Homo will
also confirm our general observations about the unity of
prayer and thought in Anselm's theology since Anselm's
"Meditatio Redemptionis Humanae" places expressions of

devotional feeling and doctrinal speculation side by side.

We shall now turn our attention to some of the indications of the devotional setting that surrounded the creation of Cur Deus Homo. Although we do not have the same rich and deeply moving account of the composition of Cur Deus Homo that we have of Proslogion, we do have Eadmer's description of the life setting in which Anselm wrote Cur Deus Homo.

Cur Deus Homo was written over a span of four years (1094 to 1098), begun while Anselm was involved in his numerous duties as archbishop of Canterbury and completed while in the solitude of his mountaintop exile. We do not have much information about the inner spiritual experience that nourished his theology of the atonement, except for Eadmer's note that Anselm's spirits rose as he took his abode on a mountain, in the province of Capua, contemplating a time of peace in which to finish Cur Deus Homo. Eadmer also tells us that Anselm ordered his life according to the routine of those years before he became abbot so that "day and night his mind was occupied with acts of holiness, with divine contemplation, and with the unravelling of sacred mysteries."32 The "acts of holiness" and of "divine contemplation" that Eadmer speaks of give us some idea of the devotional setting of Cur Deus Homo, but we must look elsewhere for more information about the spirituality that fostered Anselm's theology of redemption.

G. H. Williams's Anselm: Communion and Atonement attempts to add something more to our appreciation of the devotional basis of Cur Deus Homo. Williams tries to show that there are important liturgical references in the Cur Deus Homo and those works immediately related to it which reflect the actual life context of the Church in which this theology of the atonement arose. In fact, Williams argues that Anselm's theology of redemption must be understood as a reflection on the piety and liturgy of the eleventh century Church. In a passage from Williams's book, his concern that Anselm's redemptive theory be viewed not as an abstract, rationalistic system but rather as a meditation on the sacramental life of the Church is illustrated:

> Anselm's theory of the atonement, when seen in
> the isolation of its rationalistic formulation
> in the Cur Deus Homo, seems so to have ab-
> stracted the action of redemption from history
> and from the on going life of the church that

it appears like a vast and remote cosmic
computation whereby the merit of a certain
innocent man's death is multiplied by the
infinity of his divinity to yield up more than
enough honor to make good on the first man's
failure to obey God.

But our analysis of the liturgical and
sacramental allusions in Cur__Deus__Homo in
connection with allied writings makes it clear
that Anselm's theory of the atonement is
especially meaningful in the penitential
Eucharistic context of a progressive incorporation into the universal humanity represented on the altar in a process which extends
Christ's faraway and long-ago action into each
day's struggle with willfulness and each day's
acceptance of the heavenly manna, a sacramental process whereby the "body of lowliness" is
gradually transformed into the "body of glory"
prepared to find its place amid the angelic
host.33

From his study, Williams concludes that Anselm's theory
of atonement is an important step in the theological
meditation on the changing sacramental life of the
Church. Williams is especially concerned with showing
that Cur__Deus__Homo reflects those developments in
eucharistic theology which stressed Christ's presence in
the eucharist and the increased importance of the
eucharist as the sacrament that incorporates men into
the body of Christ.

Although, Williams notes, Cur Deus Homo does not
use the terms baptism or eucharist at all, still it does
allude to the sacramental action of the eucharist
whereby men are incorporated into the heavenly body of
Christ, and it reflects at certain points the language
of the Mass. Williams says:

When Anselm, in substantiation of his basic
and characteristic emphasis that man redeemed
is superior to paradisic man as first created,
writes: ". . . God has restored human nature
even more wonderfully than He created it," he
is echoing the prayer at the mixing of the
chalice: "O God, who didst wonderfully
create, and yet more wonderfully renew, the
dignity of human nature (humanae substantiae
dignitatem).". . . From our study it is clear
that the key words of the foregoing composite

[debita, iustitia, tollere] from the Cur Deus
Homo [accipere, debita, iustitia, tollere]
reflect revealingly the phrasing of the canon
of the mass: "panem coelestem (calicem salu-
taris) accipiam," "dimitte nobis debita nostra," "Agnus Dei, qui tollis peccata mundi."34

So we see that even the argumentation of Cur Deus Homo
has a grounding in liturgical prayer. Williams has
shown not merely that Anselm's systematic theology and
his prayers have their roots in the life and worship of
the Church but also how they are so rooted. For Anselm,
theology and prayer are rooted in the liturgy, especially the eucharist. This liturgical setting represents
the motif level of the flesh complex in that it actually
evokes the transformation of the flesh that is reflected
upon in Cur Deus Homo. Hence, Williams insists that
Anselm's theological system must not be divorced from
the liturgical setting in which it arose and that even
Cur Deus Homo, a strongly "rationalistic" formulation of
human transformation, must be referred to the sacramental and liturgical atmosphere that inspired it.

We can observe most fully the prayerful-liturgical
formulation of Cur Deus Homo by studying Anselm's remarkable "Meditatio Redemptionis Humanae," the work that
Southern has termed a "devotional summary of the Cur
Deus Homo" and which we shall refer to hereafter as the
Cur Deus Homo prayer or the Cur Deus Homo meditation.
In this prayer, Anselm presents the discursive argument
of Cur Deus Homo in the form of a meditation. It is
unusual for an author to express the same ideas in two
different forms. It is perhaps proof of the distinctiveness of the levels of Anselm's system that he
decided to present the mystery of the redemption in
these two forms.

Where Cur Deus Homo lent itself particularly well
to this analysis of the concept of flesh at the discursive, or relational, level of Anselm's system, the Cur
Deus Homo meditation provides a similar service to our
examination of the flesh concept at the motif level of
Anselm's system. Roques has characterized the difference between the two approaches to the redemption (that
of Cur Deus Homo and that of the Cur Deus Homo meditation) in this way: Where Cur Deus Homo employs necessary reasons to "demonstrate" the redemption, the Cur
Deus Homo meditation presents the redemption as a mystery of love which is intensely present to the soul.35
According to Roques, the spiritual sensibility of the
latter replaces the juridico-rational demonstrations of

the former. But since it can be misleading to see a too-sharp distinction between Anselm's affective and his logical types of language, we suggest this more moderate statement of Roques's observation: while both Cur Deus Homo and the Cur Deus Homo meditation have similar rational elements, the latter also includes the vocabulary and metaphors of spiritual devotion not found in the former.

Because the Cur Deus Homo meditation utilizes this vocabulary of spiritual devotion and provides us with extraordinary instances of the flesh as a source of metaphors that evoke the motif of transformation in Anselm's theology, it is especially suited to an analysis of the concept of flesh at the motif level of his system. We shall now turn to the text of the Cur Deus Homo meditation, limiting our consideration to those passages that directly involve the flesh as a source of metaphors for Anselm's most profound expression of love and devotion.

In the opening paragraph of the meditation, Anselm uses the metaphors of the flesh to exhort the Christian to contemplate the mystery of redemption:

> O Christian soul, soul raised up from grievous death, soul redeemed and freed by the blood of God from wretched bondage: arouse your mind, remember your resurrection, contemplate your redemption and liberation. Consider anew where and what the strength of your salvation is, spend time in meditating upon this strength, delight in reflecting upon it. Shake off your disinclination, constrain yourself, strive with your mind toward this end. Taste the goodness of your Redeemer, be aflame with love for your Savior, chew His words as a honey-comb, suck out their flavor, which is sweeter than honey, swallow their health-giving sweetness. Chew by thinking, suck by understanding, swallow by loving and rejoicing. Rejoice in chewing, be glad in sucking, delight in swallowing.36

Here we encounter directly that aspect of joy which is one of the important characteristics of the deepest level of Anselm's system: Anselm urges the mind to remember and to contemplate the redemption so that it might delight in reflecting upon this liberation from sin.

We also note in this opening paragraph how Anselm uses the metaphors of the flesh to arouse the mind to contemplation and to characterize the enjoyment of meditation. In these metaphors, we see the profound unity of thought and devotion since the metaphors of eating are used to express both thinking and loving. Here he utilizes the metaphors of chewing and sucking to describe the processes of thinking and understanding: "Chew by thinking, suck by understanding." These metaphors express the activity of turning thoughts over in the mind (chewing) and drawing out the full understanding of the words of faith (sucking). Swallowing is the metaphor Anselm uses here to indicate the acts of love which unite the soul to God since the union of swallowing food, the closest physical union possible for two distinct entities, is expressed in that act. Thus, the metaphor of eating is used to express meditation and contemplation, feeling, and loving.

We should also be aware that these metaphors of eating have a special significance in the context of this meditation. Not only do they express the activities of the deepest levels of understanding and feeling, but they also reflect the actual eating process that is going on at the time when one is supposed to "chew by thinking and suck by understanding." The imagery that Anselm employs here is clearly meant to reflect the sacramental eating of the eucharist which is the life situation in which this prayer occurs and which actually effects the transformation that this prayer focuses upon. This becomes especially evident when later in this prayer Anselm says, "Let your heart feed upon these thoughts, let it chew continually upon them, let it suck upon them and swallow them whenever your mouth receives the body and blood of your Redeemer." As the Christian kneels and chews the body of Christ, he is exhorted to "chew" the saving mystery of redemption in his thoughts. The special force of the eating metaphor can be appreciated only when one understands that this metaphor is combined with and calls attention to the sacramental eating. In this way Anselm directs the meditative activity toward the physical-sacramental process that actually effects the redemption contemplated by the Christian; thus, Anselm intensifies the sacramental eating by focusing the deepest thoughts and feelings on the profound meaning and significance of the eucharist. So we see that the metaphor of eating is capable of expressing the deep unity of the physical-sacramental, the intellectual, the emotional, and the volitional aspects of Anselm's theology.

This single metaphor also provides a sense of how
the activities of the mind, heart, and will are intimately related at their deepest levels. The metaphor of
eating is particularly appropriate to express the
deepest levels of intellectual, emotional, and volitional activity because of the delight Anselm finds in
all of these activities. Not only are all of the mental
and spiritual activities related at their deepest level,
they are related in joy. The joy of profound thought,
deep understanding, and spiritual feeling is primary at
the motif level of Anselm's system. This is the point
Ott observes when he emphasizes the quality of joy as
being essential to the deepest level of Anselm's
system: "Theology has to do with giving an account to
others and to oneself. But at the same time and in
unity with this, there takes place in theology the joy
of faith beholding itself in the medium of thought."37
At this depth, or prayer, level of intellectual life,
the emotions and the will are also completely engaged in
the activity of the mind. In this opening paragraph of
the Cur Deus Homo meditation, Anselm chooses the metaphor of eating to describe this intellectual and spiritual activity because it has the power to communicate
the profound feelings of joy and the volitional acts of
love that are an integral part of Anselm's theological
project of faith seeking understanding.

In the middle of the Cur Deus Homo meditation,
Anselm again has recourse to the language of feeding to
express the level of mental and spiritual engagement
that should accompany the reception of the eucharist:

> Behold, O Christian soul, this is the strength
> of your salvation, this is what has made
> possible your freedom, this is the cost of
> your redemption. You were in bondage, but
> through the cross you have been redeemed. You
> were a servant, but through the cross you have
> been set free. You are an exile who in this
> manner has been led back home, someone lost
> who has been found, someone dead who has been
> revived. O man, let your heart feed upon
> these thoughts, let it chew continually upon
> them, let it suck upon them and swallow them
> whenever your mouth receives the body and
> blood of your Redeemer. In this life make
> these thoughts your daily bread, your nour-
> ishment, your provision. For through these
> thoughts and only through them will you remain
> in Christ and Christ in you; and only through

them will your joy be full in the life to
come.38

Here Anselm repeats the metaphors of chewing, sucking,
and swallowing which he uses in the first paragraph of
this meditation. He recalls the basic situation on
which the Christian should meditate: that mankind is
freed by Christ from bondage. Again Anselm reminds us
that the most appropriate time for the Christian to
meditate upon (to "savour") the mystery of redemption is
while feeding upon the eucharistic bread. Here, at the
motif level of Anselm's theology, human transformation
really occurs through eating Christ's glorified flesh.
In this particular passage, we also see that Anselm
singles out the cross as the central symbol which the
Christian is to contemplate while eating the "body of
glory."

Anselm focuses on the cross in this hortatory
paragraph because it immediately follows a more
discursive explanation of how Christ accomplished man's
salvation by his death on the cross. In chapter 4, we
discussed the important role of Christ's obedient
death: on the discursive level of Anselm's system,
Christ's death explains how human nature was able to
offer God something that it did not owe him (Christ was
not obliged to die since he was not a sinner; for
Anselm, death is the result of man's sin and a sinless
man would not have to die) and something which was
greater than everything else in the universe, i.e., a
gift that was commensurate with the dignity of the
Person offended by man's sin (because Christ is God as
well as man, his death had the infinite value necessary
to atone for original sin). In the Cur Deus Homo
meditation, we see that a summary of this discursive
explanation of the importance of Christ's death precedes
Anselm's exhortation to reflect on the significance and
personal meaning of that doctrinal explanation.

This provides us with an excellent example of how
the two levels of Anselm's system are related. The
logically coherent doctrinal presentations of Anselm's
system at the discursive, or relational, level are meant
to be appropriated with the feelings and the will. In
other words, the discursive level of Anselm's theological system is meant to be completed by the motif level
of that system since it is at the motif level that the
whole meaning of the system is evoked and consequently
can be appropriated at the deepest levels of feeling and
will. When Anselm speaks of the need to assimilate in
the heart and in the mouth what faith and reason teach

about God, he is referring to the ideal interrelationship of these two levels of his theological system.39

    In the Cur_Deus__Homo meditation, Anselm applies
this general need to relate doctrine to feeling and will
by saying that the doctrine of the cross must be fed
upon by the heart. He recommends that the Christian
"chew continually" on it, "sucking" the words, and
finally "swallowing" them. We have already observed
Anselm's use of these powerful metaphors to express the
deepest possible assimilation of the doctrines and
mysteries of faith by the feelings and the will. But
here they occur with direct reference to the eucharist
so that one is to "chew," "suck," and "swallow" the
doctrine of the cross at the same time the mouth
actually feeds on the body and blood of Christ. As we
have already seen, Anselm clearly intends a parallel
between the activity of the spirit and the process of
eating the eucharistic bread: "O man, let your heart
feed upon these thoughts, let it chew continually upon
them, let it suck upon them and swallow them whenever
your mouth receives the body and blood of your Redeemer." Not only are the spiritual and physical
processes parallel, but the spiritual process is
designed to carry on and make permanent the physical
act; thus, the constant "chewing" of the doctrine of the
cross is to become the spiritual nourishment that keeps
a person in the presence of Christ. In this way Anselm
shows that there is a way to perpetuate the eucharist:
the constant meditation on and assimilation of the
doctrine of redemption permits the eucharist to be a
permanent state of life rather than a discrete event.
In other words, human beings are intended to dwell at
the motif level where human transformation is effected
through the flesh of Christ.

    The important point to appreciate in this parallel
between meditation and the reception of the eucharist is
that the eucharist is primary to Anselm's theology. One
might even say that the eucharist is the archetype of
Anselm's theology and that all other acts of prayer,
reflection, meditation, and contemplation are essentially types of that fundamental archetype.

    The Cur_Deus_Homo meditation concludes with two
paragraphs that repeat the eating metaphors. The first
of these paragraphs reads:

        Consider, O my soul, peer into, O my inmost
        being, how much my entire substance owes to
        Him. Yes, O Lord, because You created me I

owe my entire self to Your love; because You
redeemed me I owe my entire self; because Your
promises are so great I owe my entire self.
Indeed, I owe to Your love much more than
myself-as much more as You are greater than I,
for whom You gave Yourself and to whom You
promise Yourself. I pray You, O Lord, make me
to taste by loving, what I taste by knowing.
Let me sense by affection what I sense by
understanding. I owe more than my entire
self, but I have no more to give; of myself I
am not even able to give my entire self. O
Lord, draw my whole self into Your love. The
whole of what I am belongs to You as Creator;
make it Yours through its loving commitment.40

In this paragraph we see how Anselm uses the same metaphor of taste to express both knowing and loving. Again
this provides us with the sense of how closely these two
activities are joined in Anselm's theology. The understanding of faith which theology seeks includes both
knowing and loving; therefore, theological understanding, for Anselm, engages the total person, not just the
mind. Consequently, he prays that God might make him
taste by loving what he tastes by knowing. Here the
metaphor of taste is utilized to express the assimilation of faith.

For Anselm, the discursive theological activity is
that of gaining insight into faith through a systematic
study and arrangement of the mysteries of faith. But
the motif level of his theology includes an even deeper
engagement of the person at the level of feeling and
will. This is what Anselm expresses when he says, "O
Lord, make me to taste by loving, what I taste by
knowing. Let me sense by affection what I sense by
understanding." Here Anselm indicates that there is an
even deeper level of theology than that of knowing.
This deeper level is the level of responding to the call
of faith by the affections and the will, and it is the
level where transformation actually occurs. This life
response is what Anselm prays for in the Cur Deus Homo
meditation.

Throughout this chapter, we have seen how the
flesh provides metaphors for the deepest levels of feeling and will. We have seen that eating is a powerful
metaphor of union with Christ, especially in relation to
the sacramental eating of the eucharist. But this is
not the only image of union with Christ that Anselm
employs. For Anselm, the Christian's relationship to

Christ is expressed not merely in eucharistic images but also in conjugal images. We not only "feed on Christ," but also "embrace and love him." He is not only our "Bread of life," but also our "Spouse." So at the end of the Cur Deus Homo prayer, we see how Anselm employs the imagery of conjugal love to express the depths of his soul:

> Behold, O Lord, my heart is before You. It strains, but can do nothing of itself; do, O Lord, what it cannot do. Receive me into the inner chamber of Your love. I ask, I seek, I knock. You who cause me to ask, cause me also to receive. You grant that I seek; grant that I also may find. You teach me to knock; open to me when I knock. If You deny him who asks, to whom do You then give? If he who seeks seeks in vain, who then finds? If You keep [the chamber door] closed for one who knocks, for whom do You open? If you withhold Your love from one who implores, what do You give to one who does not implore? You cause me to desire; cause me also to obtain. O my soul, cling to Him, cling tenaciously. Good Lord, O good Lord, do not scorn my soul; let Your tender kindness satisfy it, let Your affection make it fat, let Your love fill it. Let Your love seize my whole being; let it possess me completely, because together with the Father and the Holy Spirit You are the only God, blessed forever. Amen.41

In this passionate expression of longing and love, we see that Anselm employs imagery drawn from the Song of Solomon.42 His longing for intimacy with the Lord is expressed as a longing to enter into the inner chamber of the Lord's love, recalling those powerful verses of the Song of Solomon: "I found him whom my soul loves. I held him, and would not let him go until I had brought him into my mother's house, and into the chamber of her that conceived me."43 In this imagery of conjugal love one can see the metaphors of the flesh brought together into a forceful unity: the desire for union expressed by the various activities of the flesh (eating, drinking, panting, sighing, longing) is totally embodied in the metaphor of love. In the metaphor of human love, Anselm finds a suitable vocabulary to speak his deepest feelings for the Lord who has redeemed him; thus, in another prayer he speaks of his soul as falling in love with its Lord and being married to its God.44

We hear again the echo of the Song of Solomon at the close of the Cur_Deus__Homo meditation when Anselm prays for the Lord to revive his soul that "faints out of hunger" for the Lord's love:

He brought me to the banqueting house,
and his banner over me was love.
Sustain me with raisins,
refresh me with apples;
for I am sick with love.45

Here we see how the lover is called upon to refresh the beloved who languishes. The language of hunger and conjugal love come together so that affection and love are the food which satisfy the soul, filling it and making it fat.

This feeding metaphor repeats the eucharistic language that we have already observed in this meditation. Anselm's most intimate language of love is seen here in reference to the eucharist since this is the method by which men are actually joined to Christ; thus, the physical union that is achieved through sexual intercourse in conjugal love is parallel to the spiritual union that is achieved through eating in eucharistic devotion. In this way both conjugal love and eating have an important role as metaphors that describe the union of the soul with God, the goal of transformation.

In this chapter we have considered the motif level of Anselm's theology. At this deepest level of his theological system we have seen that the religious life was primary and that theological studies were only a continuation of and reflection upon his life of devotion. We have also observed that even the most seemingly abstract of Anselm's works should be seen in relation to his prayers which reveal the liturgical and sacramental character of Anselm's theological milieu.

We also observed that metaphor is the appropriate language for expressing the motif level of Anselm's theology because it has the capacity to evoke its whole meaning symbolically. We noted particularly the role of flesh as a metaphor evoking the motif of Anselm's theology. In this regard we saw how the flesh of Christ is a motif symbol that evokes the entire spiritual reality believed in by the Christian, namely, the redemptive death of Christ, the saving grace of God, the divine mystery of the Church, the way of transformation. We noted too that the metaphors of the flesh also express the deepest feelings of the Christian in the presence of these mysteries of faith, namely, feelings of longing, desire, passion, and love.

Finally, we examined how the two fundamental aspects of the motif level of Anselm's theology, its liturgical-devotional setting and its use of flesh as a basic metaphor, can be seen in the *Cur Deus Homo* prayer, which expresses the motif of transformation through the flesh of Christ. We studied the doctrines of *Cur Deus Homo* as they appear cast into a setting of liturgical prayer, observing how the metaphors of the flesh are used to focus on the sacramental presence of Christ in the flesh, to describe the Christian's physical, mental, and spiritual participation in the mystery of the redemption, and to evoke continuously throughout the day that divine reality that is specially present in the sacrament of the eucharist. Moreover, at the end of the *Cur Deus Homo* prayer, we noticed how Anselm joined the metaphor of Christ as our bread of life with Christ as our spouse so that the imagery of sacramental feeding and conjugal love comes together in vivid language that echoes the Song of Solomon.

To deal thoroughly with the motif level of Anselm's theology, we would have to treat the flesh not only as a metaphor but also as a sacrament. Eating the eucharistic bread is more than a metaphor for spiritual union with God; it actually effects the union that it symbolizes. Because of its special efficacy as a sacrament, the eucharist is the archetype of all prayer and all devotion for Anselm; therefore, in the next chapter we shall see how the eucharist as the flesh of Christ is the motif of Anselm's entire theology.

At the same time we shall illustrate, in relation to the eucharist, the co-presence of the three meaning levels we have already considered, namely, the denotative, the relational, and the motif levels; therefore, in the next chapter we shall observe that the eucharist is a particularly valuable example of the coinherence of these three levels of meaning since the very definition, or denotative meaning, of the eucharist is at once the metaphorical meaning, namely, the flesh of Christ. And we shall see that this definition of the eucharist as a living, enacted metaphor actually completes the relational meaning of flesh that we discovered in chapter 6.

NOTES

1.   H. Ott, "What Is Systematic Theology?" in The Later Heidegger and Theology, ed. J. Robinson and J. Cobb, Jr. (New York, 1963), p. 97.

2. R. Southern, "The Anselmian Revolution" in St. Anselm and His Biographer (Cambridge, 1963), pp. 42-47.

3. Ibid., p. 47.

4.   R. Roques, "Structure et caractères de la prière anselmienne" in SR, pp. 119-87.

5.   "Le point de vue des traités est avant tout logique, intellectuel, objectif: ils s'efforcent d'établir par des 'raisons nécessaires' et par des raisonnements rigoureusement enchaînés (concatenatio, connexio) une vérité ou un ensemble de vérités cohérent qui, de soi, ne dépendent pas de l'affectivité de lecteur. . . . Les oraisons ou meditations sont au contraire destinées avant tout à toucher le coeur, à le convertir plus parfaitement et à le remplir d'amour pour Dieu et pour les réalités saintes" (ibid., pp. 122-23).

6.   It is appropriate at this point to comment upon the relationship between metaphor and symbol. Metaphor is a type of language which utilizes the figurative sense of words rather than their literal sense.   T. Hawkes speaks of metaphor as the fundamental form of figurative language, and he describes very well the imaginative involvement necessary to grasp the meaning of metaphor: "However, when a word is used figuratively, what is established is the expectation of some sort of imaginative 'linkage' with other words similarly used. Metaphor, by means of this sense of 'linkage' leads us towards the 'target' of its meaning, but does not 'contaminate,' or predetermine that target for us, as simile does with its sense of fait accompli. Even in such a poor metaphor as 'my car beetles along' the reader is forced to make an imaginative 'completion' from within his own experience of what the metaphor figuratively suggests.   There is, after all, no simple 'comparison' or 'analogy' made between the elements involved.   In metaphor 'one constituent acts upon another almost like an X'ray.' The reader has to do

something, to join in, in order to hit the 'target'"
(Metaphor [London, 1972], p. 72). Hawkes speaks of the
active involvement of imagination as the method by which
the reader understands metaphor. We have already spoken
of "feeling" as the mode of perception by which one
grasps the whole evoked by a motif symbol. In relation
to the understanding of metaphors and symbols, imagination and feeling are closely related. In both imagination and feeling one is brought into immediate contact
with a whole reality evoked by the metaphor or symbol.
Where imagination appropriates the visual aspect of
metaphor or symbol, feeling is a more general perception
of the reality evoked by metaphor and symbol.
     In metaphor, the identity of two things is af-
firmed. The things are not merely related to one
another but they actually participate in one another,
e.g., the mass is sacrifice, the breath is spirit, the
eucharistic bread is Christ. Hawkes describes this
identity, or interpenetration, of elements by comparing
it to an X-ray. The participation of the elements in
metaphor is such that both elements are seen at the same
time. Participation is also a principal feature of
symbols. P. Tillich, for example, considers participation to be one of the defining characteristics of symbol. He defines symbol by distinguishing it from signs
in this way: While signs do not participate in the
reality to which they point, symbols do (The Dynamics of
Faith [New York, 1957], p. 42). When Tillich speaks
specifically about religious symbols, he stresses that
the power of symbols is tied up with their participation
in, and identity with, the reality they evoke. In this
regard, religious symbols are like metaphors since both
rely on participation to evoke a whole reality.
     Symbol and metaphor are also very closely related
in another way. Certain powerful religious symbols
operate on the basis of analogy which is also the foundation of metaphor. Although symbols need not involve
analogy, the richest and most fertile symbols are those
based on a natural analogy. J. M. Somerville says that
these most powerful symbols are founded on "an underlying analogy that is ontologically rooted in the nature
of things" (New Catholic Encyclopedia, 1st ed., S. V.
"symbol"). L. Bouyer agrees with Somerville in that we
must mention that the symbols which are capable of
lending themselves to an effective religious knowledge
are the natural symbols to which revelation will bring a
higher significance, which is furthermore not an arbitrary one; e.g., the symbolism of the waters of baptism,
or food in the Eucharist or again the symbols borrowed
from human relations like fatherhood" (Dictionary of
Theology [New York, 1965], p. 435). Somerville calls

such symbols "natural symbols" and suggests that baptism
and the eucharist are extremely important as symbols
precisely because they employ natural symbols for spiritual cleansing and nourishment. Somerville singles out
three general categories of symbol: arbitrary symbols,
associative symbols, and evocative symbols. He characterizes them this way: arbitrary symbols are not found
in nature but are established by decree--notation in
music or mathematics is an example. Associative symbols
are joined to their meaning by an implicit middle term
with which they are connected either naturally or his-
torically. Examples of associative symbols are the key,
which is a natural symbol for authority owing to its
association with ownership, and the dove and the olive
branch, which is a historical symbol for peace because
of the story of Noah. Evocative symbols communicate a
meaning by engendering certain attitudes and feelings
rather than by direct statement. There is, of course,
nothing absolute about this classification of symbols.
Tillich, for example, would refer to Somerville's arbitrary symbols as signs, not symbols. Somerville also
calls attention to the wide application of symbolism
during the Middle Ages, describing the fundamental conception of this use of symbolism as "a movement from the
material symbol to something in a spiritual or supra-
sensible order (New Catholic Encyclopedia, S. V. "symbol"). This is the kind of "carry over," or transfer-
ence, that we consider the essence of metaphor.
     Somerville also draws attention to the emotive
quality of religious symbols, saying that their aim is
not so much to evoke intellectual assent as to elicit an
affective response. He locates the sacramental symbols
in this category of "charged" symbols because of their
capacity to evoke a whole reality that is perceived by
feeling. According to Somerville, their power of self-
transcendence enables them to communicate a sense of the
sacred which touches the believer's feelings as well as
his mind. He attributes this power of religious symbols
to evoke spontaneous attitudes and affections to their
simplicity, their ability to avoid the complexities of
formal analogy. We shall also see how Anselm's metaphors of the flesh operate at this same level of deep
feelings.
     Metaphor and symbol are alike in these important
respects: (1) metaphor and symbol are identical with
the reality they evoke because they participate in that
reality; (2) the most powerful metaphors and symbols
operate on the basis of natural analogy. Both metaphor
and symbol are capable of evoking whole realities that
are perceived by feeling. In fact, metaphor is symbolic

language, and the deepest symbols, by representing and
evoking a whole reality, are metaphors.

7. "Fac me, domine, ita ea ore et corde percipere, atque fide et affectu sentire" (Orat. III). Commenting on this passage, Roques says that Anselm stresses the necessity of assimilating in the heart what
reason teaches about the mysteries of faith: "Le sac-
rement eucharistique et les mystères qu'il contient
doivent être reçus dans la bouche et dans le coeur:
'ore et corde.' Et ce que la raison enseigne doit avoir
aussi son retentissement dans le coeur" ("Structure et
caractères," p. 161).

8.   "Sic enim esse veritas ostendit, et tamen
affectus non sentit. Sic ratio docet, et cor non
dolet" (Orat. X; S III, 34, 41-42).

9. Roques has also observed this close relationship of the flesh to the heart in his study of Anselm's
prayers, noting that the heart or the flesh represent a
different order of experience from that of reason:
"Comme tel, en effet, le coeur est d'un autre ordre que
la raison, et il engage plus directement le corps; ses
mouvements touchent et entraînent le corps; ils s'im-
priment en lui et s'expriment spontanément par lui"
("Structure et caractères," p. 161).

10.   "Certe, si cor meum contritum fuerit, si
viscere mea commota fuerint, si liquefacta fuerit anima
mea, si rivi diu fluent ab oculis meis; tunc sperabo
quia Nicolaus adest precibus meis" (Orat. XIV; S III,
57, 69-71).

11.   "Sentiat filius tuus viscera maternae
pietatis" (Orat. X; S III, 40, 194).

12. "Enitemini, viscera animae meae, enitemini
quantum potestis--si quid potestis--omnia interiora mea,
ut ejus (Virginis) merita laudetis, ut ejus beatitudinem
ametis" Orat. VII; S III, 18, 9-11).

13.   "Utinam sic viscera animae meae dulci fervore
vestrae delectationis exardescant, ut viscera carnis
meae exarescant. Utinam sic intima spiritus mei dul-
cedine vestri affectu impinguntur, ut medullae corporis
mei exsiccentur" (Orat. VII; S III, 24, 159-162).

14.   Roques observes the ambiguous character of
the term affectus as it is used in Anselm's prayers:
"Cette prière fréquente pour demander à Dieu, au Christ

ou aux saints l'affectus vrai et l'intensité de cet affectus est d'autant plus nécessaire que l'âme est toujours sollicitée par laffectus carnalis qui l'a souvent detournée et privée de la saveur des réalités spirituelles de la contemplation des réalités intérieures et de la joie des réalités célestes" ("Structure et caractères," p. 150.

15. Adnes also points out that this direct quality of the physical senses makes them an apt metaphor for the immediate, affective experience of God, and this is in contrast to the mediated, indirect character of discursive reason: "Mais l'analogie ou la métaphore des sens, par le caractère d'expérience immédiate et non rationnelle qu'elle évoque, se trouve très bien adaptée à l'expression de pareils états (direct experiences of the Divine)" ("Goût Spirituel," in Dictionnaire de Spiritualité, vol. VI [Paris, 1967], col. 629).

16. "Sancta Maria Magdalene, quae cum fonte lacrimarum ad fontem misericordiae Christum venisti, de quo ardenter sitiens abundanter es refocillata" (Orat. XVI; S III, 64, 3-5).

17. "'Sitivit in te anima mea, quam multipliciter tibi caro mea' (Ps. 62/2); 'Sitivit anima mea ad deum fontem vivum. Quando veniam et parebo ante faciem dei mei?' (Ps. 41/3); Quando venies consolator meus quem expecto? O si quando videbo gaudium meum quod desidero! O si 'satiabor cum apparuerit gloria tua' (Ps. 16/15) quam esurio! O si inebriabor 'ab ubertate domus tuae' ad quam suspiro! Si potabis me 'torente voluptatis tuae' (Ps. 35/9) quam sitio!" (Orat. II; S III, 9, 86-92).

18. "Esuriens accedit ad ostium clementiae tuae, suppliciter mendicans eleemosinam opulentiae tuae. . . . Non sum oblitus hoc dicens, o tu iuste et misericors deus, nec sum ingratus multimodis beneficiis tuae erga me dilectionis ab initio creationis meae, sed donec satietur utraque tua dilectione, semper se pauperem et egenam clamat esuriens anima mea" (Orat. XII, S III, 45, 9-46, 24).

19. "Adiuva, ut pane caritatis satietur esuriens anima mea" (Orat. XIII; S III, 53, 107-108).

20. "O pulchra ad intuendum, amabilis ad contemplandum, delectabilis ad amandum, quo evadis capacitatem cordis mei? Praestolare, domina, infirmam animam te sequentem. Ne abscondas te, domina, parum videnti

animae te quaerenti. Miserare, domina, animam post te
anhelando languentam" (Orat. VII; S III, 21, 89-92).

21. "O tu benedicta super mulieres, quae angelos
vincis puritate, sanctos superas pietate, anhelat
moribundus spiritus meus ad tantae benignitatis re-
spectum, sed erubescit ad tanti nitoris conspectum"
(Orat. V; S III, 13, 24-14, 27).

22. "Anhelat videre te, et nimis abest illi
facies tua" (Pros. I, S I, 98, 9-10).

23. "Domine meus, creator meus, tolerator et
nutritor meus, esto adiutor meus. Te sitio, te esurio,
te desidero, ad te suspiro, te concupisco" (Orat. II; S
III, 7, 29-30).

24. Roques has also written about Anselm's metaphorical use of the body and the senses to express the
spiritual desires of man. But Roques stresses the
caution with which Anselm used the imagery of conjugal
love: "Elle exprime son affectivité spirituelle dans un
ensemble d'actes ou d'attitudes qui engagent le corps:
contritio, commotio, commota viscera, liquifactio,
compassio, compunctio, dolor, fletus, lacrimae. Plus
exactement et plus généralement, l'âme transpose ses
affections sur le registre des cinq sens corporels, du
goût en particulier; gustare mandere, sugere, glutire,
sapor, inebriari, satiari, et aussi, visus, tactus,
auditus, olfactus. . . . Par ses 'sens spirituels,'
l'âme accède à la douceur ou à la suavité de l'amour
(dulcedo, suavitas); elle s'ouvre le plus possible à cet
amour dans un désir fervent et ardent (fervor, desiderium, succendere, exardescere, consupiscere) qui, par
exemple, la fait pleurer et deposer ses baisers sur les
blessures du Christ, et qui peut emprunter les traits
soit de l'amour filial . . . soit de l'amour conjugal
(sponsus, cubiculum). Mais, il faut souligner encore,
dans ce dernier ordre de métaphores, Anselme s'est
montré particulièrement discret. Il cite certes le
Cantique des Cantiques, comme le reste de l'Ecriture,
mais avec beaucoup de mesure et de sobriété, en évitant
telles exégèses allégoriques ou telle applications
detaillées qui lui eussent paru manquer à la fois de
rigueur et de goût" ("Structure et caractères," p. 171.

25. "Utinam vel semel suggerat deo pro me et pro
cuncto peccato meo: 'Domine ne statuas' illi 'hoc peccatum!' Doce me, beata anima beati Stephani, quo sapore
iucundabaris, qua satietate aestuabas, cum eructavit cor
tuum verbum tam bonum. Quam dulce faucibus animae meae

eloquium tuum super mel et favum ori eius. Mandendo magis ac magis dulcescit, sugendo plus et plus suavissimus sapor eius affluit, plus vivendo plus fulgescit, omni modo tractatum semper ad delectationem crescit" (Orat. XIII; S III, 53, 93-100).

26.   "Quippe hoc ipsum est de maximis, de gratissimis mihi tuis beneficiis, quia per suavem gustum tui hanc in me excitasti aviditatem ut renaut 'consolari anima mea' nisi per eius satietatem" (Orat. XII; S III, 46, 24-26).

27.   "Benignissime, suavissime, serenissime: quando restaurabis mihi quia non vidi illam beatam tuae carnis incorruptionem?" (Orat. II); "non enim erit tibi difficile, quiquid volueris obtinere a dilectissimo et suavissimo domino et amico tuo, qui vivit et regnat" (Orat. XVI); "non enim es suscipienda secundum crudelium qui te mitissimo paraverunt insipientissimam impietatem, sed secundum eius qui te sponte suscepit sapientissimam pietatem" (Orat. IV); "ille, inquam, bonus deus, mitis homo, misericors filius dei, pius filius hominis venit quaerere peccatorem errantem, et tu, bona mater eius, potens mater dei, repelles miserum orantem?" (Orat. VI); "affectus carnalis infatuavit in me saporem spiritualium, intentio infimorum incurvavit animam meam ab intuitu supernorum" (Orat. XIV); "quomodo namque eructabit cor bonum odorem, unde intus non habet saporem?" (Orat. XVI).

28.   Dictionnaire de Spiritualité, cols. 629-42.

29.   In a brief way Adnes sums up the important aspects of the taste metaphor; all of his observations are applicable to Anselm's use of this metaphor: "De toutes les sensations le goût est sans doute la plus subjective, celle que l'on a le moins tendance à objectiver, à concevoir séparée du sujet qui l'expérimente, celle aussi qui est le moins intellectualisable, renseigne le moins sur l'objet, mais est capable de causer le plaisir, ou la répulsion, la plus intime, la plus organique, la plus viscérale. L'emploi de cette image, métaphore ou analogie, pour exprimer une forme particulière de l'expérience spirituelle dévoile certes partiellement la nature de cette expérience dans la mesure où elle indique que toute distance, toute extériorité est abolie entre l'objet et le sujet, dans la mesure où elle suggère une intériorisation et une imbibition de l'objet dans le sujet qui, entré intérieurement en contact avec l'objet, s'en délecte en quelque sorte vitalement" (ibid., col. 642).

30.   "L'objet propre du sens spirituel du goût est
la douceur, la suavité de Dieu, du Verbe (considere le
plus souvent comme incarné et en relation spéciale avec
l'Eucharistie), des réalités surnaturelles en général.
Ou plus exactement, Dieu, le Verbe, ces réalités devien-
nent pour l'âme le principe objectif d'une expérience
savoureuse, suave, délectable, qui definit le sens même
du goût" (ibid., col. 631).

31.   Southern, St. Anselm and His Biographer,
p. 36.

32.   VSA, p. 107.

33.   G. H. Williams, Anselm: Communion and
Atonement (St. Louis, 1960), pp. 62-63. Emphasis of
the word body is ours. Later we shall see the significance of this transformation from the "body of lowliness" to the "body of glory."

34.   Ibid., pp. 49-54.

35.   "La sensibilité spirituelle a donc ici rem-
placé, ou, du moins, submergé les démonstration de
caractère 'juridico-rationnel' du Cur Deus Homo,
rappelées par le début de la méditation. Et cette
différence de points de vue apparaît bien dans un
vocabulaire et des thèmes partiellement nouveaux, dont
on ne trouve guère l'équivalent dans les traités
didactiques et logiques d'Anselme, et qui s'imposent au
contraire tout au long des Orationes et Meditationes:
affectus, cor, desiderium, devotio, dulcedo, suavitas,
familiaritas, fervor, fovere, gaudium, sentire, gustare,
satietas, sont parmi beaucoup d'autres, les principaux
termes où s'exprime la sensibilité spirituelle d'Anselme (Roques, "Structure et caractères," p. 158).

36.   "Anima Christiana, anima de gravi morte
resuscitata, anima de misera servitute sanguine dei
redempta et liberata: excita mentem tuam, memento
resuscitationis tuae, recogita redemptionem et liber-
ationem tuam. Retracta ubi et quae sit virtus tuae
salvationis, versare in meditatione eius, delectare in
contemplatione eius. Excute fastidium tuum, fac vim
cordi tuo, intende in hoc mentem tuam. Gusta bonitatem
redemptoris tui, accendere in amorem salvatoris tui.
Mande favum verborum, suge plus quam mellitum saporem,
gluti salubrem dulcorem. Mande cogitando, suge
intelligendo, gluti amando et gaudendo. Laetare mandendo, gratulare sugendo, iucundare glutiendo" (Med.
III; S III, 84, 3-12, AC I, 137).

37. Ott, "What Is Systematic Theology?" p. 97.

38. "Ecce, anima Christiana, haec est virtus salvationis tuae, haec est causa libertatis tuae, hoc est pretium redemptionis tuae. Captiva eras, sed hoc modo es redempta. Ancilla eras, et sic es libertate. Sic es exul reducta, perdita restituta, et mortua resuscitata. Hoc mandat, o homo, hoc ruminet, hoc sugat, hoc glutiat cor tuum, cum eiusdem redemptoris tui carnem et sanguinem accipit os tuum. Hoc fac in hac vita cotidianum panem, victum et viaticum tuum, quia per hoc et non nisi per hoc et tu manebis in Christo et Christus in te, et in futura vita erit plenum gaudium tuum" (Med III; S III, 88, 129-89, 136; AC I, 141-42).

39. The necessity to assimilate doctrinal understanding at the level of feeling and will is also expressed in Oratio III and Oratio X.

40. "Considera, anima mea, intendite, omnia intima mea, quantum illi debeat tota substantia mea. Certe, domine, quia me fecisti, debeo amori tuo me ipsum totum; quia me redemisti, debeo me ipsum totum; quia tanta promittis, debeo me ipsum totum. Immo tantum debeo amori tuo plus quam me ipsum, quantum tu es maior me, pro quo dedisti te ipsum et cui promittis te ipsum. Fac precor, domine, me gustare per amorem quod gusto per cognitionem. Sentiam per affectum quod sentio per intellectum. Plus debeo quam me ipsum totum, sed nec plus habeo nec hoc ipsum possum per me reddere totum; trahe tu, domine, in amorem tuum vel hoc ipsum totum. Totum quod sum tuum est conditione; fac totum tuum dilectione" (Med. III; S III, 91, 191-200; AC I, 144).

41. "Ecce, domine, coram te est cor meum. Conatur, sed per se non potest; fac tu quod ipsum non potest. Admitte me intra cubiculum amoris tui. Peto, quaero, pulso. Qui me facis petere, fac accipere. Das quaerere, da invenire. Doces pulsare, aperi pulsanti. Cui das, si neges petenti? Quis invenit, si quaerens frustratur? Cui aperis, si pulsanti claudis? Quid des non oranti, si amorem tuum neges oranti? A te habeo desiderare, a te habeam impetrare. Adhaere illi, adhaere importune, anima mea. Bone, bone domine, ne reicias eam; fame amoris tui languet: refocilla eam. Satiet eam dilectio tua; impinguet eam affectus tuus; impleat eam amor tuus. Occupet me totum et possideat totum, quia tu es cum patre et spiritu sancto deus solus benedictus in saecula saeculorum" (Med. III; S III, 91, 201-11; AC I, 144).

42.   Roques has called attention to this imagery
of conjugal love in the <u>Cur Deus Homo</u> meditation and
other of Anselm's prayers, noting that its source of
inspiration is the Song of Solomon: "Mais nous l'avons
vu, l'amour de Deiu est aussi feu et désir ardent
(succendere,   exardescere,   concupiscere).   Sous   ce
rapport, il emprunte ses expressions à l'amour humain,
familial   et surtout conjugal. . . . Le <u>Cantique</u>
permettait à Anselme de développer ce thème sur lequel
d'ailleurs il n'a pas abusivement   insisté.("Structure et
caractères," pp. 165-66.

43. Song of Sol. 3:4.

44. <u>Orat</u>. XII; S III, 19, 28-38.

45. Song of Sol. 2:4-5.

8

ILLUSTRATIVE CASE: THE EUCHARIST AS
TRANSFORMATION THROUGH THE FLESH OF CHRIST

The Three Levels of Meaning
of Flesh

We devoted a separate chapter to each of the three
levels of analysis (denotative, relational, and motif
levels) of the concept of flesh. We wish now to bring
these three levels together by analyzing their coinherence with respect to a single key topic, namely, the
flesh of Christ in the eucharist. There will be three
parts to this analysis: (1) We shall see what the
eucharist means at the denotative level, i.e., we shall
look at Anselm's definition of the eucharistic flesh;
(2) we shall consider the function of the concept of
flesh in Anselm's doctrine of the eucharist; and (3) we
shall see how the bread that is "the flesh of Christ" is
the enacted, comprehensive metaphor that effects human
transformation.

The Denotative Meaning of
Flesh in the Eucharist

As we saw in the word study of the concept of
flesh (chapter 5), the denotative level of analysis is
concerned with the definition of words or of concepts,
i.e., how certain words denote, or refer to, particular
things. In the word study, we saw that the flesh concept denoted, among other things, the eucharist. In
this section we are concerned with Anselm's use of the
concept of flesh in his definition of the eucharist.

We are fortunate to have Anselm's letters on the
sacraments since these deal specifically with his definitions of the eucharistic sacrifice. The context of
these letters is the debate with the Greeks regarding
the use of leavened and unleavened bread in the sacrament of the eucharist: the Latin use of unleavened
bread in the sacrifice of the Mass was considered contradictory to the Greek use of leavened bread. Anselm
addressed his letters on the sacraments to Walram,

Bishop of Naumburg, who attempted to counter the Greeks arguing with him about this use of leavened and unleavened bread in the eucharist. In the correspondence between Anselm and Walram, we read that the Greeks considered the Latins to be deserving of anathema, or at least censure, because of their use of unleavened bread. The Greeks opposed the Latin custom because they considered it to be "judaizing," i.e., observing the Judaistic precept about unleavened bread.1

Anselm notes that the issue concerning which kind of bread should be used cannot simply be decided by an appeal to Scripture since the New Testament does not specify whether leavened or unleavened bread is to be used for the eucharistic sacrifice; therefore, Anselm resorts to theological reflection about the nature of the eucharist to resolve the problem. The principal tool Anselm uses to settle this issue is an analysis of the meaning of the eucharistic elements.

The principal question of this debate focuses on the particular custom of celebrating the Mass. Both Walram and the Greeks consider the type of bread used as the central issue. They suppose that the answer to this dispute lies in deciding which type of bread expresses the true meaning of the eucharist. For Anselm this question is in certain respects beside the point. Because Anselm knows that this issue cannot be resolved with reference to Scripture, he refers it to a basic analysis of the meaning of the eucharist; he is concerned with what the eucharistic bread denotes and refers to. The issue, from Anselm's perspective, revolves essentially around the denotation of the eucharistic elements, not the elements themselves. With striking clarity, Anselm cuts directly to the heart of the issue with his understanding that the eucharistic bread is, after consecration, not bread at all, whether leavened or unleavened. Rather it is the flesh of Christ.2

In Anselm's letters on the sacraments, he writes a number of phrases and sentences that indicate that the eucharistic bread is transformed into the body of Christ: "having produced his body from bread," "We eat the unleavened Flesh of Christ," "bread from which we produce the Flesh itself," "Just as he himself did, we consecrate the bread so that by divine power it may be changed into His Body," "He whose Body we sacrifice was such [unleavened]" (i.e., free from any corruption of sin).3 In these passages Anselm affirms that, after the consecration, the eucharistic bread refers to and

becomes the flesh of Christ. In getting at the essence
of what the eucharist is, Anselm distinguishes its
substance from diverse practices associated with the
sacrament.

> However, there are many differences which do
> not conflict with the fundamental importance
> of the sacrament or with its efficacy or with
> faith in it; and these cannot all be brought
> together into one practice. Accordingly, I
> think that these differences ought to be
> harmoniously and peaceably tolerated rather
> than being disharmoniously and scandalously
> condemned. For we are taught by the Holy
> Fathers that, provided the unity of love is
> preserved within the Catholic faith, a dif-
> ferent practice does no harm.4

Here we see that at the denotative level establishing
the essence of a thing is primary. Anselm's concern
with the eucharist as the flesh of Christ illustrates
the importance of establishing the basic meaning, or
reference, of even so lofty an object of theological
investigation as the eucharist.

Yet, in spite of Anselm's stress on the essential
denotation of the eucharistic bread as the flesh of
Christ, he does not completely ignore the question why
bread is used as the symbol of Christ's flesh. For
Anselm, bread is the means of physical sustenance;
therefore, bread is used in the eucharist to show that
the flesh of Christ sustains man's spiritual life in the
same way that bread sustains physical life:

> And when elsewhere He called Himself and His
> flesh bread--[doing so] because just as a man
> lives temporally by means of common bread, so
> he lives eternally by means of this other
> bread--He did not specify leavened or un-
> leavened, because both kinds are equally
> bread. For just as both the new man prior to
> sin and the man grown old in the leaven of sin
> do not differ [from each other] in substance,
> so unleavened bread and leavened bread do not
> differ in substance (as some people suppose
> they do). Hence, the Lord is seen to have
> produced His Body from bread only for the
> following reason: [to indicate] that just as
> common bread, whether unleavened or leavened,
> gives transitory life, so His Body gives

eternal life, irrespective of whether [the
bread of His Body] is leavened or unleavened.5

Although we use this text to point to the meaning of
flesh in the eucharist (at the denotative level of
analysis), we see how the symbolic meaning influences
and colors the meaning even at the denotative level.
Here Anselm stresses that the bread used in the eucharist has power as a symbol of nourishment: as bread
nourishes man's body, so eucharistic bread nourishes
man's soul. Since leavened and unleavened bread are of
the same essence, bread, either one will serve as a
symbol of this sustenance. Anselm speaks about the
symbolic value of the western Church's using unleavened
bread since it shows that Christ is pure and innocent
and that those who eat his body are also to be free from
all "leaven of malice and wickedness," but he keeps this
point about symbolism in perspective, relating it to the
most important truth about the eucharist, namely, that
it is the body of Christ.

We have already seen in Anselm's Cur Deus Homo
prayer the strikingly intimate eucharistic language he
uses when meditating on the mystery of the redemption.
Now at the denotative level, we see the eucharist in a
more objective way, without the passion expressed in the
Cur Deus Homo prayer. Yet, clearly these different
levels of theology are related: Anselm centers his Cur
Deus Homo prayer around eucharistic imagery because the
eucharist is seen as "the bread from which we produce
the Flesh itself." Anselm's reflections on the substance of the eucharist offer the metaphysical foundation that underlies his devotion to the eucharist. Precisely because there is no separation of the ontological, the logical, and the affective for Anselm, his
devotion to the eucharist in worship is the devotional
basis and the raison d'être of his reflection on the
definition of what the eucharist actually is and how it
should be celebrated.

Thus, we see that Anselm's discussion of the
meaning of the eucharist at the denotative level provides a first step in establishing the importance of
this sacrament since it clearly affirms that the eucharist is bread that is transformed into the flesh of
Christ upon being consecrated. This definition is,
logically speaking, the first step since it is on the
basis of this definition that the eucharist plays an
essential doctrinal and devotional role in Anselm's
theology. Because of the intimate connection between
the meaning at the denotative level and the symbolic-

sacramental meaning of the eucharist, one might argue that the devotional-symbolic meaning is actually before, and more important than, the denotative meaning. This follows from the view that the actual theological definition of the eucharist is a reflection upon its symbolic-sacramental role in the worshipping community since, for Anselm, theology is a continuation of, and meditation upon, his religious life in the Church. From this point of view, the symbolic-sacramental meaning of the eucharist is before the denotative meaning in terms of the contextual origin of the meaning of the eucharist, even if the denotative meaning is logically prior in that it explains the devotional significance of the eucharist by defining it as the flesh of Christ.

The Relational Meaning of
Flesh in the Eucharist

Now we move on to see how the second level of our analysis of the concept of flesh applies to the eucharist as a doctrine in Anselm's discursive system. This second level is the relational, or discursive, level of Anselm's system where the meaning of the concept is determined by its relation to other major concepts in Anselm's doctrinal system.6   In applying this level of analysis to the eucharist, we shall see how it completes Anselm's discursive system discussed in chapter 6. Recall that we left the analysis in chapter 6 at the point of trying to discover how the justice that Christ restored to the flesh in the redemption is actually extended to Christians. We asked whether Anselm considered there to be a parallel between the way Adam transmitted corruption by means of the flesh (in the act of propagation) and the way Christ transmits righteousness. We shall now attempt to show that the eucharist provides this parallel action whereby the righteousness of Christ is transmitted by means of the flesh of Christ.

In the analysis of Anselm's system at the discursive level, we saw that the flesh explained how men could be redeemed whereas angels could not. Within the structure of Anselm's argumentation the flesh was seen as the reproductive nature that joined all men to Adam, and more specifically, to the condition of Adam's will; therefore, the flesh concept not only served to represent the participatory character of the human race (the condition in which humans participate in the spiritual state of Adam or Christ) but also to specify the negative moral character of this participation in terms of the human will. In this systematic role, flesh represented two important aspects of the human condition: the flesh as man's participatory nature, and the flesh as the natural will, that disposition of will which determines the condition of the personal will. Around this dual role of the concept of flesh Anselm was able to construct a convincing case for the necessity of the God-man.

Now we shall see how Anselm's view of the will and the flesh enable his redemptive theory to explain the restoration of man's fallen nature. This restoration is a renewal of the flesh such that this flesh possesses the disposition toward justice. This follows from the notion of a natural will (a will of the flesh) that corresponds directly to the disposition of the personal will. In this view the flesh of Christ becomes the vehicle for the disposition toward justice. In his doctrine of the eucharist, Anselm takes seriously the theoretical possibility that if Adam had been confirmed in justice, his reproductive nature (flesh) would have extended righteousness to all of his race. Because Adam sinned, justice was not extended. But now, in the eucharist, justice is extended to men. In this case, however, it is not the flesh as reproductive nature which extends justice to men but rather it is the flesh as eucharist which performs this function.7

Here we see Christ as the new Adam who actually does what the old Adam was originally intended to do, namely retain for human nature (the flesh) the disposition toward justice. In this light we can see how the striking parallel between Christ and Adam is completed: both Adam and Christ cause radical changes in human flesh. Adam's act of disobedience is atoned for by Christ's act of perfect and free obedience on the cross. The transformation of the flesh caused by Adam and Christ is transferred in a physically realistic way--by the activities of propagation (in regard to Adam's corruption) and feeding (in regard to Christ's righteousness). This parallel can be seen in table 8.1.

Participation in the archetypal figures is through the flesh as a participatory nature. It is through the flesh that men are joined to Adam or to Christ; through the flesh men share in the disposition or condition of their will. From this parallel, we see that Christ, the new Adam, effects an ontological change in human nature. In the redemption Christ restores to man's nature that disposition of the will toward justice which Adam lost for human nature. This change in the

ontological   structure   of human nature is central to Anselm's theology of redemption as well as his theology of
the eucharist. It represents a philosophical description of human transformation through the flesh of
Christ.

         L. Hoedl has referred to Anselm's ontological con-
cern in his study of the eucharistic treatise "Calix

         Table 8.1. Transformations of the Flesh

         1. Archetypal figures affect the nature
             (the flesh)

             A. Adam's act of disobedience
                 (original sin) corrupts human
                 nature

             B. Christ's act of obedience (death
                 on the cross) rectifies human
                 nature

         2. The nature (the flesh) affects the
             individual person.

             A. Adamic nature inclines men toward
                 sin

             B. Christic nature inclines men
                 toward righteousness

         3. The flesh as a participatory nature
             communicates the effect of archetypal
             figures on individual persons

             A. Adam influences men through sexual
                 intercourse (flesh of Adam as
                 reproductive participatory nature)

             B. Christ influences men through the
                 eucharist (flesh of Christ as
                 sacramental participatory nature)

benedictionis" which had been falsely attributed to
Anselm until about forty years ago.8 While Hoedl has no
intention of reversing the scholarly research that removed this treatise from the Anselm corpus, he does see
that Anselm's name remains tied to the treatise for this
reason: the ontological question in the medieval teaching about the eucharist springs from and corresponds to
Anselm's theological program--Fides quarens intellectum.

Hoedl argues that the search for insight into the truth and reality of faith raises the ontological question. And he sees a parallel between the desire to understand how the biblical faith about God is true and the desire to explain how the eucharistic bread and wine are the body and blood of Christ. Hoedl sees a clear connection between the former desire as it is expressed in Anselm's ontological argument (Proslogion, chapters 2 and 3) and the latter desire as it is expressed in "Calix benedictionis."9 Hoedl perceives that Anselm's theological interest is in the ontological ground of the mind and will, emphasizing Anselm's confidence that God is actively present in the deepest structures of the soul.

What is particularly important about this observation is that it stresses Anselm's concern about the ontological basis of the real presence of Christ. The change in the bread consecrated at the sacrifice of the mass is a change in the substance of the bread. Christ's presence in the eucharist is reflected in the very structures of being so that the substance of bread becomes the actual body of Christ. But the primary importance of this substantial change is that it permits a special intimacy between the Christ who is present under the appearance of bread and the Christians who eat this transformed substance. The Church comes to participate not only in Christ's body but also in the moral and spiritual quality of his life, i.e., in the grace of God, in the redemptive death of Christ, in the divine mystery of the Church.10

The language that Hoedl uses to describe the Christian's sharing in the life of Christ is that of "participation." Teilgabe, Teilnahme, Partizipation, teilhaftig, Anteil, and Teilhabe are words that serve to emphasize that the vere of the ontological change is extended to those who eat the eucharistic bread. Christians actually participate in the body of Christ. And because the substantial change in the bread renders the reality of Christ's body present, the Christian who receives a share in the eucharistic bread shares in the life, the flesh, and the will of Christ. The result of this sharing is, in the terms of Anselm's own theological system, a transformation of the being and will of man. Because the flesh possesses a participatory, natural will, the flesh of Christ adds the disposition of justice to the will of the Christian who receives the eucharist. Just as the fallen flesh is the symbol of the human will as it participates in Adam's corrupted condition, so the body of Christ is the effective symbol

that brings about what it symbolizes, namely, the disposition of Christ's will to justice extended to the Christian who then participates in Christ's righteous condition.

This substantial change that occurs in the eucharist is directly related to the change that occurs in the
faithful who partake of the consecrated elements. The
ontological change in the substance of bread permits the
transfer of the justice that Christ won for men by his
sacrificial death to those who share in the eucharist.
The eucharist as the flesh of Christ brings to individual men that justice. They receive Christ and his
righteousness so that they can now freely maintain
themselves in a state of justice. This follows with
complete consistency from Anselm's discursive system
with its teaching about the human will and how the will
can be free and just.

The doctrine of the eucharist completes Anselm's
discursive system. At this level of Anselm's system,
the flesh is seen as a participatory nature that unites
individual men to the will of either Adam or Christ.
The flesh either lacks the disposition of the will
toward justice (the condition of Adamic flesh) or possesses this disposition (the condition of eucharistic
flesh), and therefore it determines the actual operation
of the personal will of individuals since the personal
will functions only according to the dispositions that
dwell within it. Thus, after baptism, the eucharist as
the flesh of Christ extends to men the full merit of
redemption by restoring to their personal will the
disposition toward justice.

For Anselm, eating the flesh of Christ is the
physical means of being incorporated into rectified
human nature. Such a point of contact would parallel
the physical contact of reproduction that incorporates
men into Adam's fallen state. This explains the importance of Anselm's distinguishing human nature from the
corrupted reproductive nature. It is the characteristic
of the flesh that men participate in a common disposition of the will. Yet this participatory character of
flesh is not simply identified with the power of reproduction. That was merely the way men were to participate in the justice or injustice of Adam. But that same
participatory character of the flesh is the basis for
transformation as it incorporates men into the will
disposition of the "new Adam," though in the case of the
"new Adam," the act of incorporation is the sacramental
eating of the eucharist.11

The Symbolic Meaning of
Flesh in the Eucharist

So far in this chapter we have seen the denotative
and relational meaning of the flesh concept in regard to
Anselm's view of the eucharist. But what is most important is our observation that in both of these meanings
the motif level of Anselm's theology already exerts an
influence. We observed, for example, that the life
context of Anselm's devotion to the eucharist determines
his theological definition of what the eucharist is
because the definition is a reflection upon Anselm's
religious experience as centered around the eucharist.
We also saw that to establish the role of the eucharistic flesh of Christ in Anselm's discursive system, it
was necessary to rely heavily upon his prayers and
meditations. The eucharist is, therefore, the heart and
all-pervading motif of Anselm's theology.

However, Anselm did not actually write a great
deal about the eucharist. Apart from Anselm's letters
on the sacraments, the Cur Deus Homo prayer, and the
"Prayer before Receiving the Body and Blood of Christ,"
Anselm did not devote himself to writing about the
eucharist. Yet it would be quite wrong to deduce from
this lack of explicit material that the eucharist does
not hold the decisive place in Anselm's theology. Quite
the contrary is true. The eucharist is not treated as
one doctrine alongside other doctrines precisely because
it is the context of all Anselm's doctrines. This point
can be fully appreciated only from the perspective
provided by the motif level of Anselm's theology.

The deepest level of Anselm's theological system,
we have observed, is concerned with the life context out
of which his theology developed. We have also seen that
the life context of Anselm's theology is sacramental-
devotional. Prayer is at the heart of Anselm's religious life, and we have already called attention to the
sacramental character of his prayer. It is in this
liturgical setting that we may correctly assess the
importance of the eucharist in Anselm's theology. The
eucharist, the prayer of prayers, is the archetype of
all other prayers. Thus, if we have considered the
motif, or deep, level of Anselm's theology to be the
prayer level, we may also properly consider it to be the
eucharist level of Anselm's theology.

When we considered the Cur Deus Homo prayer, we
studied a number of passages which gave clear evidence
of eucharistic imagery. At that point in our study, we
were primarily concerned with the eucharistic imagery in
terms of the eating metaphor that expressed deep
feelings of longing for union with God as well as the
commitment of the will to retain the justice commanded
by God. But the eucharist is also the form or archetype
of all Anselm's prayers; thus, when Anselm recommends
for meditation the mystery of human redemption, he does
so in the context of receiving the eucharist: O man,
let your heart feed upon these thoughts, let it chew
continually upon them, let it suck upon them and swallow
them whenever your mouth receives the body and blood of
your Redeemer. In this life make these thoughts your
daily bread, your nourishment, your provision.12 Meditating on the redemption of man is most appropriately
set in the eucharistic context because the eucharist
actually renders present the redemptive mystery upon
which the Christian meditates. The flesh of Christ in
the eucharist evokes the transformation it symbolizes.
The thoughts that the Christian is to continually keep
in mind are really only an overflow from the eucharist.
The thoughts that are to be "daily bread" and "nourishment" are thoughts about the redemptive mystery that is
reenacted in the eucharist. The eucharist is the form
of all prayer precisely because it evokes the entire
spiritual reality with which all prayer concerns
itself. The eucharist embodies in a symbolic way all
that prayer longs for: the grace of God in the mystery
of Christ's redemptive life, death, and resurrection.

We should also note here that the symbolism of the
eucharist is of a special kind: the eucharist is a sacrament and as such it is an enacted, efficacious metaphor. The eucharist actually does what it symbolizes.
It gathers up into itself all of the divine mysteries
and permits the Christian to participate in them. The
eucharist, then, is the heart of the Christian life of
devotion, and consequently it is the basis of Anselm's
motif level of theology. The "flesh of Christ" evokes
the motif of Anselm's theology in such a way that men
can participate in the whole meaning of this theology.
Just like the other motif symbols discussed in chapter 4
(verbum and rectitudo), the whole meaning of Anselm's
theology is evoked by the power of the symbol: the
flesh of Christ. We cannot say entirely what this
meaning is in a discursive explanation because it is a
lived meaning. This is precisely the reason why the
motif level of Anselm's theology cannot simply be reduced to either the denotative, or relational level, or

even both of them. As soon as we attempt to describe
the lived meaning of Anselm's theology, it ceases to be
a lived meaning and becomes a logical or discursive
translation of life into words.

This difficulty of translation cannot be overcome
by simply finding better or more accurate definitions
and relational descriptions. To reach the motif level
requires a quantum leap whereby words are no longer used
to describe the meaning of something, but rather words
are used symbolically to evoke the reality itself;
therefore, if we are asked at this point in the study
what the meaning of Anselm's theology is, we must answer
by using certain profound symbols such as verbum, rectitudo, eucharist, or flesh. When we answer in this way
our speaking has a metaphorical dimension. At this
motif level we are not using words in a reductive manner. We are not saying, for example, that the eucharist
and flesh logically explain the meaning of Anselm's
theology, rather we are saying that these words evoke
the whole reality with which his theology is concerned.

Even the most careful attempts to translate the
lived meaning of Anselm's theology into a discursive
explanation are doomed to failure. The illustration of
this paradox can be seen in chapter 7. In a sense, it
is self-contradictory to explain how flesh is the motif
of Anselm's theology. For the most part we were com-
pelled to contemplate Anselm's own words, allowing them
to evoke the motif level under consideration. At the
very best, the explanations were designed to call attention to Anselm's life and to his own prayer as the
source and the lived meaning of his theology. To the
extent that this study has actually communicated something of the life, context, and lived meaning of Anselm's theology, it was speaking symbolically, pointing
to Anselm's own theological experience.

To explain how the flesh functions as a motif
symbol, we relied on Anselm's prayers, especially the
Cur Deus Homo prayer. Now as we deal with the eucharist
as the flesh of Christ, a motif symbol, the most we can
hope to do is to participate in the profound feelings of
love that Anselm himself expresses in his "Prayer before
Receiving the Body and Blood of Christ":

> Lord Jesus Christ, by the Father's plan and by
> the working of the Holy Ghost, of your own
> free will you died and mercifully redeemed the
> world from sin and everlasting death. I adore
> and venerate you as much as ever I can, though

my love is so cold, my devotion so poor.
Thank you for the good gift of this your holy
Body and Blood, which I desire to receive, as
cleansing from sin, and for a defence against
it.

Lord, I acknowledge that I am far from
worthy to approach and touch this sacrament;
but I trust in that mercy which caused you to
lay down your life for sinners that they might
be justified, and because you gave yourself
willingly as a holy sacrifice to the Father.
A sinner, I presume to receive these gifts so
that I may be justified by them. I beg and
pray you, therefore, merciful lover of men,
let not that which you have given for the
cleansing of sins be unto me the increase of
sin, but rather for forgiveness and protec-
tion.

Make me, O Lord, so to perceive with lips
and heart and know by faith and by love, that
by virtue of this sacrament I may deserve to
be planted in the likeness of your death and
resurrection, by mortifying the old man, and
by renewal of the life of righteousness. May
I be worthy to be incorporated into your body
"which is the church," so that I may be your
member and you may be my head, and that I may
remain in you and you in me. Then at the
Resurrection you will refashion the body of my
humiliation according to the body of your
glory, as you promised by your apostle, and I
shall rejoice in you for ever to your glory,
who with the Father and Holy Spirit lives and
reigns for ever. Amen.13

On one level we may attempt to translate this prayer
into a discursive explanation about the meaning of the
eucharist. This is basically what we attempted to do in
establishing the relational meaning of the flesh of
Christ in Anselm's discursive system.

In such a discursive explanation one may talk
about the function of the flesh of Christ as incorporating men into Christ's mystical body, the Church. Such
an explanation serves a valuable doctrinal purpose,
showing the relationship between the various elements of
Anselm's discursive system. But at the motif level one
is called upon to go beyond an understanding of this

discursive   explanation;   here we are called upon to participate in Anselm's deepest feelings of devotion.

Conclusion

We   have   seen   how the   flesh   is   an   integrative
notion in Anselm's theological   system   and   that   it   is
operative   at   each   of   the   three   levels which we have
examined, namely, the denotative,the relational,   and the
motif.   At   each   of   these   levels of analysis we have
observed different aspects of the   concept   of   flesh and
how   flesh contributes significantly to the formation   of
Anselm's theology.   In this regard flesh can be considered a fundamental symbol   of   Anselm's theology   which
takes   its   place   alongside R. Pouchet's recitudo and H.
Kohlenberger's verbum.   This study has attempted to add
to that motif research as well   as   to   the   other recent
literature   on   the nature of Anselm's distinctive   theological system.

In the first   part   of   this   analysis a word study
illuminated the wide variety of meanings   associated with
the   flesh concept. This study showed the various   denotations   of   the flesh complex indicating that they range
from the common   meanings   associated   with   the flesh in
everyday language   such   as a man's body and his   bodily
appetites through the sacramental   meaning of the body of
Christ   in   the eucharist to the more   technical   meaning
that it receives   when it denotes the dispositions of the
human will. Some of these   various   meanings were negative,   others were neutral, and still others   were   positive.

The   negative meanings, alluding to moral and
spiritual corruption,   referred to the unrestrained
appetites, to those who "walk according to the flesh,"
and to the risen body as it reflects the condition of an
evil   soul. The neutral meanings denoted the body as   a
material object   that can be perceived by the senses, the
body as the locus of   perception   and sensation, and the
dispositions of the will. In these   cases   the   flesh is
neutral   in   the sense that it denotes either the morally
neutral role of   a   physical body in sensing and perceiv-
ing external reality,   or   the   moralizable   character of
the will.   In the latter case the flesh can be   either
positive or negative depending   on   whether   or   not   it
possesses   the   disposition   of   the will toward justice.
The positive meanings of the concept   of   flesh   referred
to   the   earthly   flesh   of Christ, to the risen body   of
Christ in the eucharist,   and   to   the   risen   body   as   it

reflects the condition of a righteous soul. In each of these positive meanings the flesh is associated with Christ who assumed the flesh in the mystery of the incarnation and rectified it in the mystery of the redemption. Thus in the word study we observed the flexibility of the flesh concept and saw how it was capable of being the basic common term within the unfolding of all salvation history, linking its events together as the history of the transformation of the flesh, or, put another way, the transformation of human beings through the flesh, moving from the originally righteous flesh through the corruption of the flesh at the fall of Adam to the restoration of justice to the flesh.

In the second part of this analysis we examined the role of the concept of flesh in relation to other concepts and doctrines that form the language web of Anselm's discursive system. We saw that on the discursive, or relational, level of Anselm's system flesh plays an important role in the logical explication of various doctrines. We noted that flesh also has an important systematic function in relating the following doctrines to one another: God, creation, angels, free will, grace, original sin, incarnation, virgin birth, redemption, and resurrection. From one doctrine to another we traced the vicissitudes of the flesh: it was created with original justice; it distinguished men from angels; it joined all men to Adam; it was corrupted in Adam; it was assumed by the Second Person of the Trinity whereby Christ became our brother (escaping its corruption in the virgin birth); it permitted the God-man to offer his death as atonement for Adam's sin; it was raised from death in Christ's resurrection; and men are incorporated into its glorious, risen condition through the sacraments, especially the eucharist.

Through these various functions the concept of flesh serves as a bond that gives coherence to Anselm's discursive system. We also noted that the special meanings of flesh as a natural will and as a disposition of the personal will enable it to provide continuity for Anselm's discursive system since these two meanings explain the relationship of the individual personal will to the natural will. It is this relationship that is fundamental to an understanding of the overall meaning and direction of Anselm's discursive system, i.e., it is the theological explication of evil (participation in Adam's corrupted will) and grace (participation in Christ's righteous will).

In chapter 7 we examined the deepest level of Anselm's theology, the motif level. There we saw that Anselm's thought must be related to the life context out of which it developed. Our examination of the motif level showed that Anselm's theology could not be understood fully unless it was seen as a reflection upon the religious life of the Church and of himself as a member of that living-sacramental community. We also observed that the motif level of Anselm's theology could be expressed only by the use of metaphor because the motif level concerns the whole meaning of Anselm's theology and metaphor is the figurative language capable of evoking such "wholes." We noticed that the flesh is an important source of Anselm's metaphors expressing the deepest feelings of the heart, the strongest commitment of the will, and the most profound reflections of the mind. Finally, in considering the Cur Deus Homo prayer, we saw that the flesh of Christ is a motif symbol that evokes the whole spiritual reality of which Anselm's theology seeks an understanding: human transformation through the flesh of Christ.

Thus, we have examined the role of the concept of flesh in Anselm's theology at three different levels. We have affirmed the vital interrelationship of these three levels of meaning and have stressed their complementary character. It seemed essential to distinguish these levels at which the term flesh functions to highlight the richness of this concept and to indicate the complexity of its role in the total theology of Anselm. But we do not wish to give the impression that the analytical distinction of three levels of meaning implies that a word is actually used in only one sense. All three levels of meaning are always co-present and mutually coinhering. In fact, the usefulness of the term flesh in Anselm's theology is that it unites so well the various meaning levels we have considered.

From the point of view adopted in this study, the variety of meaning levels implies the richness of a living reality. The living reality that the concept of flesh communicates is the unity of life and the transformation of human beings. Where the denotative and relational analyses have stressed more heavily the intellectual function of the flesh concept in Anselm's theology, the motif analysis has attempted to bring out the metaphorical and sacramental implications of the concept.

We emphasize the importance of sharing in the lived meaning of Anselm's concept of flesh. While we may begin to understand this concept from a word study that takes into account the basic denotations of the words _caro_, _corpus_ and _concupiscentia_, or from a study of the role of the flesh in Anselm's discursive system, we cannot finally grasp the meaning of the flesh complex until we experience it as a symbol evoking the entire meaning of his theology. We may attempt to translate the lived meaning of Anselm's theology into descriptions of what theology is about. We may also try to translate the motif level of the concept of flesh, saying that it represents the union of the soul with God, a union that can only take place in the rectitude of will through the disposition of the will toward justice (the flesh of Christ), but such a translation necessarily fails to communicate the full meaning of the concept.

It is one thing to talk about union with God and the transformation that accompanies it, but it is quite another thing to experience it. The motif, or deep, meaning of the concept of flesh is not to talk about that union, but actually to evoke that experience itself. It is for this reason that the term "transformation complex" best describes the role of flesh in Anselm's theology. Flesh is a hermeneutical principle that highlights the process of human transformation as the primary concern of Anselm's life and work. This study has attempted to return this central inspiration of Anselm's theology to the foreground. The monastic-devotional context and the transformational intent of Anselm's theology are indispensable reference points for recovering the real Anselm in this century. Hopefully, this work will have contributed to that end.

NOTES

1. <u>EDSA</u> II.

2.   We should note here that the century dominated
by Anselm's theological thought is especially important
in the development of a theology of the eucharist. The
eucharistic controversy in the eleventh century led
finally to the official acceptance of the terminology
"substantial change" to describe the sacramental change
of bread and wine into the body and blood of Christ. It
is noteworthy that the leading figure in the establish-
ment of this doctrine was Lanfranc, Anselm's teacher and
his immediate predecessor in Canterbury.
     The source of Lanfranc's position is Paschasius
Radbertus's <u>De Corpore et Sanguine Domini</u>, the earliest
extensive systematic work on eucharistic theology.
Paschasius's extremely realistic teaching on eucharistic
change set off a controversy in the ninth century; it
was also in reaction to Paschasius's work that the
eleventh-century controversy flared up.
     The eleventh-century figure who took issue with
Paschasius's "realistic" interpretation of eucharistic
change was Berengarius of Tours. Berengarius developed
the teaching of Ratramnus (Paschasius's opponent in the
ninth-century controversy) and John Scotus Erigena
(Ratramnus's teacher). Berengarius called Paschasius's
reasoning "silliness" (<u>inepta</u>) and "madness" (<u>vecordia</u>),
wishing to replace that theory with one true to the
Fathers. Berengarius considered his own theory to be
based on St. Augustine. From Augustine's distinction
between the <u>sacramentum</u> (sign) and the <u>res sacramenti</u>
(the reality symbolized), Berengarius reasoned that the
bread as the <u>sacramentum</u> (sign) was not changed, even
though that same bread acquired a new dignity after the
consecration (C. Sheedy, <u>The Eucharistic Controversy of
the 11th Century against the Background of Pre-Scholastic Theology</u> [Washington, 1947], p. 102). Thus, a change
does take place, even though the change is not by <u>cor-
ruptio subjecti</u>.
     The important point of this eleventh-century
eucharistic controversy is that Berengarius rejected
that philosophical explanation of eucharistic change
which spoke of substantial change; at the same time
Lanfranc helped to defend this orthodox interpretation
of eucharistic change. Lanfranc denied any conflict
between the simultaneous presence of Christ in heaven
and in the eucharist. He did not claim to understand

how this substantial change actually occurred but simply
regarded it as an impenetrable mystery.

Lanfranc did not develop the doctrine of transmu-
tation beyond Paschasius's position except to stress
more strongly the absolute objectivity of Christ's
presence. He went so far as to say that even sinners
and the unworthy receive the true body of Christ. The
main point of Lanfranc's teaching on this matter is that
the eucharistic body of Christ is identical to the body
of Christ, born of Mary.

It is without question that Anselm's own eucharistic theology was influenced by his teacher Lanfranc
and the Church's definition of eucharistic change. The
idea that was to be expressed by twelfth century theo-
logians as "transubstantiation" already occurs during
the Berengarian controversy. This idea is expressed by
the Roman Synod of 1079 as "substantialiter converti":
"Panem et vinum . . . substantialiter converti in veram
et propriam ac vivificatricem carnem et sanguinem Iesu
Christi" (DZ 700). See J. McCue "The Doctrine of
Transubstantiation from Berengar through Trent: The
Point at Issue," Harvard Theological Review, 61 (1968),
pp. 385-430. It is against this background of a new
precision in the description of eucharistic change that
Anselm's approach to the definition of the eucharistic
bread should be seen.

3. "Corpus suum de pane fecit" (EDSA I); "azimam
Christi carnem comedimus" (EDSA I); "pane, de quo carnem
ipsam conficimus" (EDSA I); "ipsum panem in corpus eius
divina virtute operante sicut ipse fecit sacrificemus"
(EDSA III); "talis fuit ille cuius corpus sacrificamus,
scilicet sine peccati infectione" (EDSA IV).

4. "Quoniam tamen sunt multae diversitates, quae
non in summa sacramenti neque in virtute eius aut fide
discordant, neque omnes in unam consuetudinem colligi
possunt: aestimo eas potius in pace concorditer toler-
andas, quam discorditer cum scandalo damnandas. Habemus
enim a sanctis patribus quia, si unitas servatur caritatis in fide catholica, nihil officit consuetudo
diversa" (EDSE I; S II, 240, 5-10; AC III, 246-47).

5. "Et cum alibi se et carnem suam panem vocavit,
quia sicut isto pane vivit homo temporaliter, ita illo
vivit in aeternum: non ait: 'azimum' vel 'fermenta-
tum,' quia uterque pariter panis, est. Non enim differunt azimus et fermentatus substantialiter--ut quidem
putant--, sicut homo novus ante peccatum et inveteratus
fermento peccati nequaquam substantialiter differunt.
Propter hoc ergo solum videtur se et carnem suam 'panem'

vocasse et de pane corpus suum fecisse, quia sicut iste
panis azimus sive fermentatus dat vitam transitoriam,
ita corpus eius aeternam, non quia fermentatus est vel
azimus" (EDSA I; S II, 224, 4-12; AC III, 233-34).

      6. The explanation in this section is based on
the function of the "eucharistic flesh" in the context
of Anselm's entire discursive system as set forth in
chapter 6 and therefore presupposes those prior
discussions of flesh as a participatory nature and flesh
as a natural will.
    This approach is merely an attempt to analyze the
function of the eucharistic flesh on the discursive
level of Anselm's system. The full importance of the
eucharistic flesh is only grasped when this functional
role of the eucharist is enlivened by the devotional
atmosphere communicated on the motif level of Anselm's
system. This is the point we emphasized in the discussion of the Cur Deus Homo meditation. The discussion
and texts of that part of chapter 7 should be kept in
mind as we consider the function of the eucharistic
flesh here. The living dimension of this eucharistic
function will also be highlighted in the next section
when we consider Anselm's "Prayer Before Receiving the
Body and Blood of Christ."

      7. Such an explanation of how men are justified
by Christ has been called an intrinsic, impartative
theory of justification because it emphasizes that man's
very nature is affected by redemption, that the efficacy
of Christ's sacrifice is actually imparted to the
Christians. P. Toner argued that Anselm's theory of
impartative justification could apply to the eucharist
since that sacrament is administered to adults who can
preserve the uprightness of will which constitutes
justice; but he felt that this theory could not be
applied to the sacrament of baptism. He noted that
Anselm was forced to fall back on an imputative theory
of justification when explaining the efficacy of infant
baptism because infants are incapable of preserving
their own rectitude of will by the use of reason ("St.
Anselm's Definition of Original Sin," Irish Theological
Quarterly, 3 [1908], pp. 425-36).
    While Toner was correct in that Anselm had diffi-
culty explaining infant baptism according to his theory
of intrinsic justification, he apparently did not sus-
pect that Anselm was not primarily concerned with
applying his justification theory to the sacrament of
baptism. Certain scholars have argued that Anselm's
atonement is actually a reflection on eucharistic rather
than baptismal justification. G. H. Williams's Anselm:

Communion and Atonement is the most recent study con-
necting Anselm's atonement theory to his view of the
sacraments. Williams himself cites J. Bach (Die Dog-
mengeschichte des Mittelalters vom christologischen
Standpunkte I [Vienna, 1873], pp. 362 ff.) as the first
man to suggest a relationship between Anselm's views on
atonement and the sacraments; and J. Geiselmann (Die
Eucharistielehre der Vorschoalstik [Paderborn, 1926] as
the first to suggest that Anselm's interpretation of the
eucharist was derived from his atonement system. See
Williams, Anselm: Communion and Atonement (St. Louis,
1960), pp. 52ff.
     Williams maintains that it is against the elev-
enth-century background of a more precise definition of
Christ's presence in the eucharist as well as a "theo-
logical-institutional clarification" of the role of
penance that Anselm's theology of redemption should be
understood. He shows that the old soteriological
theories growing out of the earlier stress on the sacrament of baptism gave way to a theory whose language
conformed more closely to the growing significance of
penance and the eucharist.
     Williams states that "Anselm was the first fully
and systematically to articulate this 'ecological' shift
among the sacraments in terms of the theory of redemption; and although the older views of redemption persis-
ted in unobserved detachment from the actual sacramental
life of the church, Anselm's theory in modified form was
to prevail because of its greater consonance with the
evolved sacramental system of the medieval church"
(ibid., pp. 25-26). Thus, Williams sees Anselm's impartative theory of justification primarily as a reflection
on the increasing importance of the eucharist in the
liturgical life of the Church.

     8. Hoedl describes the Ueberlieferungsgeschichte
of this treatise in "Die ontologische Frage im fruehscholastischen Eucharistietraktat 'Calix benedictionis,'" SR, pp. 90-95.

     9. Ibid., pp. 87-88.

     10. Hoedl describes this aspect of the ontologi-
cal change in the consecrated elements very well: "Die
Deutung und Bedeutung, die Jesus dem oesterlichen
Mahlhalten der Juengergemeinde gab, heben dieses Mahl
von allen anderen Mahlzeiten ab und offenbaren es als
Teilgabe und Teilnahme, als Partizipation an dem fuer
uns hingegebenen Leben Jesu Christi, weil er sein Leben,
Leib und Blut fuer uns in den Tod gab und weil er sich
uns in dieser Hingabe ganz und gar zu eigen gab, macht

er uns im Zeichen des Mahles wahrhaft und wirklich
seines Lebens teilhaftig, gibt er uns Anteil an Leib und
Blut, so dass wer in dieser Teilhabe wahrhaft und wirklich sein Leib sind. Dieses betonte vere verweist nicht
auf eine handfeste, grieïbare, starre Realitaet, sondern
auf das Umgreifende der Wirklichkeit des Leibes Christi
und der darin offenbaren Wahrheit. Dieses vere erfragt
die ontologische Frage; auf dieses vere achtete Anselm
und mit ihm die scholastische Theologie" (ibid., p.
106).

   11. Williams also recognizes this parallel
between the modes of incorporation into the archetypal
figures, Adam and Christ. Men participate in the flesh
of Adam by propagation while they participate in the
flesh of Christ by eucharistic incorporation (Anselm:
Communion and Atonement, p. 64). This study has also
indicated that baptism initiates the process that is
completed by eucharistic incorporation.

   12. AC I; p. 141.

   13. "Domine Iesu Christe, qui patre disponente,
spiritu sancto cooperante, per mortam tuam spontanea
voluntate misericorditer a peccato et morte aeterna
mundum redemisti, adoro et veneror, eo quo possum quamvis tepido affectu et humili devotione, gratias agens
tanto beneficio, hoc sanctum corpus tuum et hunc sanctum
sanguinem tuum, quae ad emundationem et defensionem a
peccatis accipere desidero.
   Confiteror, domine, quia nimis sum indignus ad
eorum tactum accedere; sed confidens de illa clementia
qua pro peccatoribus, ut iusti fierent, animam tuam
ponens ea dedisti, et pia hostia patri mactari
voluisti: illa praesumo ego peccator, ut per illa
iustificer, accipere. Supplex ergo te, pie miserator
hominum, obsecro, ut quae ad delendum peccata dedisti,
non mihi sint ad peccatorum augmentum, sed ad indul-
gentiam et tuitionem.
   Fac me, domine, ita ea ore et corde percipere
atque fide et affectu sentire, ut per eorum virtutem sic
merear complantari similitudini mortis et resurrectionis
tuae per veteris hominis mortificationem et novitatem
iustae vitae, ut dignus sim corpori tuo, 'quod est
ecclesia,' incorporari, et sim membrum tuum et tu caput
meum, et maneam in te et tu in me: quatenus in resurrec-
tione reformes 'corpus humilitatis' meae 'configuratum
corpori claritatis' tuae, secundum promissionem apostoli
tui, et in te in aeternum gaudeam de gloria tua; qui cum
patre et spiritu sancto vivis et regnas deus per omnia
saecula saeculorum, amen" (Orat. III, S III, 10, 3-23;
PAM, 100-101).

BIBLIOGRAPHY

Primary Sources

Text

Schmitt, F. S. *Sancti Anselmi Opera Omnia*. 6 vols.
   Edinburgh, 1946-61.

Translations

Fairweather, E. *A Scholastic Miscellany: Anselm to*
   Ockham. Philadelphia, 1956.

Henry, D. *The De Grammatico of St. Anselm*. South Bend,
   1964.

Hopkins, J., and Richardson, H. *Anselm of Canterbury*. 3
   vols. Toronto, 1974-76.

Ward, B. *The Prayers and Meditations of Saint Anselm*.
   Middlesex, 1973.

Selected Secondary Sources

Adnes, P. "Goût Spirituel." *Dictionnaire de Spirit-*
   ualité. Vol. VI, 1st ed. Paris, 1967. Cols.
   629-642.

Amiet, R. "Saint Anselme Liturgiste." *AA* V, pp. 283-
   95.

Assagioli, R. *Psychosynthesis*. New York, 1982.

Bainvel, J. "Anselme de Cantorbéry." *Dictionnaire de*
   Théologie Catholique. Vol. I. 1st ed., 1923.

_____. "La théologie de saint Anselme. Esprit,
   méthode et procédés, points de doctrine." *Revue*
   de Philosophie, 15 (1909), pp. 724-46.

Barth, K. *Anselm, Fides Quaerens Intellectum*. Munich,
   1931.

Bayart, J. "The Concept of Mystery According to St.
   Anselm of Canterbury." *Recherches de Théologie*
   Ancienne et Médiévale, 9 (1937), pp. 125-66.

Beorlier, E. "Les rapports de la raison et de la foi
    dans la philosophie de saint Anselme." Revue de
    Philosophie, 15 (1909), pp. 692-723.

Bourke, V. J. "Human Tendencies, Will and Freedom." In
    L'homme et son destin, ed. L. De Raeymaeker. Lou-
    vain-Paris, 1960, pp. 71-84.

Bouvier, M. "Th. A. Audet et la Théologie du Cur Deus
    Homo," SB, pp. 313-25.

Bouyer, L. Dictionary of Theology. New York, 1965.

Bynum, C. "Jesus as Mother and Abbot as Mother: Some
    Themes in Twelfth-Century Cistercian Writing."
    Harvard Theological Review, 70 (1977), pp. 257-84.

Camelot, P. "Réalisme et symbolisme dans la doctrine
    eucharistique de S. Augustin." Revue des Sciences
    Philosophiques et Théologiques, 31 (1947), pp.
    394-410.

Campbell, R. "Anselm's Theological Method." Scottish
    Journal of Theology, 32 (1979), pp. 541-62.

Cayré, F., ed. Augustinus Magister. 2 vols. Paris,
    1954.

Charlesworth, M. St. Anselm's Proslogion. Oxford,
    1965.

Chibnall, M. "The Relations of Saint Anselm with the
    English Dependencies of the Abbey of Bec." SB,
    pp. 521-30.

Choisy, E. Paschase Radbert. Geneve, 1888.

Choquette, I. "Voluntas, Affectio and Potestas in the
    Liber De Voluntate of St. Anselm." Mediaeval
    Studies, 4 (1942), pp. 61-81.

Church, R. Saint Anselm. London, 1905.

Clark, M. Augustine, Philosopher of Freedom. New York,
    1958.

Congar, Y. "L'église chez saint Anselme." SB, pp. 371-
    99.

Cousin, P. "Les relations de saint Anselme avec Cluny."
    SB, pp. 439-53.

Cremer, H. "Der germanische Satisfaktionsbegriff in der
     Versoehnungslehre." Theologische Studien und
     Kritiken (1893), pp. 316-45.

_____. "Die Wurzeln des Anselmschen Satisfaktions-
     begriffs." Theologische Studien und Kritiken
     (1893), pp. 7-24.

Crouse, R. "The Augustinian Background of St. Anselm's
     Concept of Iustitia." Canadian Journal of
     Theology, 4 (1958), pp. 111-19.

Daoust, J. "Le Janseniste Dom Gerberon, éditeur de
     saint Anselme (1675)." SB, pp. 531-40.

Delhaye, P. "Quelques aspects de la morale de saint
     Anselme." SB, pp. 400-422.

Dickinson, J. "Saint Anselm and the First Regular
     Canons in England," SB, pp. 541-46.

Dickson, M. "Introduction à l'édition critique du
     coutumier du Bec." SB, pp. 599-632.

Domet de Vorges, E. "Le Milieu philosophique à l'époque
     de St. Anselme." Revue de Philosophie, 15 (1909),
     pp. 605-17.

Draeseke, J. "Sur la question des sources d'Anselme."
     Revue de Philosophie, 15 (1909), pp. 639-54.

Duclow, D. "Structure and Meaning in Anselm's De Veri-
     tate." American Benedictine Review, 26 (1975),
     pp. 406-17.

Dufourcq, A. "Saint Anselme: Son temps, son rôle."
     Revue de Philosophie, 15 (1909), pp. 593-604.

Eadmer. The Life of St. Anselm. Edited and translated
     by R. Southern. London, 1962.

Evans, G. R. Anselm and A New Generation. Oxford,
     1980.

_____. Anselm and Talking About God. Oxford, 1978.

_____. "St. Anselm and Knowing God." Journal of
     Theological Studies, 28 (1977) pp. 430-44.

_____. "St. Anselm's Definitions." Archivum Latini-
     tatis Medii Aevi, 41 (1979), pp. 91-100.

Evans, G. R. "St. Anselm's Images of Trinity." Journal of Theological Studies, 27 (1976), pp. 46-57.

_____. "Why the Fall of Satan?" Recherches de Théologie Ancienne et Médiévale, 45 (1978), pp. 130-46.

Evdokimov, P. "L'aspect apophatique de l'argument de saint Anselme." SB, pp. 233-58.

Fairweather, E. "Incarnation and Atonement." Canadian Journal of Theology, 7 (1961), pp. 167-75.

_____. "Iustitia Dei as the Ratio of the Incarnation." SB, pp. 327-35.

Filliatre, C. La philosophie de saint Anselme. Paris, 1920.

Flasch, K. "Der philosophische Ansatz des Anselm von Canterbury im Monologion und sein Verhaeltnis zum augustinischen Neuplatonismus." AA II, pp. 1-43.

_____. "Vernunft und Geschichte. Der Beitrag Johann Moehlers zum philosophischen Verstaendnis Anselms von Canterbury." AA I, pp. 165-94.

Forest, A. "La doctrine de saint Anselme." In Le Mouvement Doctrinal du IXᵉ au XIVᵉ Siècle. Paris, 1956, pp. 53-73.

_____. "L'argument de saint Anselme dans la philosophie réflexive," SB, pp. 273-94.

Foreville, R. "L'ultime ratio de la morale politique de saint Anselme: Rectitudo voluntatis propter se servata." SB, pp. 423-38.

Froehlich, W. "Die bischoeflichen Kollegen des hl. Erzbishofs Anselm von Canterbury. Erster Teil: 1093-1097." AA I, pp. 223-67.

_____. "Die bischoeflichen Kollegen des hl. Erzbishofs Anselm von Canterbury. Zweiter Teil: 1100- 1109." AA II, pp. 117-68.

Funke, B. Grundlagen und Voraussetzungen der Satisfaktions-theorie des hl. Anselm von Canterbury. Muenster, 1903.

Gagacz, M. "La 'Ratio Anselmi' en face du Problème des
    relations entre Métaphysique et Mystique." AA II,
    pp. 169-85.

Gilson, E. "Sens et nature de l'argument de Saint An-
    selme" Archives d'histoire doctrinale et lit-
    téraire du moyen âge, 9 (1934), pp. 5-51.

Glorieux, P. "Quelques aspects de la christologie de
    saint Anselme." SB, pp. 337-47.

Gollnick, J. "The Flesh Complex in the Theology of St.
    Anselm of Canterbury." Ph. D. thesis, University
    of Toronto, 1974.

Haenchen, E. "Anselm und Vernunft." Zeitschrift fuer
    Theologie und Kirche, 48 (1951), pp. 312-42.

Haering, N. "Berengar's Definitions of Sacramentum and
    their Influence on Mediaeval Sacramentology,"
    Medieval Studies 10 (1948), pp. 109-46.

Hall, C. The Meaning of Dreams. New York, 1953.

Hammer, F. Genugtuung und Heil. Vienna, 1967.

Harnack, A. History of Dogma. Vol. VII. New York,
    1958.

Hawkes, T. Metaphor. London, 1972.

Hayden, A. "Saint Anselme et saint Thomas. La vraie
    nature de la théologie et sa portée apostolique,"
    SB, pp. 45-85.

Heinrichs, L. Die Genugtuungstheorie des hl. Anselmus
    von Canterbury. Paderborn, 1909.

Henry, D. P. "Numerically Definite Reasoning in the Cur
    Deus Homo." Dominican Studies, 6 (1953), pp. 48-
    55.

_____. "Remarks on Saint Anselm's Treatment of Pos-
    sibility," SB, pp. 19-22.

Hernandez, M. "Les caractères fondamentaux de la pensée
    de saint Anselme." SB, pp. 9-18.

Herrera, R. "St. Anselm: A Radical Empiricist?" AA
    II, pp. 45-56.

Herrera, R. "St. Anselm's <u>Proslogion</u>: A Hermeneutical Task." <u>AA</u> IV/2, pp. 141-45.

Heyer, G., Jr. "Anselm Concerning the Human Role in Salvation." In <u>Texts and Testaments</u>. Edited by W. March. San Antonio, 1980, pp. 163-72.

Hoedl, L. "Die ontologische Frage im fruehscholastischen Eucharistietraktat 'Calix benedictionis,'" <u>SR</u>, pp. 87-110.

Hopkins, J. <u>Anselm of Canterbury</u>. Vol. IV. Toronto, 1976.

_____. "Anselm's Debate with Gaunilo." <u>AA</u> V, pp. 25-53.

_____. <u>A Companion to the Study of St. Anselm</u>. Minneapolis, 1972.

Hufnagel, A. "Anselm's Wahrheitsverstaendnis in der Deutung Alberts de. Gr." <u>SR</u>, pp. 19-33.

Jones, R. <u>Sancti Anselmi Mariologia</u>. Mundelein, Ill., 1938.

Jung, C. <u>The Symbolic Life</u>. Princeton, 1976.

Jungmann, J. <u>The Early Liturgy</u>. Notre Dame, 1959.

Kane, G. S. <u>Anselm's Doctrine of Freedom and the Will</u>. New York, 1981.

Kelly, J. N. D. <u>Early Christian Doctrines</u>. London, 1958.

Kohlenberger, H. <u>Similitudo und Ratio</u>. Bonn, 1972.

_____, ed. <u>Sola Ratione</u>. Anselm Studies for F. S. Schmitt on his seventy-fifth birthday. Stuttgart, 1970.

Koyré, A. <u>L'idée de Dieu dans la philosophie de st. Anselme</u>. Paris, 1923.

Kuss, O. <u>Der Roemerbrief</u>. Regensburg, 1959.

Lampe, G. "The Eucharist in the Thought of the Early Church." In <u>Eucharistic Theology Then and Now</u>. London, 1968, pp. 34-58.

Laporte, J. "Saint Anselme et l'ordre monastique." _SB_,
    pp. 455-76.

Leclercq, J. "Une doctrine de la vie monastique dans
    l'école du Bec." _SB_, pp. 477-88.

Lefevre, Y. "Saint Anselme et l'enseignement systéma-
    tique de la doctrine." _SB_, pp. 87-93.

Levasti, A. _Sant' Anselmo_. Bari, 1929.

Lewicki, J. "Saint Anselme et les doctrines des Cister-
    ciens du XIIe siècle." _AA_ II, pp. 209-16.

Lohmeyer, E. _Die Lehre vom Willen bei Anselm von Can-
    terbury_. Lucka, 1914.

Lottin, O. "Libre Arbitre et liberté depuis saint An-
    selme jusqu'à la fin du XIIIe siècle." In _Psy-
    chologie et Morale aux XIIe et XIIIe Siècles_.
    Vol. I. Louvain, 1954, pp. 11-14.

_____. "Les Théories sur le péché originel de saint
    Anselme à saint Thomas d'Aquin." In _Psychologie
    et Morale aux XIIe et XIIIe Siècles_. Vol.
    IV. Louvain, 1954, pp. 11-14.

Mason, J. "Saint Anselm's Relations with Laymen:
    Selected Letters." _SB_, pp. 547-60.

Mazzarella, P. _Anselmo d'Aosta_. Padova, 1962.

McCue, J. "The Doctrine of Transubstantiation from
    Berengar through Trent: The Point at Issue."
    Harvard Theological Review, 61 (1968), pp. 385-
    430.

McIntyre, J. "_Cur Deus Homo_ The Axis of the Argument."
    _SR_, pp. 111-18.

_____. "Premises and Conclusions in the System of
    St. Anselm's Theology." _SB_, pp. 95-101.

_____. _St. Anselm and His Critics_. Edinburgh, 1954.

Merton, L. "Reflections on Some Recent Studies of St.
    Anselm." _Monastic Studies_, 3 (1965), pp. 221-34.

Merton, T. _The Monastic Journey_. Kansas City, 1977.

Michaud-Quantin, P. "Notes sur le vocabulaire psychologique de saint Anselme." SB, pp. 23-30.

Murphy, L. "Martin Luther's Marginal Notes To The Sentences of Peter Lombard on the Transmission of Original Sin." Science et Esprit, 33 (1981), pp. 55-71.

Nédoncelle, M. "La notion de personne dans l'oeuvre de saint Anselme." SB, pp. 31-43.

North, R., Holsti, O., Zaninovich, M., and Zinnes, D. Content Analysis. Northwestern University, 1963.

Olsen, G. "Hans Urs von Balthasar and the Rehabilitation of St. Anselm's Doctrine of the Atonement." Scottish Journal of Theology, 34 (1981), pp. 49-61.

Ott, H. "What Is Systematic Theology?" In The Later Heidegger and Theology. Edited by J. Robinson and J. Cobb, Jr. New York, 1963. Pp. 77-111.

Ottaviano, C. "Le basi psichologiche dell'argomento ontologico in un importante brano dei 'Dicta Anselmi.'" SR, pp. 57-70.

The Oxford English Dictionary. Vol. IV. Oxford, 1933.

Plagnieux, J. "Le Binome iustitia-potentia dans la sotériologie augustinienne et anselmienne." SB, pp. 141-54.

Porcelloni, E. "Le problème de la dérivation du monde à partir de Dieu chez Scot Erigène et chez saint Anselme." AA II, pp. 195-208.

Porée, A. "L'école du Bec et saint Anselme." Revue de Philosophie 15 (1909), 618-38.

Pouchet, J. "La Componction de l'humilité et de la piété chez saint Anselme d'après ses 'orationes sives méditationes.'" SB, pp. 489-508.

Pouchet, R. "Existe t'il une 'synthèse' anselmienne?" AA I, pp. 3-10.

_____. La rectitudo chez saint Anselme. Paris, 1964.

Powers, J. Eucharistic Theology. London, 1967.

Principe, W. _Alexander of Hales' Theology of the Hypo-
static Union_. Toronto, 1967.

Richardson, H. _Toward an American Theology_. New York,
1967.

Rigg, J. _Anselm of Canterbury_. London, 1896.

Riviere, J. "Contribution au _Cur Deus Homo_ de saint Augustin." In _Miscellanea Agostiniana_. Vol. II,
ed. D. G. Morin. Rome, 1931, pp. 837-51.

_____. _Le dogma de la rédemption chez saint Augus-
tin_. Paris, 1933.

Roberts, V. "The Relation of Faith and Reason in St.
Anselm of Canterbury." _American Benedictine
Review_, 25 (1974), pp. 494-512.

Rondet, H. "Grâce et péché: L'Augustinisme de saint
Anselme." _SB_, pp. 155-69.

Roques, R. _Pourquoi Dieu s'est fait homme_. Paris,
1963.

_____. "Structure et caractères de la prière an-
selmienne." _SB_, pp. 119-87.

Rule, M. _The Life and Times of St. Anselm_. 2 vols.
London, 1883.

Salmon, P. "L'ascèse monastique dans les lettres de
saint Anselme de Cantorbéry." _SB_, pp. 509-19.

Schmaus, M. "Die metaphysisch-psychologische Lehre
ueber den Heiligen Geist im _Monologion_ Anselms von
Canterbury." _SR_, pp. 189-219.

Schmitt, F. S. "Anselm und der (Neu-) Platonismus." _AA_
I, 39-71.

_____. "Anselm von Canterbury." _Lexikon fuer Theo-
logie und Kirche_, 1 (1957), pp. 592-94.

_____. "Die Chronologie der Briefedes hl. Anselm
von Canerbury." _Revue Bénédictine_, 64 (1954),
pp. 176-207.

_____. "Cinq récensions de _l'Epistola de Incarna-
tione Verbi_ 'de S. Anselme de Cantorbéry." _Revue
Bénédictine_, 51 (1939), pp. 275-87.

Schmitt, F. S. "Eine dreifache Gestalt der 'Epistola de Sacrificio azimi et fermentati' des hl. Anselm von Canterbury." Revue Bénédictine, 47 (1935), pp. 216-25.

_____. "Eine fruehe Rezension des Werkes de Concordia des hl. Anselm von Canterbury." Revue Bénédictine, 48 (1936), pp. 41-70.

_____. Eine neues unvollendetes Werk des hl. Anselm von Canterbury (Beitraege zur Geschichte der Philosophie und Theologie des Mittelalters, 33/3). Muenster, 1936.

_____. "St. Anselm of Canterbury." New Catholic Encyclopedia. Vol. I, pp. 580-83. New York, 1967.

_____. "Ein weiterer Textzeuge fuer die I. Rezension von de Concordia des hl. Anselm." Revue Bénédictine, 48 (1936), pp. 318-20.

_____. "Die wissenschaftliche Methode in Cur Deus Homo." SB, pp. 349-70.

_____. "Zur Chronologie der Werke des hl. Anselm von Canterbury." Revue Bénédictine, 44 (1932), pp. 322-50.

_____, ed. Analecta Anselmiana. 5 vols. Frankfurt, 1969-1976.

Sheedy, C., The Eucharistic Controversy of the 11th Century against the Background of Pre-Scholastic Theology. Washington, 1947.

Soehngen, G. "Die Einheit der Theologie in Anselm's Proslogion." In Einheit in der Theologie. Munich, 1952, pp. 24-62.

_____. "Rectitudo bei Anselm von Canterbury als Oberbegriff von Wahrheit und Gerechtigkeit." SR, pp. 71-77.

Somerville, J. M. "Symbol." In New Catholic Encyclopedia. Vol. XIII. Washington, 1967, pp. 860-61.

Southern, R. Saint Anselm and His Biographer. Cambridge, 1963.

Southern, R. "St. Anselm and Gilbert Crispin, Abbot of Westminster." Mediaeval and Renaissance Studies, 3 (1954), pp. 78-115.

Southern R., and Schmitt, F. S., eds. Memorials of St. Anselm. London, 1969.

Steiger, L. "Contexe syllogismos. Ueber die Kunst und Bedeutung der Topik bei Anselm." AA I, pp. 107-43.

Stolz, A. "Anselm's Theology in the Proslogion." In The Many-Faced Argument. Edited by J. Hick and A. McGill. New York, 1967, pp. 183-206.

_____. Anselm von Canterbury. Munich, 1937.

Stone, P., Dunphy, D., Smith, M., and Ogilvie, D. The General Inquirer: A Computer Approach to Content Analysis. Cambridge, Mass., 1966.

Thonnard, F. "Caractères augustiniens de la méthode philosophique de saint Anselme." SB, pp. 171-83.

Tillard, J. The Eucharist. New York, 1967.

Tillich, P. The Dynamics of Faith. New York, 1957.

Toner, P. "St. Anselm's Definition of Original Sin." Irish Theological Quarterly, 3 (1908), 425-36.

Tonini, S. "La Scrittura nelle Opere sistematiche di S. Anselmo." AA II, 57-116.

Urry, W. "Saint Anselm and His Cult at Canterbury." SB, pp. 571-93.

Vagaggini, D. "Rationes Necessariae de S. Anselme et S. Thomas." SB, pp. 45-63.

Vignaux, P. Philosophy in the Middle Ages. New York, 1959.

Watson, G. "Karl Barth and St. Anselm's Theological Programme." Scottish Journal of Theology, 30 (1977), pp. 31-45.

Williams, G. H. Anselm: Communion and Atonement. St. Louis, 1960.

Wilmart, A. Auteurs spirituels et textes dévots du moyen âge latin. Paris, 1932.

_____. "Les homélies attribuées à saint Anselme," Archives d'histoire doctrinale et littéraire du moyen âge, 2 (1927), pp. 5-29.

_____. "Le premier ouvrage de saint Anselme contre le trithéisme de Roscelin." Recherches de Théologie Ancienne et Médiévale, 3 (1931), pp. 20-36.

_____. "Une prière ancienne à sainte Anne." La Vie spirituelle, Supplement, 2 (1924), pp. 18-26.

_____. "Une prière inédite attribuée à saint Anselme." Revue Bénédictine, 35 (1923), pp. 143-56.

_____. "Les prières envoyées par saint Anselme à la comtesse Mathilde en 1104." Revue Bénédictine, 41 (1929), pp. 35-45.

_____. "Les propres corrections de saint Anselme dans sa grande prière à la Vierge Marie." Recherches de théologie ancienne et médiévale, 2 (1930), pp. 189-204.

_____. "Textes attribués à saint Anselme et récemment édités." Revue Bénédictine, 48 (1936), pp. 71-79.

_____. "La tradition des lettres de S. Anselme." Revue Bénédictine, 43 (1931), pp. 38-54.

_____. "La tradition des prières de saint Anselme," Revue Bénédictine, 36 (1924), pp. 52-71.

TEXTS AND STUDIES IN RELIGION

DATE DUE

FEB 4 '04			

HIGHSMITH   #LO-45220